Special Treatment

BOOKS BY ALAN ABRAMS

Journalist Biographies Master Index
Media Personnel Directory
Why Windsor? An Anecdotal History of the Jews of
Windsor and Essex County
Special Treatment: The Untold Story of Hitler's Third
Race

Special Treatment

The Untold Story of Hitler's Third Race

by ALAN ABRAMS

Lyle Stuart Inc.   Secaucus, N.J.

FIRST EDITION

A portion of the material in Chapter Six appeared
in slightly different form in the *Detroit Free Press*.

The excerpt from *This Quiet Dust and Other Writings*,
by William Styron, copyright © 1982 by William Styron,
reprinted by permission of Random House, Inc.

Published by Lyle Stuart Inc.
Published simultaneously in Canada by
Musson Book Company,
A division of General Publishing Co. Limited
Don Mills, Ontario

Queries regarding rights and permissions should be
addressed to: Lyle Stuart, 120 Enterprise Avenue,
Secaucus, N.J. 07094

Manufactured in the United States of America

Library of Congress Cataloging in Publication Data

Abrams, Alan E.
  Special treatment.

  Bibliography: p.
  1. Jews—Germany—History—1933–1945. 2. Marriage,
Mixed—Germany. I. Title.
DS135.G33A36 1984   943′.004924   84-8823
ISBN 0-8184-0364-0

For SHARON ABRAMS
1943–1983

You didn't have to do it.
Didn't you know I always loved you?
This book is yours.

Contents

Acknowledgments

But for a terrible tragedy, this book would bear a warm and heartfelt dedication to Professor Klaus J. Herrmann of Concordia University in Montréal, Québec. Without his help, there would not have been any book. It is as simple as that, and I hope he will not be too displeased by the result of his counsel and support.

There were many others who helped me along the way during these past three years, and they all deserve far more than just this brief mention. In addition to those who consented to my interviewing them either in person, by mail or by telephone, the following went out of their way to help me in myriad ways:

Serge and Beate Klarsfeld in Paris; David Lawrence, Jr., Alexander B. Cruden and especially Bill Roberts—all of the *Detroit Free Press;* Bill Schiller of the *Toronto* (Ontario) *Star* and Ute Hertel— for their translations; Pierre Assouline of *France-Soir;* Heinz Höhne of *Der Spiegel;* Grant Black of the *Windsor Star* for his photographic services; the late Dr. Albert Speer; Bob McAleer and Marty Gervais of the *Windsor Star;* Ben Fiber and Joy Kogawa of Toronto; Benton Arnovitz; Lionel Koffler; Barbara Rinehart; Cecilia Lorenz; David Bianco; John Harnett, M.S.W.; Philip Slomovitz of the Detroit *Jewish News;* Marilyn Vasily; Jean-Luc Bodin, Press Attaché of the Embassy of France in Canada, Ottawa; Ekkehard Fahldieck of the Internationales Pressezentrum in Berlin, German Democratic Republic; Erasmus Antiquariaat en Boekhandel in Amsterdam and Anacapa Books in Berkeley, California; Alex Berman; Charles R. Stern, Ph.D.; Howard M. Goldberg of Howard Studios in Cincinnati; the staff of the United States Embassy Guest House in Bonn, Federal Republic of Germany.

I most gratefully acknowledge the assistance and cooperation extended to me by the staff and directors of the following archives and libraries: Rijksinstitut voor Oorlogsdocumentatie (the Netherlands State Institute for War Documentation), Amsterdam, the Netherlands; Yad Vashem, Jerusalem, Israel; Bibliothèque Nationale, Paris, France; Bundesarchiv, Koblenz, Federal Republic of Germany; Berlin Document Center, Berlin, Federal Republic of

Germany; Deutsches Zentralarchiv, Potsdam, German Democratic Republic; Deutsche Staatsbibliothek, Berlin, German Democratic Republic; Bibliothek der Jüdischen Gemeinde, Berlin, German Democratic Republic; Bibliothek, Jüdische Gemeinde zu Berlin, Berlin, Federal Republic of Germany; DEFA-Studio für Spielfilme Archiv, Potsdam, German Democratic Republic; National Archives and Records Service, GSA, Suitland, Maryland; Center of Military History, Dept. of the Army, Washington, D.C.; Leddy Library, the University of Windsor, Windsor, Ontario (Canada); Purdy Library, Wayne State University, Detroit, Michigan; Libraries of the University of Michigan, Ann Arbor, Michigan.

My sincerest thanks to the Ontario Arts Council for the initial grant which made possible my research for this book, and especially to Lyle Stuart for believing in it. And special thanks to Allan J. Wilson and Arthur Smith of Lyle Stuart Inc. for their help.

For Elizabeth Scala Abrams, and Barbara Sharron—who each shepherded me through a year of intense turmoil and somehow always managed to keep me writing—there will never be enough ways to say thank you.

In many ways, the best came last. And it is appropriate that my final acknowledgment be made to Judy Cameron, who stayed awake for a series of summer nights to insure that these three years of hard work were not spent in vain.

Milford, Michigan
July, 1984

"Better to cause a scandal than to be less than truthful."

HEINRICH LEO,
Prussian historian

"Hush! hush! Don't say anything which might be used against us."

Admonition quoted by
GEORGE E. SOKOLSKY in
the introduction to his
We Jews.

Foreword

The story of the Mischlinge Jews—the children of Jews in interfaith marriages who became Hitler's Third Race—has never been fully told. Instead, there exists a veritable litany of misconceptions centering upon the legal amount of "Jewish blood" an individual could carry in one's veins and still stay alive in Nazi Germany. With very few exceptions, if you were a Jew in a mixed marriage, you weren't necessarily sent to your death in a concentration camp. If one of your parents was a Jew, you didn't have to die. Nor were you sent to the ovens if you had two Jewish grandparents. The facts are that many of these Jews survived. But years of popular literature, Hollywood films, television shows, journalism and plain old-fashioned ignorance have combined to create and perpetuate a myth so powerful that it is taken for the truth.

Beyond this, there were full-blooded Jews who, in order to survive, worked for the aims of the Nazis and their followers not only in Germany, but in most of Nazi-occupied Europe as well. Sometimes they did so because they really believed in the fascist cause. Others were just "useful."

The numbers of these groups of special survivors is surprisingly high, considering that most people have managed to hear or read nothing about them. To receive any exemption from Nazi racial laws meant receiving an exemption from death. And the Nazis liked nothing better than to play God. When the number of these Jews who received the Nazi gift of life is tabulated, even conservatively, the total staggers close to the half-million mark. Surely, they are one of the Holocaust's best-kept secrets.

From the moment I began my research on this subject, I was amazed to learn that although the core of the material has appeared in various scattered sources over the last forty years, no one has ever looked at the human stories of suffering hidden behind the cold statistics. What was it like to be a Mischling in Nazi Germany? Or to be a Jew in a mixed marriage in a country officially without Jews? How did you feel when your Jewish parents, brothers, sisters, the lovers you might have married, your friends, neighbors, and even your schoolmates were all murdered—by the very people who chose to let *you* live?

One reason the world has almost ignored this compelling story—even though there is enough emotion and drama in it to fill a sixteen-hour television mini-series—must lie in the highly volatile nature of the material itself. There is a latent and long-smoldering fuse in clear sight which awaits but the merest hint of flame to ignite. This book is not designed to give the anti-Semites of the world yet another stick with which to beat the Jews—they can find plenty of their own in the forest. Nor is this book meant to be either an attempt to humanize the Nazi mentality or to minimize the horrors of the Holocaust. Yes, these Jews did survive, but not without their own set of horrors.

By its very nature, this book raises many deep, dark and basic questions about the instinct for human survival. And they are uncomfortable questions to answer. Many depend upon a mythical "right" or "wrong" that is as old as the Talmud itself. If you are looking for a finger of blame to point you down this path, you won't find it here. Those concepts of "right" and "wrong" lost their validity the day the Nazis killed their first Jew. Is it right to protect your spouse and your children? Is it wrong to save your own life? Or even to want to live? These are among the most basic of human concerns. Are we not all survivalists? What *is* so wrong with wanting to survive? Isn't it something we all desperately try to do every day of our lives? Why then does it suddenly become so terribly "wrong" whenever Jews do it—especially in the worst of all possible times?

What I find to be really immoral is to look at the participants—and even the bystanders—in an era of history as tragic and painful as this epoch was, and be somewhat disappointed when we don't find the measurable levels of remorse we have come to expect from the voices of those who survived.

Long before the conquering Allied armies in their sweep through the Third Reich liberated the pathetic survivors of the concentration camps, they found the mixed marriage Jews. In fact, the first Jew in the ruins of Nazi Germany encountered by the American army was a Jew in a mixed marriage.[1] Now, almost forty years later, all of the other surviving Jewish groups have had their day and their share of media attention. The Jews in hiding have become the erroneously called "Last Jews in Berlin," and the concentration camp survivors are often frequently assumed to be the only "Survivors of the Holocaust," a designation that the mixed marriage Jews and their Mischlinge children certainly have a legitimate claim to sharing.

The history of the Holocaust has somehow overlooked this third group of Jewish survivors. No one ever talks about them. It is almost as if they have become the unmentionables of the Jewish world. Their very survival is even seen as an embarrassment to the memory of those who perished. It is time for them to tell their story.

"... the Nazis went on to say that a man was
Jewish even if only one of his eight great-
grandparents had been Jewish and even if he was
not considered Jewish by other Jews."

DR. ERNEST van den HAAG
in his *The Jewish Mystique*

Chapter One

Mongrels

ONE NIGHT IN 1935, Werner Goldberg went to bed as a Jew. When he awoke the next morning, he was a Mischling. Overnight, Goldberg had changed his race. Adolf Hitler, and not God, had worked a miracle.

"Before then," recalls Goldberg,[1] "I was a Boy Scout and my life was Scouting. We had seen a lot of the world—as a boy I was in Poland, Sweden, France, the Netherlands. But then came 1933. I was then fourteen. One day the leader of our Boy Scout group said to me, 'I have heard that your father is a Jew, and I have the impression in the last weeks that you are not so integrated in our group as you were before. We are now awaiting word that we will become part of the Hitlerjugend [Hitler Youth] and with a member like you we'll have problems. So I think it is better that we separate. Think it over. I will not throw you out, but think it over and tell me if you agree.'

"I went on my bicycle and drove around the Bahnhof [train station]. I couldn't go home. I did not know what to tell my parents because they were the reason this was happening to me. I did not know what this meant—this business about my father being a Jew. To me, he had always looked like Goethe. At last I went to my father and told him what had happened. He told me that 'if somebody doesn't want you, don't run after them.' And so I left the Scouts."

A few months later, Goldberg was asked to join the Hitler Youth. He did, and remembers that "after a short time somebody said to me, 'I have heard you are a Jew. You cannot come here again.' And so I left there too. The same thing then happened in my school. One day the director came and ordered me to get up in front of my entire class. 'Are you an Aryan?' he demanded. I replied that I didn't know. 'Well, see that you know tomorrow,' he said angrily and stormed out. That night I told my father and asked him what I should say. He said, 'Tell them you are not a Jew—you are Christian.' My father, who was a full-blooded Jew, had been baptized in the Protestant faith in 1900, when he was nineteen. My mother, who he married in 1918, was from a Protestant Silesian family. Her maiden name was Christ.

"The next day I went back to school and the director came into my classroom again. I told him 'I asked my parents. I am a Christian.' The director glared at me and said, 'I didn't ask for your religion. I asked for your race.' "

For Werner Goldberg, "the problem was that the Nuremberg Laws which created the new racial classification of Mischlinge for people like me with one or two Jewish grandparents didn't come into effect until 1935. And in that time between 1933 and 1935, nobody knew what position he was in. Is one a Jew or not a Jew? The children in such families knew nothing about this. But they learned it quickly enough when they had to make their family tree to prove they were Aryan and immediately saw they weren't—they were Jewish. And in this situation a lot of people tried to tell the authorities 'This is not my father—I am illegitimate. My mother has another friend,' and such things."

The April 1933 laws and regulations issued by the German Interior Ministry, specifically for the purpose of retiring officials of "non-Aryan descent," were the first attempts of the Nazis to define the Jews. If you had a Jewish parent or grandparent, it meant that you were of "non-Aryan descent." If your parent or grandparent belonged to the Jewish religion, it was assumed that they and you were Jews. And in 1933 Nazi Germany, there were only two races: "Aryans" were those without any Jewish ancestors and thus with generations of pure "German blood" in their veins, while "non-Aryans" were those whether Jewish or Christian (like Werner Goldberg and his father) who had at least one Jewish parent or grand-parent.

Although the Nazi propaganda apparatus called the April 1933 regulation a racial law (a misconception unfortunately perpetuated by popular history), the sole criterion for inclusion in either the "Aryan" or "non-Aryan" camp was religion. And it wasn't even your own religion that mattered. It was that of your ancestors.

Almost from the beginning, the need for the German bu-reaucracy to further define the Jews was evident. The racial definitions of 1933 made necessary the Nuremberg Laws of 1935. But the flood of Nazi racial laws did not end there. Sub-sequent commentaries on the Nuremberg Laws continued to be issued until 1943, even as the last of the German Jews were being deported.

But what happened along the way to change the most racist and inhumane laws ever written by man into a virtual life-saving device for some of its intended victims? The answer is at once terribly complex and predictably simple.

If there are rules, then there must be exceptions. It has always been that way and that's the way it will always be. So why do we believe it was different when it came to deciding the ultimate fate of the Jews at the hands of the Nazis? Even the most unspeakable of horrors rarely affects the way human nature works. Who shall live and who shall die was not de-termined by God. Those decisions were made by men. The Nazis relied upon laws to guide them in making their consid-erations. These man-made laws contained a series of compli-cated loopholes big enough for almost half a million Jews to slip through. These are the Jews this book is about. It is often said that even God could not save the Jews of Europe. But these laws did.

Some among them were full Jews. And they were called

"privileged." To an outsider looking in on Nazi Germany, it seems absurd. What possible privileges could a Jew have under Hitler? One was the right to continue living their lives virtually the same as other Germans did. This gift of life was a surprise present that the "privileged Jews" never asked for, except perhaps in their dreams. Had they ever dared suggest such a thing, the Nazi hierarchy might have died laughing.

But these are the facts: At the end of World War II, there were still more than 28,000 registered full Jews living in Germany.[2] And they were not hiding in attics, forests and piles of rubble. Nor were they awaiting their turn to die in a Nazi concentration camp. Technically, Germany had already been proclaimed "Jew-free." But these Jews were free too. They could walk about the streets of Berlin and other German cities ducking Allied bombs with the rest of the civilian population. They did not have to wear the identifying yellow Star of David, (the six-pointed "Mogen David" imprinted with "Jude") as had other Jews. Those other Jews were now all gone to "the East," and these Jews remained behind—free and alive.

Almost all of these 28,000 "privileged Jews" lived as partners in mixed marriages. That is what saved their lives. A handful among them, those we would today call "single parents," were deported near the end of the war, but not to death camps. And almost all came home again.

It was only this large number of surviving Jews that prevented the total annihilation of European Jewry. For even the children of these mixed marriages (the Nazis called them Mischlinge, some historians prefer Mischlinge Jews) were spared by the Nazis.

A conservative tally shows 107,000 children of mixed marriages in Germany and Austria in 1939.[3] Higher figures also exist, but they include those Mischlinge being raised as Jews— a group which did not survive. Four years earlier, journalist George E. Sokolsky thought[4] the "fifty-percenters numbered between two and three million" in Germany. The number for the Czech Protektorat (which may also include the mixed

II. <u>Juden in Mischehe.</u>

a) <u>Jüdische Ehepartner.</u>

Im Gesamt-Judenregister war ursprünglich nur die Tatsache
einer Mischehe ohne Angabe, ob mit oder ohne Nachwuchs,
verzeichnet. Auf Grund der Ende letzten Jahres anlässlich
der Rückstellungsaktion erfolgten Neuanmeldungen von Misch-
ehenzugehörigkeit konnte die Zahl der Misch ehen mit Kindern, der bestehenden Schwangerschaften und der Jüdinnen
in kinderlosen Mischehen erfasst werden. Nicht dagegen erfasst wurden die männlichen Juden in kinderlosen Mischehen,
deren Zahl nur geschätzt werden kann.

Es ergibt sich zur Zeit folgendes Bild:

Mischehen	Ehemann jüdisch	Ehefrau jüdisch	Summa	
mit Kindern	3748	2290	6038	(davon 3080 mit Sperrstempel)
mit derzeitiger Schwanger-schaft	236	55	291	(ohne Stempel)
ohne Kinder	schätzungs-weise ca. 2000	1024	ca. 2000-3000	(ohne Stempel)
Summa	ca. 5000-6000	3369	Gesamtsumme der Juden in Mischehe ca. 8000-9000	

Die Voraussetzungen und damit die Zahlen ändern sich in
schwer festzuhaltender Weise fortgesetzt durch folgende Tat-
sachen:

Auflösung von Mischehen durch Tod oder Scheidung,
Abgänge durch Straffälligkeit,
Tod oder Geburt von Kindern.

Um die Weiterbehandlung der Mischehen möglichst wenig zu
komplizieren, empfiehlt sich, die bestehenden Schwangerschaften zunächst hinsichtlich der Rückstellungsfähigkeit
den Mischehen <u>mit Kindern</u> gleichzusetzen. Der ursprünglich

A page from Frau Slottke's list of Jewish Stay-Behind Groups in the Netherlands (see note 6). This sheet tabulates Jews in mixed marriages with
and without Mischlinge children. *(Photograph courtesy Rijksinstituut voor
Oorlogsdocumentatie, Amsterdam)*

marriage Jews) is estimated at 30,000.[5] In 1941, the last year
the Nazis even bothered to count them, there were nearly
21,000 Mischlinge in the Netherlands[6]—although one SS officer serving there thought the number might be as high as
300,000! And these early tabulations of Mischlinge population
are as good as later ones, for their numbers were never greatly
reduced by the Nazi terror.

Add to these figures the number of mixed marriage Jews
who survived at the end of the war; we already know of the
28,000 in Germany and there were close to 9,000 more in the
Netherlands.[7] That makes almost 200,000 lives saved just in
the Reich, the Protektorat and the Netherlands. And how
many more survived in Italy? Or in Bulgaria?[8] Indeed, their
numbers may never even have been totalled. Generally
speaking, the Nazi exemptions for Jews crossed European
frontiers with the first wave of goose-stepping shock troops.
If a captive nation were ever in doubt as to what official policy
to follow, they had only to look to the Reich example for guid-
ance. In most countries that saved Jewish lives. But not in
Poland; the Nazis considered all Poles racially inferior and
certainly wouldn't save a Jew just because he or she was married to a Pole. Yet the exemptions were extended to occupied
Russia by 1943,[9] although by then it was far too late for them
to do much good.

Almost certainly, had the intermarried Jews and their children not survived, their numbers would have been added to
the long columns of Jewish dead and we would today mourn
seven million Jewish victims of the Holocaust.

But are these children of mixed marriages really Jews? As
we shall see, the Nazi Party always thought they were. In
1983, the Central Conference of American Rabbis agreed to
recognize as Jews children with one Jewish parent of either
sex—thus ending a twenty-five century tradition[10] of defining
a Jew solely as the child of a Jewish mother. The American
Reform rabbinate[11] will now "presume" that a child of an
inter-married couple is Jewish if either of the parents are of

that faith. The two other major branches of contemporary Judaism, the Orthodox and Conservative movements, continue to adhere to the stricter definition.

Examining the reasons why the Nazis enabled a half-million Jews to survive while they coldbloodedly slaughtered six million others leads to a myriad of ironies. Only a generation before the Holocaust, the nucleus of this group of surviving Jews—the Jews in mixed marriages—had been perceived by their fellow Jews as being the greatest threat to the continued existence of German Jewry. Interestingly enough, that same concern about intermarriages, albeit from the opposite perspective, was first expressed by German Christian church leaders as early as the eleventh century. With contemporary figures for intermarriage in the United States estimated at 40 percent, some American Jewish leaders have a similar fear. Orthodox Rabbi Naftali Halberstam of Brooklyn's World Jewish Genealogy Organization, in a January 1984 open letter, wrote "intermarriage has done to Our People [sic] the same damage our enemies sought to inflict four decades ago." That same month, a news report placed current European intermarriages even higher—at 50 percent![12]

In 1911, the Jewish author of a widely read book, *Der Untergang der deutschen Juden (The Decline of the German Jews)*,[13] predicted there would not be a single German Jew alive by the year 2000. He was almost right, but for all the wrong reasons. The author wasn't prescient enough to forecast the Holocaust—no one could have done that. Instead, he saw intermarriage and conversion as the tools of destruction. A generation later, conversion alone couldn't save the lives of Jews, as it so often had done in times past. The Holocaust wasn't the Spanish Inquisition, and many converted Jews— even some who had become Christian priests—were sent to concentration camps because they were still considered to be racial Jews.[14] But it was intermarriage, the second of the author's twin evils, that kept his prediction from premature birth.

During 1933, the first full year of Nazi rule, 44 percent of all marriages[15] contracted by Jews in Germany were interfaith—a higher estimate than even the current estimate for such marriages in the United States. Just the very thought of intermarriage between German and Jew was enough to bring out the worst in the Nazis who saw it as the embodiment of Rassenschande (racial defilement), the most terrible of sexual sins. The Law for the Protection of German Blood and Honor, one of the group of Nuremberg Laws enacted on 15 September 1935, officially prohibited Jewish-Aryan marriages, but did nothing about those in existence. Yet there were already far too many of these for the Nazis not to notice. Consider these statistics: a 1938 tally showed one out of ten Jews in Germany[16] living in a mixed marriage. A year later, other figures claimed that 25 percent[17] of all existing marriages involving Jews were mixed. At least one-third of Berlin's Jews[18] were married to Christians. As far as the children of these mixed marriages—the Mischlinge—were concerned, only 9.9 percent[19] were being raised as Jews. The mixed marriage Jews in these later surveys were apparently reconciled to living under the constraint of the Nazi regulations: after six years of the increasing hostility of the regime, they had not emigrated.

As long as there were Jews remaining in mixed marriages, the long-range Nazi plan to totally isolate the Jews from the general population was frustrated. But the Nazis would find a way to get around this delay much easier than they could solve another related problem. The large number of intermarriages was beginning to have an effect upon blind acceptance of a basic tenet of Nazi ideology—the alleged racial inferiority of the Jew. German spouses were already beginning to ask, "If the Jew is supposed to be such a subhuman species, why do I find being married to one so enjoyable?" Fortunately, few minds were swayed by the Nazi response.

However, it wasn't an attack of belated concern over the plight of racially confused Germans like the Goldberg family that brought about the 1935 definition of what comprised a Jew in the eyes of the Nazis and made possible the many exemptions from that interpretation. Of all things, it was the Japanese! The Nazis were hardly prepared for the official reaction of the Japanese to the 1933 "Aryan" laws. The cement on the foundation of the future fascist Axis was hardly dry when Japan lodged a none-too-subtle indication of her intense displeasure over the clear implication that non-Aryans (the Japanese, for example) were inferior to Aryans (the Germans).[20] The Foreign Office held several meetings with Interior Ministry representatives during 1934, but no one could come up with an explanation that was satisfactory to the Japanese.

This unexpected side effect of the anti-Jewish decrees served to focus the attention of the bureaucrats upon what many saw as the real problem with the laws. The term "non-Aryan" was being used to define not only full Jews—those with four Jewish grandparents—but three-quarter Jews, half-Jews and even one-quarter Jews. The bureaucrats knew what the future held for the Jews; they were already hard at work planning it. To include these fractional Jews in the more drastic measures to come would create difficulties which no bureaucrat wished to face. To narrow the target group, a precise and clear-cut definition of just what was meant by "Jew" was mandatory. The task for the bureaucrats was to succeed where centuries of Talmudic scholars had failed. Dr. Hans Globke of the Interior Ministry later claimed that the subsequent laws were designed "to protect those Jews most like us."[21] (By this, Globke meant those Jews who were close to the way of life of the bureaucrats—as well as those married to people in their circle.) And he was right!

By the beginning of 1935, the issue was being widely discussed in Nazi Party circles. At one meeting, Dr. Kurt Blome,[22] the secretary of the German medical association, loudly opposed any plans for the creation of a "third race." His suggestion was that one-quarter Jews be counted as Ger-

mans and half-Jews be relegated to the Jewish column. Blome
believed that "among half-Jews, the Jewish genes are notoriously dominant." The Nazi Party officially endorsed and
adopted Blome's view, but it never succeeded in imposing that
policy on the Interior Ministry. Fortunately for the Mischlinge,
it was there that the bureaucrats were writing the Nuremberg
Laws.

The Interior Ministry bureaucrat with responsibility for the
drafting of the laws was Ministerialrat (Administrative Advisor to the Ministry) Dr. Bernhard Lösener, who had been
transferred to the Ministry after long service in the customs
office. Lösener worked directly under Staatsekretär (Under
Secretary) of Constitution and Law Dr. Wilhelm Stuckart.
While both Stuckart and Lösener were officially assigned to
the fractional Jew question, Lösener can unquestionably be
considered as being both father and savior of the Mischlinge.
It was Lösener who rejected the Nazi Party proposal to equate
half-Jews with full Jews, and this decision ultimately saved
the Mischlinge. Lösener successfully employed twisted Nazi
logic to argue that such an equation would instead strengthen
the Jewish side because "in principle, the half-Jew should be
regarded as a more serious enemy than the full Jew because,
in addition to Jewish characteristics, he possesses so many
Germanic ones which the full Jew lacks."

To counter this genetic threat, Lösener proposed sifting the
half-Jews into two groups. Those who belonged to the Jewish
religion or were married to a Jewish person would be counted
as Jews. The others wouldn't.

This was the basis of the First Regulation to the Reich Citizenship Law, issued on 14 November 1935. The long period
of uncertainty experienced by Werner Goldberg and thousands
of others had officially come to an end. Now, not just Goldberg
but *everybody* would know exactly where they stood in the
Nazi racial structure.

Described as Jews were:
1. those who were descended from at least three Jewish
   grandparents (e.g. full Jews and three-quarter Jews).

2. or were descended from two Jewish grandparents (e.g. half-Jews) *and* met any of these all-important requirements:
   (a) belonged to the Jewish religious community on 15 September 1935 or joined it subsequently.
   (b) *or* were married to a Jewish person as of that date, or subsequently.
   (c) *or* were the offspring of a marriage with a three-quarter or full Jew after the 15 September 1935 law prohibiting new intermarriages went into effect.
   (d) *or* were the offspring of an extramarital relationship with a three-quarter or full Jew and born out of wedlock after 31 July 1936. (This was one of the very few restrictions placed upon an illegitimate child by the Nazis. It was designed to even further remove the half-Jews from the sexual and social circles of full Jews.)

The half-Jews in the above categories became the nucleus of what are known as the Jewish Mischlinge. Very few of their number survived the war. As we shall see, most parents of Mischlinge opted to protect their offspring by raising them as Christians, when given the choice.

The vital determination of the status of the grandparent, so very important in both the full or three-quarter Jew and half-Jew classifications, was based upon the "presumption" (again!) that if a person formally belonged to the Jewish religious community (paid taxes to and was registered at the Gemeinde,[23] the administrative office of the Jewish community), that person was a Jew.

Now defined for the first time not as a Jew (although still not an Aryan either) but as an "individual of mixed blood" (the actual category was not named at the time the law was announced) was any individual who:

1. was descended from two Jewish grandparents (thus, half-Jews) who did not adhere to or had left the Jewish religion as of 15 September 1935 and did not subsequently rejoin it.

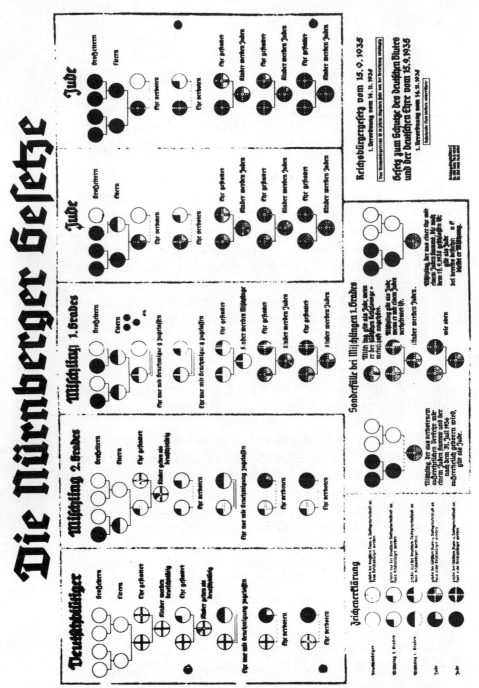

In case there was ever any doubt about a person's status, all one had to do was consult this handy chart of the Nuremberg Laws' racial classifications. This particular example once hung on the wall of Gestapo headquarters in Amsterdam. *(Photograph courtesy Rijksinstituut voor Oorlogsdocumentatie, Amsterdam)*

2. *and* was not married to a Jewish person on 15 September 1935 or subsequently.

Eventually, the half-Jews who met these requirements would be called "Mischlinge of the First Degree." The bureaucrats at the Interior Ministry thought of the name afterwards. They must have been particularly pleased with their choice, for "Mischling" means "mongrel."[24]

But this mocking term, better suited to a barnyard, did not disappear from our world with the fall of the Third Reich. "Mischling" is still used today by the white supremacist government of the Republic of South Africa to denote the offspring of mixed racial marriages.[25]

The Interior Ministry ruling that gave the Mischlinge their name also created "Mischlinge of the Second Degree" status for those descended from only one Jewish grandparent.

What would all this have meant had it occurred in the United States in early 1981 and not in Nazi Germany in 1935? Many prominent Americans, children of mixed marriages like authors J. D. Salinger and Nelson Algren, actress Goldie Hawn, historian James Thomas Flexner, San Francisco Mayor Dianne Feinstein, former presidential advisor Theodore C. Sorensen and United States Senator William S. Cohen of Maine, would be classified as Mischlinge of the First Degree—members of a third race.[26] Also placed in that category would be the children of well-known personalities in mixed marriages, like those of actors Paul Newman and Tony Curtis (including his daughter, actress Jamie Lee Curtis), singer Eddie Fisher (although his daughter, actress Carrie Fisher, would have automatically been reclassified as a Jew when she later married singer Paul Simon), author William Styron, songwriter Irving Berlin, and actress Lauren Bacall. How the racially crazed Nazis would have classified the three daughters of black singer Diana Ross by her marriage to a Jewish publicist is anybody's guess.[27]

Contemporary American Mischlinge of the Second Degree would include Secretary of Defense Caspar W. Weinberger and his predecessor James R. Schlesinger, and former pres-

idential candidate Senator Barry M. Goldwater. One can play
this same game of "what if" in virtually any nation on the
globe. It has been conservatively estimated that there are
today over two million children of Jewish-Christian mixed
marriages throughout the world.

Thus, what Ministerialrat Lösener had succeeded in doing
in 1935 was to split the non-Aryans legally into two distinct
groups: Mischlinge and Jews. From this point on, the Mischlinge were removed from the destruction process. All of the
subsequent measures of destruction were to be aimed solely
at the Jews. At least on paper, the Mischlinge were not Jews.
And with only very few exceptions, the Mischlinge were fated
to be left alone. (But, as we shall later see, a Mischling could
be denounced for acting, in some way, "like a full Jew." And
it could cost his life.)

The amount of Jewish blood in one's veins was not the issue—a subsequent generation of popular mythology to the
contrary. It was the amount of *German blood* that counted.
The Nazis were reluctant to spill it needlessly, and it became
a prime factor in saving Jewish lives.

But if you are looking for something even more extraordinary, consider the wording of Article Seven of the 14 November 1935 ordinance. In its entirety it gives "The Führer
and Reich Chancellor" the right to grant exemptions from the
ordinances.[28]

There it is again—exemptions. This time it meant that Hit-
ler, with a mere stroke of his pen, had the power to elevate
Mischlinge of the First Degree (should they ever become an
endangered species) to a higher and safer racial classification.
Since the Nazis had made up all this racial foolishness to begin
with, all the Führer was really doing was pretending to play
God by deciding whether to make a worthy Mischling of the
First Degree into either a full Aryan or a Mischling of the
Second Degree.

Article Seven became the basis for the Honorary Aryan
classifications, which are dealt with in detail later. Apparently

even Hitler knew at least 340 "first-rate Jews"[29] (as Hannah Arendt has called them) whom he either raised to the status of Germans or granted the privileges of half-Jews. Either action was sufficient to keep them alive. There were 260 other Jews[30] on Hitler's waiting list for this "honor," having received the Führer's personal promise of elevation. What did it take to qualify? When Marshal Ion Antonescu, the Rumanian dictator who suffered from the same stomach trouble as Reichsführer Hitler, sent the Führer his Jewish cook, a Fräulein Kunde, Himmler was livid. After the Gestapo chief questioned the propriety of having a Jew prepare the Führer's food, Hitler turned furiously to an aide and said, "Aryanize the Kunde family!"[31]

Laws can be revoked, but death can't. And once the destruction process became irreversible, the bureaucrats were kept busy creating additional laws to further expand the Nuremberg guidelines. With one hand, the civil servants were signing orders snuffing out millions of Jewish lives across Europe. And with the other, they were writing laws to save the lives of Jews—the parents of the Mischlinge.

In many cases, the non-Jewish partners in mixed marriages often came from circles that were close to the Nazi Party leadership, the upper echelons of the civil service, and even the army. Or they belonged to these groups themselves. These were the spouses of Hans Globke's "Jews most like us." One reason that the Nazis hesitated to use force against the Jewish partners in mixed marriages was a desire not to risk the displeasure of the powerful families and friends of Germans married to Jews. After all, the Nazis didn't want to get into any more internal squabbles than necessary.

Even if the Nazis had succeeded in forcibly dissolving all existing mixed marriages, what would they then do with the younger children from these marriages? Who would educate and look after them? What would be the responsibility of the state toward them?

These were weighty considerations, and they concerned

those in the decision-making capacities of the Nazi hierarchy.
As late as 1944, Artur von Seyss-Inquart, German high commissioner of the Netherlands (later hanged at Nuremberg as
a war criminal), wrote Hitler's deputy Martin Bormann:

"The following is to be considered with respect to (mixed)
marriages in which there are children. If one parent is brought
to a concentration camp and then probably to labor in the East,
the children will always be under the impression that we took
the parent away from them. As a matter of fact, the offspring
of mixed marriages are more troublesome than full Jews. In
political trials, for example, we can determine that it is pre-
cisely these offspring who start or carry out most of the assassination attempts or sabotage. If we now introduced a
measure that is sure to release the hatred of these people,
then we will have a group in our midst with which we will
hardly be able to deal in any way save separation."[32]

One is truly amazed to find such heartfelt concern expressed
by the Nazis at a time when they were working overtime
cramming the bodies of full Jewish children into the ovens of
the "East."

The ultimate solution to the Mischlinge dilemma in Germany
did not call for the forced separation of the parents of the
Mischlinge. Instead, it protected them. Six months before the
Nazi invasion of Poland, a decree issued by Reichsmarschal
Hermann Göring created the category of "privileged mixed
marriages." The determining factor as to whether a mixed
marriage was to be considered privileged or non-privileged
was the current religious affiliation of the couple's children.

In the case of a German man with a Jewish wife, the marriage was considered privileged if the children (the Mischlinge)
of the couple were not raised as Jews (like Werner Goldberg)
or if the pair were childless.

However, it was somewhat more difficult to obtain privileged status if a German woman had chosen to take a Jewish
husband. If their children were not being raised as Jews, the

marriage was privileged. But if the couple were childless, they were classified as non-privileged. This sexist distinction on the part of the Nazis placed many of the childless Jewish husbands in mixed marriages in jeopardy, but only for a short time—until the guidelines for privileged and non-privileged status began to overlap. Until that happened, the only life insurance for a Jew in Nazi Germany was an Aryan wife and Mischlinge children.

The continuing trend toward exempting even more mixed marriage Jews from the anti-Jewish measures eventually resulted in Jews whose marriages had been terminated by divorce or death receiving privileged status, provided they were the parent of a Mischling child who had been killed in action. Even the Jewish husband in a childless mixed marriage would be classified as privileged if he had lost his only child in the service of the Fatherland. In the gray area of privileged mixed marriages, there was always room for further exceptions.

Once the deportations of Jews began in the fall of 1941, the Jews in non-privileged mixed marriages learned that they would be receiving a special gift from the Nazis. Just like the Jews who held privileged mixed marriage status, they were to be spared from deportation to the death camps. Although the distinctions between the privileged and non-privileged classifications occasionally became blurred, the Nazis always maintained both as separate entities.

In Göring's original classifications, bringing up Mischlinge children as Jews meant that the marriage was not privileged. So it wasn't really surprising that the privileged mixed marriages outnumbered the others by three to one.[33]

For a Jew, privileged mixed marriage status became a virtual courtesy card—entitling the lucky holder to receive special treatment.[34] The first of these benefits was the exemption from the Jewish Tenancy Law. It was this decree which "legally" enabled the Nazis to uproot Jewish families from their homes and move them into Judenhaüser—apartments already

occupied by other Jews—thus closely confining them within
the ghetto. By being exempt from this procedure, the Jews
in privileged mixed marriages were not only separated from
the "other" Jews, but they were removed from the isolations
under which those Jews were now placed and which subsequently made easy their identification and deportation.

The Jews in privileged mixed marriages were also exempted
from compulsory membership in Die Reichsvereinigung der
Juden in Deutschland (The Reich Association of Jews in Germany).[35] It was this tool of the Nazis, nominally headed by
Rabbi Dr. Leo Baeck, that compiled the lists of Jews for deportation and collaborated with the Nazis in dispersing the
Jews from the ghettos to the death camps. This exemption
helped save the lives of the privileged mixed marriage Jews.[36]

But of all the exemptions, the most important was that from
the decree ordering all Jews to wear the yellow star. Although
they were issued the yellow Star of David, the Jews in privileged mixed marriages did not have to wear it on their clothes
or fasten it to their doors. They were not outwardly identified
as Jews, either by confinement to the ghetto, appearance on
the internally compiled official lists of Jews, or by the immediately recognizable sight of the yellow star sewn to their
outer garments. These exemptions effectively removed the
privileged mixed marriage Jews from each stage of the process
that would only end with the deaths of those Jews who had
chosen to marry within their own faith.[37]

The only restrictive measures which the privileged mixed
marriage Jews were not exempted from were those which already were in effect. Thus, they were still required to carry
the identification card marked with a "J." In some countries,
notably the Netherlands, the degree of shading of the rubber
stamped "J" determined the status of the Jew carrying the
card. The identity card for a full Jew married to another Jew
bore a closed "J" stamped in blue ink. A full Jew in a mixed
marriage carried an identical card save for the fact that the

letter "J" was open and stamped in red ink. It was to be one of history's simplest but cruelest distinctions[38] between life and death.

The Jews in privileged mixed marriages were required to show their identity card to every civil servant they were dealing with before being asked to verify their status. They also had to give their identity number on all correspondence. Further, they had to have either an acceptable Jewish name (a list was available) or add Israel or Sara to their first name. Thus, Werner Goldberg's father would receive mail addressed to "Herrn Albert Israel Goldberg" and bearing the ironical closing salutation of "Heil Hitler!"

But they were exempted from all the other degrading, humiliating and harmful measures which made life before deportation a living hell for the rest of the Jews. On a day-to-day level, the lives of the privileged Jews hardly differed from those of other Germans. They received the same food as non-Jews: meat, poultry, fish, eggs, white bread, milk and fruit. They also received clothes and cigarette stamps, even shaving cream—all things denied to those who had to wear the yellow star. Their food stamps were not marked with a "J," nor were they restricted to specified short shopping hours or limited to certain approved shops.

Unlike the other Jews, they were allowed to leave their places of residence without special authorization by the police and could sit wherever they liked on trains, streetcars, subways or elevated trains without restriction. They could enter the waiting rooms and were not forced to relinquish their seats to every Nazi. They were allowed to use public telephones and automatic ticket vending machines. They could go to any hairdresser and buy any book or newspaper they pleased.

These Jews had control over their own property and were not forced to give up their gold, silver or jewelry. They could own typewriters, cameras, furs, woolens, skiing outfits and textiles. The Nazis allowed them to keep and wear medals and badges of honor given to them. They could have pets (dogs, cats, birds) and they were free to go to restaurants, theaters, concert halls, and to the movies.

They did not have to pay the Sozialausgleichsabgabe (Social Equalization Tax), the special income tax levied on Jews on top of the regular income tax, which amounted to 15 per cent of a person's income. Jewish fathers were allowed to claim their Mischlinge children as tax exemptions, and all privileged mixed marriage Jews benefitted from the same tax exemptions as non-Jews.

The Jews in this category were neither separated from others at their workplace or at air raid shelters. They received the same pay, special bonuses, extra pay, and support as did other workers, and were subject to the same period of notice of dismissal as they. In short, they shared full rights and benefits with German workers. But why shouldn't they? After all, they were loyal Germans—an important point to remember. Their sons could even serve in the German armed forces during the first year of the war.

There was always a fear that one day these privileges would come to an end. That fear was almost realized when just two months after the January 1942 first Final Solution Conference, Nazi Party hardliners worked out a law which would have immediately dissolved all existing "racially" mixed marriages. At the last minute, the Catholic archbishop of Berlin (later named a cardinal), Count Konrad von Preysing, raised his objections. The Catholic Church would not be delighted with the prospect of so many enforced divorces, which would be seen by the Vatican as a direct violation of one of the most basic tenets of the Church. This left the Nazis with a dilemma: How would they now accomplish their purpose if the divorces were restricted to Jews who had married Protestants, while those married to Catholics would still remain legally wed? To continue with the entire divorce plan, over the objections of von Preysing, might even—God forbid—provoke the otherwise silent Pope Pius XII. Was it worth risking a statement by the

Pope, perhaps calling attention to the deportation of the Jews, just to be able to catch another 28,000 Jews in the Nazi net and make Germany totally Judenrein (free of Jews)?[39]

Apparently not, for a jurist, perhaps somewhat relieved by this almost divine intercession, quickly pointed out that the German courts would become hopelessly clogged by attempting to process this large number of simultaneous divorces. Indeed, it may even have been the Justice Ministry's opposition to the proposed law that somehow prompted von Preysing to take a last-minute stand on the issue. And so the plan, if not the idea, was temporarily shelved.

Since instant divorce would also have meant an instant death sentence for the Jewish partner in the mixed marriage, the Nazis may have feared having more than just a legal battle on their hands. Eventually the bureaucracy submitted the entire mixed marriage question to Hitler for a decision, but the Führer refused to even consider it.[40] Thus, Hitler, by his inaction, and von Preysing, by his courageous action, became the highly unlikely twin saviors of the Jews in mixed marriages.

28,000 Jews walking around Germany without their yellow stars! Didn't any top Nazis notice? One day Dr. Joseph Goebbels did. He even wrote a letter to Heinrich Himmler about it. Reichsführer SS Himmler may have thought it a bit odd to have come from Goebbels, for wasn't the stepfather of the Propaganda Minister's wife, Magda, a Jewish pharmacist named Friedländer?[41] Regardless, Himmler responded with an order that Jewish spouses in mixed marriages be rounded up in what was to become known as the Fabrik Aktion. It was the only time that the Nazis moved against the mixed marriage Jews, and in turn, it precipitated the only known instance in the history of the Third Reich of a public protest demonstration by Germans against the Nazi arrests (or even treatment) of Jews.

Werner Goldberg's father was among those arrested. Werner is perhaps the only living eyewitness to the protest demonstration.[42] "One day there came what I feared the most," remembers Goldberg. "They took my father. He got a paper that he should report to the Arbeitsamt [work office] in Berlin-Neukölln on Fontane-Promenade. When I came home from work my mother said, 'Father went at 8:00 A.M. to the work office and he has still not come back.'

"I took a taxi to the building. It was evening, but not yet very cold. It was March [1943] and I asked some people sitting there in the park if they had seen anything. One of them told me that in the morning 'there came a lot of cars, gray SS cars, and they took the people who were there away with them.' 'Do you know where they went to?' I asked. 'No,' they said, 'but it was an awful sight.'

"I went on foot through the area asking everyone whether they had seen anything. Finally one person told me that earlier that evening, he had seen many people brought to the 'Clou' on the Leipzigstrasse at the corner of Mauerstrasse. And so I went there. The 'Clou' had once been a popular ballroom but now it was a Gestapo prison. There were a lot of people standing outside but none of them could tell me if this was the only station where people were brought or who was being held inside. I did see an officer in a Luftwaffe uniform. He was shouting very loudly for the release of his wife.

"Finally a soldier told me that 'there are also people in the Rosenstrasse, in the former administration building of the Jewish community. Here there are only wives. The men are at the Rosenstrasse. If you search for your father, go there.'

"It was now very late in the evening and when I got to the Rosenstrasse the street was sealed off. On one side stood the police. And in front of them were about 200 or 300 civilians, mostly women. Of course I did not know it at the time, but this was the beginning of the massive protest by hundreds of Aryan spouses against the arrests of their Jewish husbands.

"For the first time, Jews in privileged mixed marriages had been arrested and now they were awaiting transport to concentration camps. But the people outside were all waiting for their relatives to be set free. 'Surely this must be some sort of administrative mistake,' they were saying. 'We live in privileged mixed marriages!' But this was also the first time that German citizens had ever staged a mass protest against the Nazis. The women began to chant 'Gebt unsere Männer frei!' ["Set our husbands free"] demanding that their husbands be returned to them. Some of the women, in pairs of two, silently walked down the street to the Reichluftfahrtministerium [Air Force Ministry] where Reichsmarschall Hermann Göring had his office. There they stood, just staring into the lighted windows. After all, it was Göring who had created the privileged mixed marriage status, and now look at what was happening! But throughout this the police did nothing. They took no action against the women. They too were Germans.

"I went to a pay telephone and called my brother Günther. He is a year younger than me and he lived at home with us. I told him that since it was impossible to get any information now, we should take turns watching here, hour by hour, to see what would happen. I told him I would stay through the night. 'You come at 6:00 A.M.,' I said, 'and then I go home.' Günther came and stayed through the afternoon. Then I came back. We continued to take turns for two days. One of us was always there. Watching. Waiting.

"On the second day the Nazis came with the closed moving vans, the type they used for carrying away the Jews. We could not see what was going on inside of them. Later, two cars came and parked in front of the building. I crossed over and saw an SS man. I gave him a letter and asked him to give it to the officer in charge. He said he would do it and that he would give me a sign when it was done. I waited. But there was nothing. I still did not know if my father was even in this building.

"In the afternoon of the third day, there came a military vehicle, an open car with four SS officers. I thought I recognized one of the men in the front of the car as being Gerhard Wolff, one of my former classmates. I crossed through the

police lines and grabbed the end of his jacket. It was him—
and he recognized me!

"I told him that I believed that my father was inside this
building. 'You are in luck,' Gerhard replied, 'I am the chief
of this Aktion. But I can't speak to you here. Call me in the
evening.' And he gave me a card with his telephone number.
That evening he confirmed my worst fears: 'Yes, your father
is in the building. But don't be afraid. I will arrange his coming
out.'

"That was the last time I talked with Gerhard. The next
morning, very early—about five or six—the doorbell at our
house was ringing and my father was there. That night there
had been a big air raid, many bombs had fallen all over Berlin.
As my father later told us, when the air raid alarm was sound-
ed, every light in the building was turned off. A man wearing
a uniform, and with a headlamp, came into the room where
my father was being held and cried out 'Goldberg!' Of course,
my father thought this meant the end for him. The man ordered him to come out and my father was very scared. He
took my father down the stairs, opened the front door, and
shoved him outside. Then the door clanged shut behind my
father. As he stood there on the street, the night sky was
brightly lit from the bombings. The air raid continued all during the time it took my father to walk the twenty kilometers
[about twelve miles] from the Rosenstrasse in Berlin-Mitte to
our home in Grunewald. But by morning it was over and he
was home safe. The only papers my father had on him were
those which said he had been under arrest but was now free.
They were signed by the SS.

"Later that day the Nazis freed the other men in the building. Some said that Göring had personally stopped this Aktion.
Maybe it was because of that Luftwaffe officer with the Jewish
wife? If Göring had paid no attention to the women outside
his office, he may have listened to the pleas of this officer.
But it was already too late for some of the men who had been

in the room with my father. They had been transported to the camps—probably in the two vans which I had seen.

"As to Gerhard Wolff: some years ago I heard from somebody who had been on a Caribbean island and had seen Wolff there. They said you would hardly know it is him because his face is so badly disfigured—probably from a bomb. But they did speak to him. He is one of those who can not come back to Germany because he has committed so many war crimes. Later I inquired about him at the archives of the war criminals. But there are so many Gerhard Wolffs in their files that it is difficult to find the right one."

The Fabrik Aktion was to be the only Nazi action taken against those in privileged mixed marriages to result in deportation of the Jewish spouses. How many were arrested? One can only guess, but even though only a relative handful died in the camps, the lesson was not lost upon those who were freed. The gift of life as a privileged Jew was not to be taken for granted. The privileges could be revoked at any time and without warning, solely upon the whim of the Nazis. The many pleas to Göring to return the few who had already been deported fell upon deaf ears. The SS was allowed to have their human sacrifice, and the propaganda value to the Nazis should not be underestimated. Spread by word of mouth throughout the Jewish mixed marriage families, it was a chilling reminder of how the fate that had befallen the rest of the Jewish side of the family would be shared by the Jewish spouse if he or she didn't toe the fine line of acceptable behavior tolerated by the Nazis.

Most of the time, the pressures upon the Aryan spouse in a privileged mixed marriage were far from subtle. Civil servants, party hacks and functionaries, and even women's groups threatened, cajoled, jeered and otherwise humiliated the Aryan spouse (almost always the German woman) in a concerted effort to make her divorce her Jewish husband. To their everlasting credit, very few succumbed to the pressure. To do so would mean serving their former spouse with both divorce and death papers. For the Jewish spouse, a divorce would mean a full lifting of all privileges, making him just another Jew in Hitler's Jew-free Germany, with absolutely no official protection. By remaining loyal to their husbands, these Aryan women saved a significant number of Jewish lives. Yet, unlike other heroic Christians, they have never been memorialized on Jerusalem's Street of the Righteous Gentiles, the road of honor near the Yad Vashem Holocaust Memorial.

One situation where pressure was placed upon the male Aryan was in the case of German Army Generalmajor (equivalent of a U.S. brigadier general) Riemann. His superiors gave him an ultimatum: either divorce his Jewish wife or resign his military commission. The General chose to resign, although conceivably he could have appealed all the way up to Hitler. Riemann not only continued to live with his wife throughout the war years, but also hid his full Jewish brother-in-law in the cellar until the liberation of Berlin.[43]

The options open to the Nazis were becoming limited. Pressure was not effective and the use of force to eliminate mixed marriages was all but ruled out after the Fabrik Aktion. Yet, almost two years earlier, the Nazis had seriously considered a far deadlier method for removing the thorn in their sides. The fate of the Jews in mixed marriages was always closely linked to that of the Mischlinge of the First Degree simply because they were the parents of the Mischlinge. As Adolf Eichmann put it, both problems "were surrounded by a forest of difficulties." Fortunately for the Mischlinge and their parents, the Nazis were never able to see beyond the trees.[44]

Toward the end of 1941, Nazi Party circles began a campaign to equate the Mischlinge with the Jews. The Final Solution was imminent, but the degree of its finality remained unresolved. The Nazi Party wanted to subject the Mischlinge to the same Final Solution as the Jews, but the civil servants did not want to see the Mischlinge killed. The same bureaucrats who fought the Party to create the Mischlinge in 1935, now had to fight to keep them alive. To the bureaucrats, the Mischlinge were the children of those Jews "most like us."

The delegates to the first Final Solution conference, held at Am Grossen Wannsee, a suburb of Berlin, on 20 January 1942, devoted considerable discussion to the proposal to equate Mischlinge of the First Degree with Jews. (By comparison, the decision to exterminate the Jews of Europe totally was made in a matter of minutes.) Staatssekretär Dr. Wilhelm Stuckart pleaded that "deporting the half-Jews would mean abandoning that half of their blood which is German." As can be expected, the Nazis would provide exceptions for this new Mischlinge-Jew equation. These would be granted to Mischlinge of the First Degree married to Germans who had children (their offspring would be Mischlinge of the Second Degree) and to those Mischlinge who "by reason of services rendered to the German people, had been accorded liberation permits."

At the second Final Solution conference, chaired by Adolf Eichmann, the Nazis laid their trump card on the table. A proposal was submitted which called for the voluntary sterilization of all Mischlinge of the First Degree. Once rendered unable to reproduce, after a while the Mischlinge would just cease to exist. It was argued that "the Mischling, facing the choice of evacuation [read deportation] or sterilization, would prefer sterilization." Stuckart, who would rather see Mischlinge not breed than dead, agreed with the proposal, although he must have considered it a setback. Earlier, citing "the half-Jews' intelligence and excellent education," Stuckart said he would "prefer" to see them "die a natural death" even though "three to four decades may be necessary to achieve this purpose." Although it would require a major medical effort, sterilization would be quicker.

At the third Final Solution conference, the participants were told that the Mischlinge could be sterilized without disrupting the war machinery. It was agreed that a sterilization program would be implemented "without further ado." Voluntarily submitting to sterilization was to be the price paid by the

Mischling "for graciously allowing him to remain in Reich territory"—quid pro quo. A duly sterilized Mischling could then live out the rest of his or her life in peace, if not in fecundity.

First, a cost-effective method for the mass sterilization of the 39,000 Mischlinge of the First Degree still of childbearing age had to be found. That plum assignment went to Dr. Josef Mengele. Thus the gruesome and hideous operations performed by Mengele and his crew of butchers upon helpless Jewish inmates of concentration camps were originally conceived to find the cheapest method for sterilizing other Jews— the Mischlinge who would then be allowed to live. Mengele could never convince Eichmann that his surgical procedures were cost efficient, so the entire Mischlinge sterilization plan was abandoned, but not before horrible disfigurements and deaths had been inflicted upon thousands of innocent victims. Even so, doctors at Auschwitz continued their barbaric experiments upon Jewish women until late 1944.

There were some in the Nazi hierarchy who felt the sterilization plan should be salvaged for those Jews in mixed marriages still capable of bearing children, a group much smaller in number than the comparable Mischlinge. Eichmann, by now preoccupied with the killing process—a system that worked cheaply and effectively—decided to let the privileged mixed marriage Jews die off naturally. As for the Mischlinge, he would deal with them as he was now dealing with the Jews— but only after Germany had won the war.

But the sterilization concept wasn't dead yet. It found a new home in Nazi-occupied Holland, where a Jew in a mixed marriage had to produce a certificate of sterilization before being issued the open red "J," the identity card stamp they needed to stay alive. Unfortunately, many Jews needlessly subjected themselves to the sterilization procedures. Needlessly? Indeed! A booming trade selling phony sterilization certificates quickly sprang up. These bogus certificates were of such good quality they invariably fooled the authorities. Where could the Jews buy them? From agents of the Gestapo

who made a comfortable living peddling paper protection to
the Jews.[45]

Of the two major surviving groups of Dutch Jewry at the
end of the war, by far the greatest number is comprised of
the Jews who lived in mixed marriages. The remainder con-
sists of those Jews who successfully lived in hiding, the Anne
Franks who were never discovered.

*Once Heinrich Himmler set out to have a first hand
look at the efficiency of the Nazi mobile killing
units. He requested that one of the commanders
shoot a batch of one hundred Jews so that Himmler
could see what a "liquidation" looked like. His host
consented and rounded up the victims. All but two
were male. Seconds before the shooting was to
commence, Himmler raised his hand. He had
spotted in the group a young boy, about twenty, who
had blue eyes and blond hair. While the
executioners stood by with their loaded guns,
Himmler approached the youth.*

"Are you a Jew?" asked Himmler.

"Yes."

"Are both of your parents Jews?"

"Yes."

*Himmler thought for a moment, and then asked,
"Do you have any ancestors who were not Jews?"*

"No," replied the youth.

*Himmler shrugged his shoulders. "Then I can't
help you!" he said as he walked away.*

The firing began.

As told by RAUL HILBERG in
The Destruction of the European Jews.

Chapter Two

The Sound of Blowing Grass

IT WAS A CLASSIC piece of war propaganda designed to inspire those on the home front, and it virtually fell from heaven into the lap of the Nazis. A few weeks after the start of World War II, a young German soldier in his Wehrmacht uniform sat casually for a series of photographs in a civilian photographer's studio in a small German village just a few kilometers from the Polish frontier. The finished prints were to be sent to the soldier's family in Berlin, but the photographer had a better idea. In a burst of pride and patriotism, he sent a negative to the Reich Ministry of Propaganda and Public Enlightenment. The minions of Dr. Joseph Goebbels also thought they knew a good thing when they saw it, and within days a photograph of the young soldier began to appear in newspapers throughout Germany.

The caption on the photograph read "The Perfect Aryan Soldier,"[1] and so indeed he appears to be. What a great joy it must have been for the Nazis to find this idealized, almost mythological representation of the German fighting man— truly a worthy addition to the depictions in the official Nazi gallery of racially pure Aryan types. Only months before, Paul Keck's painting of the ideal German girl had been the stellar attraction at the 1939 Exhibition of German Art—and now here was her mate! This soldier of Hitler's Germany, blond hair peeking from beneath his Wehrmacht helmet, blue eyes staring sternly and yet somewhat dreamily ahead as if he had seen the true vision of the Thousand Year Reich. A real Nordic

Hero, he looked as if he had stepped off the cover of *Neues Volk*, the calendar of the Nazi Office of Racial Politics. He was the *new* Germanic Race.

Perhaps fortunately for everyone concerned, the Nazis never learned that their "Perfect Aryan Soldier" wasn't an Aryan. He was Private Werner Goldberg of the Wehrmacht, and he was a Mischling, the son of a Jew.[2]

Goldberg was one of nearly 45,000 male Mischlinge of the First Degree. Like so many other children of mixed marriage Jews, Goldberg wore the swastika and fought for Hitler during the successful 1939–40 Blitzkrieg campaigns which rapidly conquered Poland, France, Belgium, Luxembourg and the Netherlands.

Some say there was another reason, one much more sinister and hardly altruistic, for making the half-Jews into Mischlinge and sparing them from the fate of the full Jews. They may have been saved only because they could eventually fight for Germany. The expansionist plans of the Nazis required men for her armies, and this potential pool of part-German bodies was too good to toss upon the rubbish heap of history. The Mischlinge could be useful! They would make ideal German soldiers, able to follow orders without question. After all, were they not both German and Jew—with the innate respect for authority so common to both cultures?

Whatever the true motive, the virtual total acceptance of the Mischlinge into the Wehrmacht (armed forces) meant that the Mischlinge would eventually feel safer in the army than they would as civilians at home. It wasn't until after the British and French evacuation of Dunkirk, which signalled the end of the campaign in France in June 1940, that a secret order signed by Field Marshal Wilhelm Keitel, Chief of the High Command of the Armed Forces, was put into effect.

Keitel's order, dated 8 April 1940, ostensibly transferred "Mischlinge who are 50 percent Jewish or men who are married to a Mischling" to the Reserve or Militia Units which were stationed outside battle zones. However, each Mischling was to have his papers stamped "n.z.v." That meant "nicht zu verwenden"—"not useful." This was done to "clearly distinguish them from the other conscripts in this category." But even this attempt at isolation and identification would once again result in typical Nazi indecision over what to do with the Mischlinge.[3]

There was also the by now standard exemption clause. It stated that "The Führer reserves the right to make exceptions in special cases, applications for which are to be filed with the High Command of the armed forces (the OKW—Oberkommando der Wehrmacht.)" Attending to this flood of applications probably kept the Führer busy for a while. Apparently this was the type of appeal made on behalf of Klaus Peter Scholz, whose story appears in Chapter Four.

Mischlinge of the Second Degree were not discharged. In fact, they continued to be drafted as conscripts—especially after 1941. Both they and members of the armed forces who were married to Mischlinge of the Second Degree could be "promoted and used as senior officers."

A year later, with the invasion of Russia less than a month old but already a smashing success for the Nazis, the German High Command did an apparent about-face. Realizing they had lost a valuable supply of manpower by divorcing the Mischlinge of the First Degree, they now sought a hasty reconciliation. The OKW decided that some Mischlinge were good enough to fight and die in the Wehrmacht after all. So a new order, issued "On Behalf of Keitel" (as Chief of the Supreme Command he apparently did not have to eat his own words), on 16 July 1941 made it official.

Of course by then most of the "not useful" Mischlinge had been sent home. However, an application for their continuation in active service could be made by their senior officers provided that the Mischling had "proven himself by extraordinary valor and military readiness during the war and has been awarded honors by the Third Reich (especially the Iron Cross, the SA [storm trooper] badge of honors, wound stripe or war service cross)." Until the application was decided upon, the Mischling was to remain in active service. Provisions for reinstatement were also specified for those already discharged. The order even applied to those who were married to Mischlinge of the First Degree and had already been transferred to the Reserve or Militia. No effort was ever made to draft back into military service those Mischlinge who had been sent home. By the time this order made the rounds, the attention of the High Command was focused upon the Eastern Front, and if the Mischlinge were even being thought about at all, it was in terms of their Final Solution.

There has been some confusion over the status of Mischlinge of the First Degree who were high ranking officers in the armed forces. Were they also removed by Keitel's 1940 order? An order of 13 March 1939, which was not made public, allowed Mischlinge officers "to remain in the standing army by decision of the Führer." But how many Mischlinge officers could there have been in the army by that time? After all, non-Aryans were subject to dismissal from the army just as they were from all other facets of German life. A decree signed by Hitler on 21 May 1935 had stipulated Aryan descent as a prerequisite for remaining in active service. This was still some months before non-Aryans were divided into Jews and Mischlinge. But wait—the 1935 decree also contains a provision for exceptions! The recipients of these are presumably the individuals the 1939 order was directed toward.

Those Mischlinge who entered the army after 1935 apparently did not rise to the higher ranks, although most of them weren't kept in the service long enough to do so. That could further explain why the 1940 order affected mainly conscripts. If indeed the High Command's official policy did lean toward using the Mischlinge as cannon fodder, it was borne out by not promoting them above the rank of common soldiers. Some of the Mischlinge, like Klaus Peter Scholz, were not even permitted to advance to the rank of Gefreiter (an acting corporal, the grade between private first class and corporal). Scholz's highest promotion was to Oberschütze (private first class infantry rifleman), although as we shall soon see, Werner Goldberg received an impromptu promotion to officer rank.

Every application for exemption made to the Führer was to contain a short account of the applicant's military career and qualifications and "one photograph each of the member of the armed forces concerned or of his wife of non-German blood, [photographed] from the front and the side." In addition, there should be a "declaration of whether the Jewish relatives are still alive and of what nature their relationship is to the person concerned." Conceivably, some of the 340 Honorary Aryanships personally granted by Hitler could have gone to these applicants from the military. If the Führer did not elevate a military Mischling to full German status, he could just as easily raise the worthy applicant to the rank of Mischling of the Second Degree, which was enough to keep him in the military service. The number of these internal Mischlinge upgradings may never have been tabulated, since the recipient essentially remained a Mischling. In many ways, the procedure was the same as for a routine military promotion which required final approval by the Führer. Like the appointment of Mario Heil de Brentani (editor of Rommel's field newspaper) as a Sonderführer (Special Officer), it had to be personally signed by Hitler.

Since the 16 July 1941 order cancelled that of 8 April 1940, there can be no doubt that some Mischlinge of the First Degree (either still in that status or in a higher racial classification granted by the Führer) served in the German armed forces *throughout* World War II.

Werner Goldberg recalls "my school friend Hans-Jürgen Fuhrmann. In his family, the father was Aryan and the mother Jewish. She had been a singer and coached actors in singing, pronunciation and speaking. She taught Curt Goetz and his wife, Valerie von Martens.

"Hans-Jürgen's father had been a member of the Prussian parliament in the 1920s and was a director of Knorr-Bremse [the Munich-based brake manufacturers]. There were five children in the family, and my friend did not like to know that his mother was Jewish. To himself, he *was* an Aryan. He served in the Heer [army] until 1945, having reached the rank of Feldwebel [sergeant]. He fought on the Eastern Front and was a prisoner of war until 1948, when he returned to Berlin. He owned a big store here and died about 1979."

Arthur Müller, now known as Arthur Miller, a Mischling who recently returned home to Germany to retire after spending twenty-five years as a General Motors assembly line worker in Flint, Michigan, remembers another "fellow who was a pilot. And he flew some very important persons during the war although he was half-Jewish. There were always exceptions."[4]

Author and journalist Rolf Vogel thinks the expulsion of the Mischlinge from the German armed forces was "the best idea Hitler ever had." Vogel, a Mischling, entered the army in March 1940 but was "pushed out" five months later. "I could not have survived had I stayed in the army," says Vogel. "I would have been sent to the Russian front and there I would have been killed."[5]

Grimly, Werner Goldberg underscores Vogel's fear. Says Goldberg, "When I left my division in France it was July of 1940. At that time, there was not yet an Eastern Front. That was not to come until 22 June 1941—the day we invaded Russia. My division was sent there. Of my company, I know only five who survived. They fought in the cold winter, under siege in a big castle. Many of them froze to death. The whole battalion was destroyed."

But even with "n.z.v." stamped on their identity cards, Mischlinge like Rolf Vogel could still do many things to aid their Jewish parent. Basically, the Mischlinge had received the equivalent of a dishonorable discharge, and as Vogel points out, "only a specialist would know the meaning of 'n.z.v.' on a military paper. So when we got bombed out of our flat, I would wear the leather coat of an officer, without epaulets, and go to the office for people made homeless by the bombings. I would say 'Heil Hitler!' and show them my military passport. After I told them that our flat had been bombed, they gave me a new apartment—with three rooms—as well as 6000 Reichsmark [well over $2,000] and a lot of papers to sign. But when I went from there to the food office, two people walked in right ahead of me to get their allocations. A man who had been standing off to the side came up to the table and told them, 'I'm from the Gestapo. I want to see your papers.' I quietly went back out and came back another day."

Dr. Hans Salomon, the noted World Health Organization parasitologist, believes that his fellow soldiers had great sympathy for the plight of the Mischlinge among their ranks.[6] "You know that they were not all Nazis," says Dr. Salomon, who himself was a Mischling, "and they would say, 'Hans, how can they treat your mother like that and still keep you in the army?' Once my mother wrote to me that she was being made to go to the separate Jewish air raid cellar. [Jews in privileged mixed marriages were allowed to use the same shelters as other German civilians.] So I wrote a really strong letter of protest to the commander of my division. I told him that I could not tolerate this any longer, that I am a German soldier and now one of my parents is being treated like this! Well, they summoned me to the captain and he asked me, 'Why do you protest against the Führer's laws?' And I said that I didn't know whether the Führer had personally ordered that, but if he had, I would also protest against the Führer. He jumped up and said, 'You cannot do that!', and a month later I was discharged. They must have known something like that was coming."

Journalist Hans Faust, son of a Jewish mother, believes the attitude of officers of the German Army toward the Mischlinge should not have come as a surprise.[7] He points out that at the time of Heinrich Heine, many would-be officers of the Prussian Army eagerly sought out and married wealthy young Jewish maidens in order to get enough money to purchase a military commission. Faust believes that many of the aristocratic Prussian military had Jewish wives, but by the third or fourth generation, their descendants, still carrying on the tradition of military service, could not remember that their foremothers had been Jews. In Faust's own case, "When I went to the army, I was assigned to a very conservative regiment in Frankfurt an der Oder, the 8th Infantry Regiment. This was the regiment that had been called in to quell the revolution of 1848. Most of the officers were aristocrats with some knowledge of their personal family histories, and thus they even had a little love towards the Jewish people.

"I was not badly treated in the army. When the war with Poland broke out in September 1939, they said 'No, no, you stay in Germany.' And when my regiment came back, they were sent to the border with France and they took me along. When war broke out there in May 1940 they sent me back home, but afterwards, when they came to the coast of the Atlantic poised there awaiting the word to invade England, they had me join them once again and were very kind to me. Then came the secret order to put out all the Mischlinge. And the officer in charge of my division said to me, 'All Jewish people must get out of the army now. But let me think. One of your grandparents *could* be an Aryan. What was your grandfather's name?'

"I told him my grandfather's name was Salomon Lewy, that he had been the baker of matzoh for the Jewish community in Posen, Poland, and that I did not think he would ever find an Aryan who is named Lewy.

" 'No, no,' the officer said, 'I mean your grandmother.'

" 'Oh yes, my grandmother Johanna. She was born Wittkowski.'

" 'Oh that's good,' said the officer as he clapped his hands, 'A Polish name! That should at least be a little Aryan.' "

"I said to him, 'You are very kind, but I don't believe that my grandfather, a Jewish man who was very strong in his faith, would be married to an Aryan woman.' And I protested that the name Wittkowski was not really the same name as an Aryan would have. But he said, 'Oh, don't worry. We will prove it.'

"I had to say to him, 'No, no, just let it go.' But it shows that at that time there was no man who was as bad as you may have thought he might be."

That same theme surfaces in the recollections of Werner Goldberg, who in 1939 at the age of twenty, also found himself in the Wehrmacht. "It must have been in March or April of 1940 that there was an action against the Jews in Berlin," he remembers, "and my mother wrote me a letter. I was then at the front, in the western part of Germany, as a soldier with the 23rd division of infantry, the Brandenburg Division. Our home stations were Spandau, Brandenburg and Potsdam. In the letter my mother said 'Help! Father gets no food cards. He is just out of the hospital and has been sent with a work crew to lay railroad tracks. We have many difficulties here.'

"I went with this letter to the chief of my company and he said, 'What can I do about this? Go see the chief of the battalion.' The chief of the battalion looked at the letter too and said I must go to the chief of the regiment. And the chief of the regiment said it was impossible that such things could happen. He said I must tell this to the General of the division!

"Our General was Walter Graf von Brockdorff-Ahlefeldt. Later, when the 23rd infantry was known as the Potsdam Division, he was actively involved in the 20th of July affair— the unsuccessful 1944 assassination plot against Hitler.

"The next day there came a military vehicle to fetch me to the General at headquarters. I was very nervous, but the General told me to sit down. 'I have time,' he said. 'I want

you to tell me about this.' So I told him. Then he stood up.
When the General gets up, I too must stand up. 'No,' he told
me. 'Take your seat.' Then he started to run up and down the
room. Finally he told me, 'Go back to your company. As of
today, you have a promotion. You go to the quartermaster in
the commissary and let him issue you a pass. Then in the next
hour you will take a pistol and you will climb into a car and
drive to Berlin. You have four weeks, and I will wait to see
that you have brought all this into order. And if the four weeks
are not sufficient for you, then you will send me a telegram
and say how much longer you need.'

"To the men of my company, the General was always a very
remote figure. You never saw him nor spoke to him. But for
a moment I had the feeling—here is a *Mensch*." ("Mensch" is
the word used both in German and Yiddish—the latter pro-
nounce it as "mentch"—to denote a *real* human being.)

"And I did as the General said. I went to Berlin and took
care to go to all of the necessary offices wearing my uniform
and pistol. And so it could be done. My father was set free
from his hard labor and he had his food cards once again. Nobody could stand up against me in my gray uniform. It was
for me an important device. It was the power of the Wehrmacht. I had seen that it was so and that it worked. The people
with the authority to handle rations and jobs who had squeezed
my father were now being squeezed themselves. From the
moment I came in with my uniform, they knew it was time
for them to make a new decision. They could always defend
themselves later by telling their superiors, 'But he was a soldier, we could not do anything.'

"One day I had to report to the office of the military commander. In this office was a chief of staff of the army. In civilian life, he had been the president of the Reich Lawyer's
Organization. When I told him my story he asked, 'Who has
allowed you to have this pistol?'

"I told him that he must ask my General. He said he could

not understand, and I told him that I couldn't either, but that he must still ask my General. Then he told me, 'It's not necessary to speak about this. In a short time you will be out of the army.' He must have already known about Field Marshal Keitel's order. I told him that my General had not told me anything about this, and he told me that I could be the one to tell my General.

"And it wasn't many days before the change came about. One morning my father rushed into my room and said, 'Get up. The German troops have gone into the Netherlands, Belgium and Luxembourg. I think you too must go to the front.' I told my father, 'Why should I go to the front? No, they tell me that I have to leave the army anyway.' Besides, I had already served on the front in Poland and on the border with France. I did not like explosions and bombs. Even though I was now an officer, having been so promoted by my General, I decided I would not go. I knew that the chief of my company was in Berlin, so just to play it safe, I gave him a call and asked if I should drive back.

"The first thing he said to me was, 'You are in Berlin? Haven't you heard the news on the radio?' and I said, 'You are in Berlin too.' But he said that he had to handle some things here for a few days. I asked him if it was possible that we could drive back together, and he told me that I had to leave Berlin that morning. 'One moment,' I said to him, 'but I heard from the chief of staff here that I would have to leave the army. And now you want me to drive toward France?'

" 'Yes,' he said. 'I know that always you hear the sound of blowing grass. I don't know anything about this business. I have no order in this direction. And I tell you—you *have* to leave Berlin this moment and go to the front.' So I stayed in Berlin two days longer. And when I thought there was no possibility to extend it, I went West. But the troops were in combat and I could not reach them. I went to the commandant at every little village along the way and asked if they knew where my division was. They only knew it was in the direction I was heading, but they always had some work that they wanted me to stay and do, and that would take two or three days at each place. And in this way, it was about two months later that I came to my company. When I arrived, the first thing I saw was the chief of my company sitting in a foxhole. 'Where were you?' He demanded. 'Eight weeks ago I told you to come to the front! I've been here six weeks already!'

" 'Ah yes, but you—you are a captain', I replied and explained about the delay. Then he said, 'I told you over the telephone you always hear the sound of blowing grass. I have here an order to ask you how the problem is with your family?' I told him that he knew the answer but he asked anyway. They were the same questions I had been asked so many times before.

" 'Your father is a Jew?'

" 'No. He's a Christian.'

" 'A racial Jew?'

"I told him it was so. Then he asked if my mother was Jewish and I said she was not. Then he asked if I was fifty percent [Jewish]. When I replied that I was, he said he had an order to ship me back to Potsdam. I asked on what grounds and he said he did not know, but he thought I would be leaving the army. Lowering his voice he asked, 'Is this a good thing for you?' I said I didn't know, the army had been a very bad thing for me, and it may be that what could come now would be better. He said that if I wanted, I could stay there for another three or four weeks. And I remembered what my father had told me when I had to leave the Boy Scouts: if somebody does not like you, don't run after them. I told that to my chief and then I added, 'And you told me that you don't like me, so I'll go back home.' And I went to Potsdam. It was not easy for me to go away from the army. I did not know where I would go. I did not like the discipline of the army, but the army provided security for me, and I had seen what protection the uniform had provided for my father."

That protection extended beyond instances of Jewish parents being shielded by their Mischlinge sons. Mario Heil de (later "von") Brentani was editor of Field Marshall Erwin Rommel's Panzer Army newspaper, *OASE (Oasis)*, during the Tunisan and African campaigns of 1942–1943. He served as a Sonderführer (special officer) and National-Socialist Führungsoffizier, a post for which he was recommended by Goebbels' second-in-command, Alfred Ingemar Berndtt. That meant de Brentani was a political officer in the army whose duty was to infuse the rank and file soldiers with Nazi ideology. For this, he received the German Order of Merit with crossed swords, the equivalent of the Iron Cross for non-combat duty. (Counterparts of de Brentani in the Soviet Red Army were known as Political Commissars. The late Leonid Brezhnev first came to the attention of the Communist Party hierarchy through his work as a political officer during those same years.)

Following Rommel's participation in the 20 July 1944 plot against Hitler, de Brentani was attached to the 14th Armee-Oberkommando unit in Occupied Italy. That de Brentani was a high Nazi Party official is beyond doubt. He identifies himself as such on the title page of a 1944 book he wrote.[8] His Nazi Party rank also appears in the Library of Congress National Union Catalogue listing of the book. Yet his wife was half-Jewish, and de Brentani used both his uniform and his position in the Nazi Party to save her from deportation.

When the Brentani family emigrated to Canada, they left the "Heil" behind them.[9] It was just enough of a variation in name to slip them successfully past any Canadian Immigration Department official checking lists of "banned" Nazis. Mario Brentani was apparently the highest ranking former Nazi Party functionary to have legally entered Canada as a postwar emigrant. The family left Germany in 1952, shortly after Brentani was called before a tribunal of West German journalists investigating allegations of professional misconduct made against him.[10] In later years, von Brentani would main-

**Der Führer und Oberste Befehlshaber
der Wehrmacht**

Ich genehmige, daß der

Unteroffizier Mario H e i l de B r e n t a n i

Propaganda Ersatz Abteilung Ia

während des Krieges weiter als Vorgesetzter im aktiven

Wehrdienst verbleiben und bei entsprechender Eignung

befördert werden kann.

Führerhauptquartier, den 12. Okt.   1941

524

The appointment of Mario Heil de Brentani as a propaganda officer in the German army—personally signed by Adolf Hitler. De Brentani was a high ranking officer in the Nazi Party. It was his job to infuse the soldiers with Nazi Party ideology. *(Photograph courtesy Ruth von Brentani)* tain that he emigrated to Canada because of a resurgence of anti-Semitism in Germany.

From 1954 until 1975, von Brentani edited and published one of the largest circulating German language newspapers in Canada, *Montrealer Nachrichten*. At first von Brentani was subsidized by the West German government. Switching his allegiance, he was then subsidized by the East Germans to the extent of receiving free vacations in East Germany and free flights thereto. Certainly the bureaucrats at Canada's federal Ministry of Multiculturism must have been unaware of von Brentani's covert East German subsidies while they pumped Canadian government funds into his newspaper. (Funding grants to Canadian foreign-language newspapers are a staple of the ministry.)

Meanwhile von Brentani was also acquiring a major international reputation as a painter of the Canadian Eskimo. His paintings received showings and acclaim in Switzerland, Austria and East Germany. An exhibition of von Brentani's art toured the U.S.S.R. for eight months during 1972.[11] Canadian Prime Minister Pierre Trudeau was one of von Brentani's admirers. In a cordial 1978 letter, Trudeau expressed his thanks "on behalf of all Canadians for your beautiful and thoughtful recordings of our Eskimo people."[12] But this acclaim for von Brentani's artistic talent was not universal. Professor Klaus J. Herrmann of Concordia University in Montréal commissioned von Brentani to paint a portrait of the Herrmann children. Herrmann thought the result to be "awful garbage," and the two men never spoke again. However, the Herrmann children are not Eskimos.

The emergence of von Brentani as a painter of Canadian native peoples bears a striking similarity to the amazing postwar resurrection of Nazi documentary filmmaker Leni Riefenstahl as a highly respected photographer of primitive Stone Age-like aboriginal tribes, but with a big difference. There's a school of thought which believes that von Brentani has even faked this—that in fact he never visited the Arctic or met the Canadian Eskimos in their natural habitat. Indeed, they claim that von Brentani's "art" involves nothing more than merely copying photographs of Eskimos made by his son.

In 1972 von Brentani claimed to have acquired over 20,000 signatures on a petition calling upon Canada to establish diplomatic relations with East Germany. In reality, the petition bore only thirty-six signatures. Von Brentani claimed that the other signers were all members of the proletariat and thus he had to sign their names for them. When the story reached the pages of the West German newsmagazine *Der Spiegel*,[13] it became a source of major embarrassment for Prime Minister Trudeau. Marc Lalonde, then Trudeau's secretary and, later, federal Minister of Finance, said that Canada would most likely now be the last country on earth to recognize East Germany. (Fourteen years later it still hasn't done so.) But somehow, the East Germans managed to overlook this rebuff, for in 1978, von Brentani became the first (and thus far the only) non-resident of East Germany to receive one of that nation's highest awards: the Stern der Völkerfreundschaft in Gold.[14] The award commemorates international friendship, and the presentation was made by East German President Erich Honecker, who presumably is not a regular reader of *Der Spiegel.*

The state-controlled East German press gave von Brentani's death prime coverage in September 1982, but it passed unnoticed by the Canadian press. Ironically, only six months earlier, many Canadian dailies carried a lengthy obituary of former SS Captain Otto von Bolschwing, reading in part: ". . . he was on a 'liquidation list' of the Gestapo after marrying a woman in Vienna whose mother was Jewish."[15] (Although one may wonder why, since marriages between Aryans and Mischlinge of the First Degree could be arranged with special consent.) Although Mario von Brentani never made it onto a hit list, he had committed the same crime.

Ruth von Brentani's mother was a Jew. Her name was Sophie Hacker and she had been married twice, first to another Jew named Heimann, and then to Georg Lütjens. The latter, an artist and photographer, was Ruth's father. Ruth also had a half sister—sixteen years younger than she—and a half brother who were, of course, full Jews. Ruth, who was born in Berlin-Charlottenburg, was twenty when she married Mario Heil de Brentani in 1931. He was already a member of the Nazi Party, having joined the NSDAP on 1 September 1930. His Party membership number was 293635.[16]

The "de Brentani" was taken from his mother's name—de Brentani di Tremezzo. Mario was given special permission by a Weimar era court to use the hyphenated "Heil-de Brentani" as his surname. The hyphen was chucked out with the Republic and the "de" followed after the war when it too was conveniently discarded in favor of the more aristocratic sounding "von." Mrs. von Brentani claims this was done because "we used to receive every day beggar letters from Italy."[17] As von Brentani was born in Italy in 1908 (although his records give three different villages as his birthplace), the letters could conceivably have come from bona fide destitute relatives.

Leipzig journalist Gerhard Moest, the *Nachrichten*'s onetime East German correspondent (and possibly liaison), asserts that Mrs. von Brentani continued as late as 1970 to sign bank checks as "Ruth H. de Brentani." That is virtually the same form of her signature (except that she spelled out "Heil") which she used to sign her husband's 1941 German income tax form. (He earned 5000 Reichsmark that year, or about $2,000. If a Jew had owned property worth that much, it would have undergone Aryanization.) Doubtless it is one of the few tax forms ever signed for a Nazi Party official by someone the Party would consider a Jew. Ruth was an acceptable name (along with Adam, David, Raphael, Debora, Esther and several others) for Germans during the Nazi era despite its obvious Hebrew origin as the chief character in the Old Testament Book of Ruth. It had been officially "Aryanized" in 1938. That decree was drafted by Hans Globke, the names expert of the Interior Ministry.

On 28 August 1939, five days before the invasion of Poland, Mario Heil de Brentani made an official application to the

Propaganda Ministry of Dr. Goebbels. Mobilization had begun on 24 August, and with war imminent, de Brentani took the opportunity to stress his record of long service and personal loyalty to the Nazi Party—even though he had been forced out of the Party for several years because of some undisclosed infraction. A little over two years later, on 12 September 1941, de Brentani was personally appointed by Hitler as a propaganda officer with the army. Although de Brentani's rank was only that of an Unteroffizier (a noncommissioned officer), Hitler would have had to sign such a document giving de Brentani permission to serve with the regular army even though he was married to a Mischling of the First Degree. The Keitel order of 1940 had transferred those with Mischlinge wives to Reserve or Militia units, but the order of 16 July 1941 would have allowed de Brentani to make an application to the Führer for this special permission. Even his 1939 letter to Goebbels would have come in handy here to prove his worth. To Mrs. von Brentani, Hitler's approval was "for me, for our family, a good thing. Without the army it would have been very difficult for us. I didn't have to wear the star. Nor did my sister because she too was married to a Christian. But I had to consider myself a Jew."

An almost eulogistic biography of de Brentani issued by one of his book publishers around 1941 (the type face is still Gothic; the total of his children is the same as on his tax form for that year) refers to his membership in a "federation of front soldiers" under the direction of Nazi theoretician Alfred Rosenberg. De Brentani is also listed as being available for "patriotic readings" under the auspices of another Rosenberg "cultural" organization. The obligatory quotes from book reviewers (some things never change) are, as can be expected, all highly laudatory. They congratulate him for expounding upon the joys of having a large family. (At that time, the de Brentani's had six children. Ultimately they had nine.) Apparently, de Brentani would often use his children as models for his fictional characters. This lends a touch of wry humor to one of Mrs. von Brentani's recollections of prewar Germany:

"There were these so-called Mutterehrenkreuze," she remembers, "the Mother's Cross of Honor. It was a Nazi decoration which each German mother received if she had four or more children. Suddenly one evening there came to our apartment these men from the Party and they told my husband, 'You have four children. Your wife is entitled to receive the Mutterehrenkreuze.'

"My husband knew that Hitler would not have liked to present this award to anyone of Jewish descent, so he said, 'Oh no, we are not eligible.' The Party men looked very surprised and asked, 'Oh! Why not?'

"Now usually my husband could think very quickly and he always knew exactly what he must say. But this time, he looked a little worried. Then he replied, 'My wife is not well. She is very sick.'

" 'What is wrong with her? She does not look like she is very sick,' the Party men demanded to know. In a hushed voice my husband explained, 'She suffers from a hereditary disease. It is one that is passed down directly from one's forefathers.' For what seemed like a very long time, the Party men remained silent. Then they looked at each other and one said, 'Oh, we are so sorry.' They expressed their condolences and left.

"We decided it was best not to be in Berlin on the first of May when the award was given out. So we took a little vacation and went to Mecklenburg. That is the only time I can remember when perhaps it was a little dangerous. But it was also very, very funny—and we laughed about it a good deal that week."

Ruth von Brentani's brother-in-law, Emil Lappe, was a former director of the *Frankfurter Zeitung*. Although he had served as a police officer and jail warden, he was sent to an Organization Todt work camp in 1944, and his wife Beate,

Ruth's sister, was sent to Theresienstadt. "There was nothing I could do for her," Ruth maintains. "I could not help her. I was not very scared of being sent away. If ordered to go with some rations to a certain station, I would not do it. I would disappear instead. I had an address in Switzerland where I could go. It was a place where I could go underground and I would have done this. I would never go the way my sister did—just like a little sheep." (Beate survived Theresienstadt and died at the age of 80 in 1975.)

"I remember once during the war my husband was on leave," continues Ruth, "but when he came home, he went back out right away. I didn't know why. Later he told me that a card had come telling me I should report to a certain place in two days. It was the same kind of card my sister received. But my husband took this card and went there instead. It was Gestapo headquarters. He went there wearing his Sonderführer uniform and demanded, 'What do you want from my wife?' And the Gestapo man stammered, 'How . . . how . . . can it be that you are a Sonderführer and your wife is half-Jewish?'

" 'I don't know,' shrugged my husband, 'but I have this special permission [to be married to a Mischlinge of the First Degree and serve in the army] issued by the Führer who has appointed me a Sonderführer and I want to know what do *you* want with my wife?'

"The Gestapo man hesitated and then snarled, 'Well, nothing. Give the card back to us and go.' And my husband did. But he never told me anything about this until later—after the war was over. Without my husband's uniform, he would have been nothing. At this time, the uniform was for him— and for us— a form of protection."

Mrs. von Brentani recalled that an article by her husband in *OASE* had prompted someone to ask his superior officer " 'Why is this de Brentani writing for you? Do you know that he is married to a Jew?' His chief suggested it would be wise if my husband now wrote under a different name. So from that time on, he signed his stories only with an initial."

Just how well deserved was the Nazi reputation for efficiency? Mrs. von Brentani's next tale casts doubts upon the thoroughness of the system. "If my husband went to speak on the radio," she says, "he had to sign a paper that he was Aryan. And he also had to sign that I was Aryan. He would leave this part blank and no one would ever say anything to him about it. Maybe they never even noticed it?"

Charlotte "Lotte" Lehmann (not to be confused with the famous German-American soprano) was the illegitimate daughter of a Hungarian Jew and a German mother.[18] Because she legally only had to document one-half of her family tree, the safe Aryan side of her mother, she was able to work in a highly sensitive post in the German Foreign Office throughout the war. She was present at many historic events including the 6:00 A.M. 22 June 1941 press conference of Foreign Minister Joachim von Ribbentrop announcing that Russia had been invaded earlier that morning. Although she saw many of the American foreign correspondents covering such conferences before December 1941 (including William L. Shirer, Henry W. Flannery and Pierre J. Huss), they in turn apparently never noticed Lehmann's distinctly non-Aryan appearance and remained unaware of her unusual background.

Her father, Ludwig Stein, had married a Jewish former opera singer named Valerie and they had a young son, Herbert. After the Nazi racial laws cost him his job as an auditor at the famous Darmstädter und Nationalbank, Mr. Stein gave private lessons in business administration from his home. Eventually, the Stein family was forced to move to an apartment in the Jewish ghetto where they shared four cramped rooms with seven other families.

On a particularly uncomfortable hot and humid afternoon late in August 1942, Stein left their apartment to go for a short walk through Berlin to get some fresh air. He wore the yellow Star of David as he was required to, hiding it just a bit under the satchel he carried. As he went through the streets, he was accosted by a German soldier, a major, in the gray Wehrmacht uniform. "Hello Mr. Stein, how are you?" asked the soldier. It was one of his former pupils. "You ask me how I am?" he replied, showing him the yellow star he had been trying to conceal, as if to say—well, how can I possibly be? Then he added, "Lest you get discovered talking to me, we better say goodbye. It might be dangerous for you if someone from the Nazis sees a German soldier talking to a Jew."

"Well, let's walk on for a bit," said the soldier. Stein asked what he was doing now and the soldier replied, "I am assigned to the alien registration department here in Berlin, and, well, Mr. Stein, as far as I can remember, you are, uh—Hungarian-born?" Stein nodded his head. "Well then," said the soldier, "promise me upon your word of honor that you will say nothing—even to your wife, and I will ring up the Hungarian Embassy to give Hungarian passports to both of you tonight. There is a Red Cross transport leaving for Berne, Switzerland, from the Bahnhof Zoo. Be at that station and you will get your passports. And the Red Cross train will be waiting for you."

Stein went back to the apartment and calmly told his wife—as if nothing unusual had happened to him—"Valerie, it's so nice outside, let's have a walk." When they got to the street he told her, "We can't go back up there. We have to go to the Bahnhof Zoo." Valerie protested, "I have no handbag! I have no hat! I have nothing!" But they went to the station and from there by train to Switzerland. Afterward, they were transported to the Swiss Embassy in Budapest, which was extraterritorial. And there they waited for the war to end. Raoul Wallenberg, the Swedish savior of many Hungarian Jews, was another who made good use of the Swiss Embassy as a safe haven for Jews. (Herbert Stein had earlier been sent to a labor camp. He escaped and successfully went underground.)

Were elements of the German army actually sympathetic to the plight of the Jews? Werner Goldberg maintains that the attitude of some officers made possible the decisions to perform individual acts of mercy.

"Before Christmas of 1939," Goldberg remembers, "I was picked to arrange a Christmas program for all of the soldiers, and I said I would do so. But when I went to the commander, I told him that many of my comrades who had entered the army at the same time as I were going to be promoted at Christmastime, and I would have to obey their orders. I would have to stand and salute them only because I was not an Aryan. And I said that if in the eyes of the German army I was not good enough to receive a Christmas promotion, then certainly I am also not good enough to arrange their Christmas program.

" 'What?' yelled my commander. 'That's impossible. In the German army there is no difference between soldiers. Here nobody is a Jew or Christian. They are all the same. If you are eligible, you will get your promotion.' And so I did. And the chief liked the poem that I wrote for the program so much that he came to get a copy for his wife."

Goldberg's poem, "Brief aus der Heimat an die Soldaten, Weihnachten 1939" (A Letter to Soldiers from Home; Christmas 1939"), also was a big hit with the troops. Spread at first only by word of mouth, it quickly became the unofficial Wehrmacht Christmas poem.[19] It was the first time in twenty-two years that German soldiers in uniform were spending Christmas away from home. It was far from being the last.

Another Goldberg anecdote indicates that the German army was not always goose-stepping in perfect time with Nazi Party ideologues like de Brentani. Goldberg remembers that "there came an order one day to the military that the greeting used by soldiers was no longer to consist of putting one's hand on the cap, but instead was to be the outstretched arm—the 'Heil Hitler' salute. But our officers made a compromise that this would only apply if one was not wearing his cap at the time.

When the whole company was assembled the next morning, the major announced, 'From today on, without a cap, you must greet each other with the long outstretched arm salute. But with the cap, it will remain the same as it has been until now. And let me tell you that if I catch anybody without their cap, I will give them three days in the brig.' "

Arthur Miller's brief stint in the Luftwaffe emphasizes Hans Faust's theory that the often compassionate treatment the Mischlinge received from the German army was a direct result of the Jewish heritage of many of the officers. Miller argues that placing the Mischlinge in the military was one of the best ideas the Nazis ever had. "Thus," he says, "we were able to survive." But unfortunately for Miller, the officer class of the Luftwaffe was not comprised of Prussian aristocrats with generations of military service on their family trees and remnants of centuries of Jewish blood in their veins. Instead, things were quite different. In Miller's own experience, "The treatment was not so nice. I remember once we all had to stand at attention and our commanding officer said to me, in front of everyone, 'You can not have a pass for Saturday night because you are half-Jewish.' "

Throughout history, there has probably never been a young serviceman wearing the uniform of any nation who wouldn't think that being deprived of a Saturday night pass wasn't cruel and unusual punishment. But it could have been a lot worse for Miller, and it almost was. The following week, another Luftwaffe officer called the assembled group to attention and asked who among them was half-Jewish. This time, Miller remained silent. And so did his comrades. It was good that they did. The officer was looking for a Mischling to step forward and "volunteer" to undertake a particularly hazardous assignment.

But hazardous is hardly the proper adjective to describe the assignment that a Major Bloch, an officer of Jewish descent, undertook for the Abwehr, the German secret service. Throughout Europe, Joseph J. Schneersohn, Grand Rabbi of

Warsaw and spiritual leader of the worldwide Lubavitcher Chassidic sect, was called the "Wunderrebbe" (Wonder Rabbi)—because he was said to work miracles. When the Germans invaded Poland in September 1939, the rabbi's followers became alarmed over his fate. Some Chassidim in the United States were successful in getting the ear of President Franklin D. Roosevelt, who then spoke out against the invasion. This in turn alarmed the Nazis. Fearing that American sympathy for the plight of the Polish Jews might undercut the supporters of American isolationism, whom the Nazis were counting on to keep the United States out of the war, the Nazis came to a startling conclusion: They had to rescue the Wunderrebbe.

The assignment went to the Abwehr. There, the director, Admiral Wilhelm Canaris, called in two of his most trusted officers: Major Horatzek and Major Bloch. The two men reached Warsaw along with the first wave of German soldiers to enter the beleaguered city. Following a series of pre-arranged signs, they rescued the rabbi, spirited him across the front lines and back to Germany, then across a neutral border where they delivered him to an American consulate official. The officers on the daring mission were careful to evade discovery by either the rabbi's followers or by regular German army units, either of which would have triggered attention to the rescue scheme.

When the rabbi ultimately arrived in New York harbor, he was met by thousands of his cheering followers who hailed his deliverance as further proof of his already miraculous abilities.

Rabbi Schneersohn died in 1950.[20] The fate of Major Bloch is not known, but Major Horatzek is said to have continued to help Jews throughout the war and is believed to have died while on yet another secret mission for Admiral Canaris.[21]

Others have told stories of Jews being smuggled out of Poland while disguised in German army uniforms. Indeed, there were illegal resistance organizations formed within the Wehrmacht and the Reichsarbeitsdienst (the compulsory pre-military service organization) as late as summer 1939 with the express purpose of aiding the Jews. Among those arrested when the Nazis smashed these groups in December 1939 was Dr. Michael Jovy, a postwar German ambassador who has been honored by Yad Vashem.[22] Could the participation of Mischlinge in such covert activities during the early months of the war have been one of the factors behind Field Marshal Keitel's decision to sever them from the military service?

Dr. Hans Salomon doesn't think so. He believes that "once the Nazis had decided to kill the Jewish people, they could hardly allow their sons to continue to fight in the German army."

Whatever the reason, Keitel's order ended one of the more bizarre aspects of the often stormy relationship between Jew and German in Hitler's Reich. But it also ushered in a new era of danger for the Mischlinge. Werner Goldberg remembers that once he returned to civilian life he was faced almost daily with questions like "Why aren't you a soldier?" and "What are you doing here in Berlin?" Finding the right answers was a tricky process. It meant the Mischlinge had to be always prepared to justify their very existence.

Fortunately, the Feodor Schmeider company, the leather clothing manufacturer for whom Werner Goldberg worked, was able to maintain an impressive level of wartime production making military uniforms. (The company was originally called Schneller und Schmeider—Schneller, a Jew, was deported, but not before the SS used him to arrest other Jews.) Thus, Goldberg's tenure, both at the company and as a "useful" member of German society, seemed assured. One day it brought him an invitation to speak before a large gathering of engineers. As he awaited his turn to go to the front of the packed hall, Goldberg was once again confronted with a familiar refrain. "Someone" had told the Party functionary who organized the meeting that they had heard Goldberg was not an Aryan. Goldberg admitted he wasn't, and was told, "Then you can not speak before this group." As usual, Goldberg began to leave. Only this time, the Party man shouted after him, "Where are you going? Come back here. You can't leave now. There are 600 people out there and we have no other speaker. You must speak before them today, but you are never to come back here again." Although Goldberg's speech was a smash hit with his audience, he never got to play an encore.

"They didn't care very much to be Jews then—or not to be Jews. But who can blame them? I wouldn't fault them for their behavior then. No one should, except he who has been in that same place. There is a line in Pirkej Avot *(Sayings of the Fathers, II, 4): 'Do not judge another till you yourself have come into his circumstances or situation.' You can't fault them. In that period, you can't fault anyone."*

JÜRGEN LANDECK, Librarian
Jüdische Gemeinde zu Berlin[1]

Chapter Three

Wanted for My Sister

TO GET AN IDEA of how it felt to be a Mischling, one has to look at the Nazi attempts to regulate everyday contacts between the Mischlinge and Jews or Germans. The Mischlinge were the Third Race, and like the third sex, they were considered outcasts, literally in a class by themselves. In order to bring about the separation of the three official races, the Nazis implemented a plan for the enforced social and sexual segregation of the Mischlinge that must have made even white American racists turn—well, maybe green—with envy.

The Nazis originally saw the Mischlinge as a living bridge between the German and Jewish communities. Since a Mischling was neither a Jew nor of "German or related blood," he or she was technically free under the Nuremberg Laws to marry or have extramarital relations with either Jews or Germans. But bridges of that nature are made to be burned. It wasn't long before the Nazi Party hardliners realized that in order to prevent what bigots of another national stripe would call miscegenation, they would have to prohibit Mischlinge of the First Degree from marrying and mating outside of their own race.

Laws were created to regulate Mischlinge marriages, but strangely the Nazis never officially proscribed Mischlinge extramarital sexual relations. If a male Mischling were to bed down either a Jew or an Aryan, he would not have been accused of Rassenschande (race mixing), presumably because he was already a symbol of this vilest of sins in the Nazi canon.

Hitler noticed this bizarre loophole and in 1941, six years after the promulgation of the Nuremberg Laws, requested an amendment to the Blood and Honor Laws to close it. This law would have banned extramarital sex between Mischlinge and Germans, but when Hitler's aides convinced him of the difficulties involved in enforcing it, the Führer backed down and the bedroom doors of Germans remained open to Mischlinge.

It was the official duty of a German male to inspect the racial identity papers of a prospective sexual partner before commencing intercourse, in order to make sure she was not a Jew. However, as several (male) former Mischlinge jokingly recalled, a Mischling could legally get directly to the matter at hand.

Here's how the law on Michlinge marriages stood:

Allowed were marriages between:

1. Mischlinge of the Second Degree and Germans.
2. Mischlinge of the First Degree. (The only kind of marriage they could make.)

Strictly forbidden were marriages between:

1. Mischlinge of the Second Degree and Jews.
2. Mischlinge of the Second degree.

Prohibited except by special consent were marriages between:

1. Mischlinge of the First Degree and Germans.
2. Mischlinge of the First Degree with Mischlinge of the Second Degree.
3. Mischlinge of the First Degree and Jews. Any Mischling in this situation would automatically be reclassified as a Jew.[2]

Thus neatly confined by law within their own group, few of the Mischlinge of the First Degree mixed socially with Germans; fewer still with Jews. To get around the obstacle of this enforced isolation from both the Jewish and German cultures of their parents, the Mischlinge had to establish their own social structures and organizations. With the option of belonging either to the Hitler Youth or to Hans-Joachim Schoeps's Deutscher Vortrupp, the Zionist youth group, not available to younger Mischlinge males, they had to advertise just to find Mischlinge partners.

Some of the Mischlinge joined a group known as the Paulus-Bund, named after Saint Paul, the Jew of Tarsus, apostle to the gentiles and a convert to Christianity. But most gravitated toward the Vereinigung 1937 (the Society of 1937)[3], which was established with the official sanction, if not under the total control, of the Nazis. Werner Goldberg was one of the first members.

Arthur Miller believes, "We were practically forced to belong to the Vereinigung 1937. Without it, we would have stood alone among the rest of the population. There was no other way to become acquainted with or to marry someone of the other sex." Indeed, the endless columns of lonely hearts ads— they appear even more forebidding set in old Gothic type— which fill the association's newsletter underscore Miller's contention.[4] (Four years later, the old German Gothic script would quickly disappear from sight after Hitler branded it as being of Jewish origin. A new generation of grateful postwar German publishers made absolutely no attempt to resurrect it.)[5]

Many of the Mischlinge lonely hearts ads express a quiet despair. One is struck by the almost terrible sense of urgency—an emotion which the writers of modern day "Companions Wanted" ads would go to great lengths to camouflage. Perhaps sex and love have never been more of a life and death issue than they were to the Mischlinge.

"Suche für meine Tochter" (Sought for my daughter), reads one ad headline. Another searches for a suitor "Für meine Schwester" (For my sister). Some ads describe the Mischlinge as being "schwarz" (dark) or "blond." According to Werner Goldberg, those Mischlinge who most resembled their Aryan parents would have an easier path to follow. His younger brother Günther, darker and more Jewish looking, was frequently stopped with challenges to produce his identity papers. "Everybody would say he was Jewish," says Goldberg. Günther did not resemble the Perfect Aryan Soldier. Near the end of the war, he was sent with many other Mischlinge to an Organization Todt labor camp. He almost died there from untreated tuberculosis.

There are also ads for non-sexual sports. One seeks members for a "Ping-Pong-Gruppe," another wants a "Tisch-Tennis-Spieler" (Table-tennis player). A large ad, headed in bold type "Mischling 1 Grades," extols the virtues of a 46-year-old member of the DAF (Deutsche Arbeitsfront, the German Labor Front) with four years of service as a "Front Soldier" during the First World War. Mischlinge were allowed to be members of non-political Nazi Party organizations like the DAF and the NSV (Nationalsocialistische Volkswohlfahrt, the National Socialist People's Welfare League). It was the latter group that usually received the leftover valuables, those no one else wanted, taken from deported Jews.

Arthur Miller[6] notes that "We couldn't even get our parents into the Vereinigung 1937. Originally, in the Paulus-Bund, such a thing was possible. But not now. We had to print in our newsletter that we were not helped in any way by the Jewish community." The rules of the organization left no doubt of this. They flatly stated that the members of Vereinigung 1937 are "not inclined toward Judaism."

Miller warmly recalls the camaraderie of the organization's social activities and how they provided a sense of belonging for an adolescent male Mischlinge legally denied his regular place in German society. He remembers, "We had a secret lake, actually nothing more than a former construction site, and we would go there in groups for small hikes and to swim. But if on our way home we would step into a restaurant, we had to say . . ." He broke off the sentence by extending his hand outward in the "Heil Hitler" salute. His lips remained silent.

Arthur Miller, Hans Faust and Werner Goldberg agreed that the main function of Vereinigung 1937 was to try to help other Mischlinge in the same situation. A theme often repeated today is that the Mischlinge received no help from the Jewish community. As Werner Goldberg put it, "To the Nazis we were practically the same as Jews. But to the Jews, we were goyim." ("Goyim" is the Yiddish term for gentiles. Although not necessarily a pejorative, it often contains an element of derision.)

Jürgen Landeck, librarian of the West Berlin Jewish Community Center and a leading spokesman for West German Jewry, claims that "the Mischlinge are the best friends the Jews in Germany have today." Yet it hasn't always been a two-way street. After the war, Arthur Miller and his mother were sponsored for emigration to Flint, Michigan, from Germany by the Flint Jewish Community Center. They were met upon arrival by the center's director. After briefly talking with them he wrung his hands in despair and loudly exclaimed, "A Jewish woman and her goyische son! We could have had a whole Jewish family for what it cost us to sponsor you!"

Eventually the Gestapo moved against the Mischlinge social organizations, seizing their membership rosters in search of unreported Jewish Mischlinge. Miller remembers that some Jewish children were "passing" as Christian Mischlinge but were eventually discovered and sent to Theresienstadt. "I had our membership book and hid it in the window frame," says Miller. The Gestapo never found it.

In the months of angst before the announcement of the Nuremberg Laws, many Jews in mixed marriages, sensing that the decision on the racial status of their children had already been made by the Nazis, began what was to become a Rush to Conversion. One of those affected was Hanns Rehfeld.[7] He explains, "I am from a family where my father was Jewish and my mother was Christian. And I was baptized at the very last moment. In 1935, when the Nuremberg Laws came, everybody not baptized by then was considered a Jew. My brothers were thirteen and eleven and I was six. My parents didn't want us to be either Jews or Christians. They said, 'When they are eighteen, then they should decide.' A very liberal thought to be sure, but by then Hitler had already decided for us. When the Nazis came to power, my father thought much the same as many other German Jews: It was an understandable government and anti-Semitism always occurs from time to time. But my mother Johanna, with much less university education but with better instincts for the coming danger than my Jewish family, believed otherwise. She felt this was a very dangerous regime and that in order to protect her children, they must be baptized. And so just before the deadline, we were all baptized in the Lutheran faith of my mother."

Rehfeld's father died in 1939. Although the cause was officially given as "heart failure," Hanns believes his father was beaten to death following his arrest for failing to give his name as "Martin Israel Rehfeld" on a ration card. All Jews, even those in mixed marriages, were required to add "Israel" or "Sara" to their names. Obviously, the penalty for disobedience was death.

European opportunists soon began supplying phony baptismal papers for Jews, just as they would later provide the Dutch mixed marriage Jews with bogus sterilization certificates. Indeed, the Jews in the Netherlands were offered their choice of baptismal certificates from fourteen different Christian denominations. Most in demand were those from the nonexistent Synodal Church, because they featured a multitude of rubber stamps that impressed German bureaucrats enough never to question the authenticity of the church.[8]

The brisk trade in specious baptismal certificates was eventually supplanted by the rising demand for the services of cooperative Aryans ready to swear in court that they were the real fathers of Jewish children. While this charade must have provided many expressions of "I told you so!" from those Nazis who had always maintained that Jewish women were notoriously lewd, immoral and promiscuous, it also saved many full Jewish children by officially making them into Mischlinge.[9]

Now even baptism, the well-traveled road so widely used for centuries by German Jews as a certain escape route from the ghetto, was becoming a cul-de-sac. Some churches had gone so far as to say that "by Christian baptism, nothing is altered in regard to a Jew's racial separateness, his national being and his biological nature. . . . The racial Jewish Chris-

Für Zahnarzthaushalt

in der Nähe Berlins wird saub. tücht. Hausmädchen mit guten Kochkenntnissen per sofort od. später verlangt. Offerten mit Zeugnisabschr. u. Gehaltsanspr. an Dr. M. Bluhme, Herzfelde i. M., Möllen Str. 9.

Hausmädchen

christlich, am liebsten mit Zeugnissen, für Haushalt von 3 Personen und 1 Säugling in Stadt Westfalens gesucht. Wäsche außer dem Haus. Evtl. Familienanschluß, guter Lohn. Angebote erbeten unter H. L. 1.

Für mein

Papier- u. Schreibwarengeschäft suche ich möglichst sofort junges Mädchen (Anfäng. od Lehrling). Oskar Philippion, Berlin W 15, Lietzenburger Straße 7.

Erf. Sprechstundenhilfe

gewandt im Umgang mit Patienten, auch massieren, sucht Tätigkeit zum 1. 1. 38. S. L. 19.

Für Nachmittag

sucht Dame Beschäftigung bei Arzt, Kind od. Betreuung alter Dame. T. E. 26.

Manicure

Pedicure, Gesichtsmassage, langjährige Praxis, preiswert Elsa Tull, Tel. 26 2836.

Mischling 1 Grades

46 Jahre alt, Mitglied d. DAS, 16 Jahre Bankfach, 4 Jahre Frontsoldat, 11 Jahre in leitender Stellung in der Textilindustrie, wünscht sich irgendwie zu verändern Befindet sich in ungekündigter Stellung. Zuschriften unter W. R. 10.

Tuchmacher

(Handweber) 30 J., Mischling 1. Gr., Mitglied der DAS, sucht Stellung in Betrieb od. Büro, per sofort Vertraut mit Buchführung, Kalkulation, Muster. usw. Zuschriften unter B. L. 59.

Dame

Krankenschwester, Staatsexamen (Kriegsdienst) Stenografie 130 Silben, Schreibmaschine, tüchtig im Haushalt, sucht Tätigkeit gleich welcher Art. P. S 63.

Ehemaliger

Tabakwaren-Händler, auch Spezialist d. privaten Krankenversicherung, evgl Mischling 1. Gr., Front- und Freikorpskämpfer, 14 J., fleißig u arbeitsfreudig, unbescholten, sucht sof. Stellung bei bescheidenen Ansprüchen. Büroarbeit auch angenehm Zuschriften erbittet Max Sophar, Kolberg, Pomm., Kummerstr. 19.

Burroughs-Kalkulator Rechnerin

perfekt auch auf Brunsviga u. and. Maschinen, vertraut mit Buchhaltung Statistik, Maschinenschr. 35 J., ungekündigt, sucht sich zum 1. 2. 38 zu verändern. Zuschr. unter C. S 2.

Junges begabtes Mädel

16 J., evgl., sucht Lehrstelle in seinem Modesalon. Schneidert gut, näht Kleider, Kostüme und Mäntel, ist eine flotte Zeichnerin und hat eine gute Schulbildung. Zuschr u. J. P. 12.

Suche

bei bescheidenen Ansprüchen Stelle als Wirtschafterin im Geschäftshaushalt, wo ich gleichzeitig meinen 16j. Sohn als Lehrling unterbringen kann. Gleichviel welche Branche. Zuschriften an M. 37.

Kaufmann (Jurist)

35 J., Mischl. 1, 4 Jahre Buchhalter, Korrespondent etc., perf. im Mahn-, Zahlungs- und Rechnungswesen usw., jetzt Süddeutschland (Stuttgart) sucht Stellung gleich welcher Art. Angebote unter R. S 12.

Aerztin, Dr. med.

in Prag approbiert, evgl., sucht Tätigkeitsfeld, am liebsten in chem. oder pharmaz. Industrie. F. S. 19.

Vertrauensstellung

sucht vielseitig geb. Dame speziell registratorische, Kartei- u. lohnbuchh. Kenntnisse. Gewandheit im Briefwechsel, auch als Bibliothekarin tätig gewesen, zum 1. 1. 38, G. S. 7.

Sprechstundenhilfe

mit etwas Hausarbeit (Staatsexamen in Hauswirtschaft Mischling 1. Gr., sucht Stellung zum 1. 1. 38. R. L. 15.

Stenotypistin

tüchtig, in ungekünd. Stellung, möchte sich zum 1. 1. 38 verändern. Mitglied der DAS. Zuschriften unter K. 8.

Sprachunterricht

Englisch, Französisch, Spanisch, Italienisch. Fernruf 260147,

Kaufm. Unterricht

Kurzschrift, Maschinenschreiben, Buchführung, kaufm. Korrespondenz, kaufm. Rechnen-Einzelunterricht. Beginn jederzeit. Kurzschriftkursus mit geringer Teilnehmerzahl. Beginn Anfang Januar. Fernr. 260147.

2 Zimmerwohnung

Bad, Diele, Küche, Gas, elektrisch in 2-Familienhaus, Berlin-Lichtenrade an ruhigen Mieter zum 1. 4. 38, evtl. früher abzugeben. RM. 55.—. Zuschriften an M. A. 8.

Komfortzimmer

Möbliert, incl. Heizung, Licht, Bad, RM. 50.—, Kaiserdamm, möglichst an berufstätige Dame zu vermieten per 1. 1. 38. Telefon 93 62 65.

2 große Leerzimmer

Höchstkomfort, zum 1. 4. 38. oder früher in kultiviertem Hause mit Bad und Küchenbenutzung Gegend Breitenbachplatz gesucht. Evtl. Tausch 4½ gegen 2½ Zimm. Tel.: 76 0978.

Ping-Pong-Gruppe!

Wir spielen auch in diesem Jahre wieder regelmäßig. Interessenten wenden sich an: Helmut Stern, Berlin W 92, Bayreuther Str. 40, Tel.: 25 6221.

Mediziner

Staatsexamen ohne Approbation, jetzt Kaufmann der Pharmazie, Mischl. 1. Gr., 31 J., 1,73 gr, wünscht nette gebild. Kameradin in Berlin kennen zu lernen, um gute engl Sprachkenntnisse besitzt und Interesse für Wanderungen, Sport und Theater hat. Zuschriften erbeten unter K. C. 5.

Erfahrener Augenarzt

(Kassenarzt) übernimmt Vertretungen. Aug. u. Dr. M. 5.

Gutaussehender

26 jähriger Bürokaufmann, Halbarier, evgl., 1,65 gr., sehr allein, möchte sympathische Dame mit Eigenheim kennen lernen. Nachricht erbeten an Lagerkarte 122, Berlin W 15.

Wessen Sohn od. Tochter

soll Zahntechniker werden? Gründliche Ausbildung durch Zahntechnikermeister gewährleistet. Einlage von RM. 5000 für Lehrzeitdauer. (4 Jahre) Zuschriften erb. unter O. B. 24.

Ich übernehme das

Papier- u. Schreibwarengeschäft von P. Lesch, Berlin W 15, Lietzenburger Str. 7. Reizende Geschenkartikel f Weihnachten. Ich bitte um Besichtigung meiner Auslagen Oskar Philippion, i. Fa. P. Lesch Nachf., Lietzenburger Straße 7.

Größere Freude

und Ueberraschung können Sie kaum auslösen, als wenn Sie mich zu Ihrer Weihnachtsgabe bestimmen. Mein Nutzungswert beträgt das Dielsache des zu zahlenden (Raten-) Preises, und ich wüßte nicht, wem ich als Geschenk nicht sehr willkommen wäre. Die Kleinschreibmaschine". Allen meinen Kunden die besten Weihnachtsgrüße und Neujahrswünsche! Gerhard Salinger, Tel.: 42 1064. (Sie erhalten durch mich sämtl. Systeme).

Gutes Welt-Radio

Gleichstrom gesucht gegen Barzahlung. 24 6485.

Klavier

gutes kreuzsaitiges von Hoflieferant Adolf Lehmann & Co. tauscht geg. Welt-Radio (Gleichstrom) 246485.

Uebersetzungen

Englisch, Französisch, Italienisch schnell, sicher, billig. Zuschrift. unter M. K. an die Geschäftsst.

Geiger (Dr. phil.)

auch Sänger (Tenor) sucht geübten Klavierspieler zu gemeins. Spiel; Violinsonaten- u. Konzerte etc. W. S. 35.

Junge geb. Bayerin

25 J., Mischl. 1. Gr., wünscht Anschluß bzw. Briefwechsel mit nettem Herrn, da, an kleinem Ort wohnend, Mangel an geselligem Beisammensein. Bildzuschriften unter M. S. 48.

Tisch-Tennis-Spieler!

Täglich von 12—24 Uhr. Treffpunkt: Berlin W 62, Bayreuther Str. 40, Tel.: 25 6221 (3. Haus vom Wittenbergplatz).

Justizrat Fritz Ladewig

Bad Blankenburg Thür. Bähringstr. 18, Fernruf 242 36 Jahre lang Nachlaßpfleger zur Ermittlung unbekannter Erben bei dem Großberliner Amtsgerichten, übernimmt Ausarbeitung von Ahnentafeln, Stammbäumen und Sammlung von urkundlichen Unterlagen aller Art (Ehegenehmigung etc.)

Für meine Nichte

ev., Mischling 1. Gr., Aerztin, 31 J., hübsche vornehme Erscheinung mit größerem Vermögen, suche auf diesem Wege gesundenLebensgefährten, mögl. Akademiker, Chemiker bevorzugt, unbedingte Diskretion verlangt und zugesichert. Ausführl. ernstgemeinte Zuschriften mit Bild erbeten unter A. R. 11.

107

These columns of Gothic lonely hearts ads are from the Mischlinge association membership newsletter in 1937. The Mischlinge were restricted by law to social contacts with members of their own "Third Race." Some of the ads seek ping-pong players! *(Photograph courtesy Werner Goldberg)* tian has no place or right in the German Evangelical Church."[10] While Werner Goldberg's father lamented his new official status as being "neither black nor white," the Nazis were quick to label him black in a shadow world.

Werner Goldberg, like all healthy eighteen-year-old German males, served his compulsory six-month term in the Reichsarbeitsdienst. "They had a uniform," recalls Werner, "a military look, and we wore the swastika on our arm."

Did Goldberg wear the swastika at home? "Yes," he replied. "It was part of the uniform." What was his father's reaction to it? "Most of the time," said Goldberg, "I took it off when I came into the house. But I had so few civilian clothes that fit, I had to wear my uniform even on the weekends." Several of the photographs Goldberg supplied for this book show him in his uniform, with the swastika arm band visible. He is posed with his mother. There are none taken with his father.

Yet others among the Mischlinge have a different perception of this time. Hanns Rehfeld sees himself as a victim. Says Rehfeld: "I might have been a Nazi, but I never had the chance. They would not take me into the Hitler Youth.

"The difficult thing to explain," Rehfeld says, "is the choking feeling for a child like myself who felt that with every day, death was coming nearer. First my father's death. Then the destruction of his family.

"My uncles and aunts were full Jews," he continues. "My father had two sisters and they were both married: one to a lawyer, another to a judge. In the spring of 1943 they were all sent to the concentration camp Majdanek—the Lublin killing center. We didn't know it was Majdanek at the time. They were told they were being sent to work camps and we pretended it was so. 'Well,' we said, 'by now they're bringing them new shoes.' And later we said, 'Well, they don't write, but let's hope they are well.' But everybody knew they weren't being sent to a work camp. Everybody was lying to each other and nobody admitted the truth. But everybody knew. We didn't dare admit the truth. It was impossible.

"My grandmother—my father's mother—was 86. On 27 May 1944 she was to be sent to Theresienstadt, which was also a camp but a little bit milder. It was where old people were sent. After she had practically seen the death of all three of her children, she was aware of what deportation meant. She was a very conservative Jew, always praying, a very devout Jew. And she committed suicide. For a Jew who believed as deeply in her faith as she did, suicide could not have been an easy thing.

"I could feel death come nearer and nearer. Every railroad boxcar I saw, I felt there were Jews inside, and I felt one step closer to death. And that experience, in those formative years from the age of seven or eight, has shocked me for life in ways that I know I can never overcome."

Werner Goldberg's father was the only one to survive from his immediate family. Werner remembers that "My father's sister and his mother were brought to Theresienstadt. From there we received once a post card and we sent them parcels. But then one day the parcel was returned. After the war I found their names on the Auschwitz lists.

"There were other relatives too. I had an uncle. He was Jewish. He had no children. In the First World War he had been a decorated officer. When the Nazis came to power he said, 'I can not believe they will do anything to me.' Once, when I was in the Reichsarbeitsdienst, I went to see him for a weekend. I was then in my uniform, the one with the swastika. Later we heard that one day he and his wife were taken away. I found their names at Auschwitz too.

"We had a lot of relatives. There was a brother of my father's father. He lived in Berlin with his wife and three children. They were brought first to Theresienstadt. Then to Auschwitz. Not one survived.

"The daughter of another sister of my father had married a Jewish man in Belgium who worked in the iron and steel industries. One day he was summoned to come to Berlin because the Nazis hoped to get a patent from him. He was here for two weeks, but he wouldn't give them what they wanted. When the Germans came to Belgium, they fetched him one day and he was never seen again."

Some of the Mischlinge even saw their Jewish parent sent to a concentration camp. The Mischlinge interviewed were luckier than most. Their parents survived.

Dr. Hans Salomon tried to keep his mother, Gertrud Salomon, from being deported to Theresienstadt in 1943. "I was able to keep her free until then," recalls Dr. Salomon, "by joining the DAF—the German Labor Front. They told me, 'If you enter, you might save your mother.' Well, I entered. But they summoned her to Theresienstadt anyway."

Fortunately, through his job in a factory, Salomon was able to get enough extra rations so that each month he could send his mother "500 grams of sausage, half a pound of butter, some other food, even coffee, which, although it was forbidden, I would put anyway into a small tin. Then I would just send the parcel through the normal mails. Officially, Theresienstadt was never called a concentration camp. It was just a town. It was in the so-called Protektorat of Bohemia and Moravia. Some of the people there were artists. Others were heroes of World War I. Auschwitz you could never send a parcel to. But Theresienstadt was different. They made quite a thing of it. There was a preprinted card to which my mother could only add her name, but which I would receive from her in acknowledgment. When I wrote to her I used a code we had arranged to let her know if Hitler's fortunes were up or down. If I wrote 'Liebe Mutter!' like this—with the exclamation mark—it meant everything was going normal, or the bad way for us. But when I wrote 'Liebe Mutter,' this way, with a comma the way the Americans do, it meant things were said to be turning out badly for the Nazis.

"I was allowed to send her parcels every four weeks. After November 1944, I received no further confirmation from her that she had received the food I had sent. But I kept on sending food parcels and she told me later that she continued to receive them until March 1945. Then suddenly everything at Theresienstadt was closed. The Russians came in from the east. The Americans had already taken part of Saxony but unfortunately they didn't penetrate as far as Theresienstadt. The Russians discharged her in July and soon afterward we were together again."

Had there been any danger of Dr. Salomon's mother being sent to Auschwitz as were so many other inmates of the so-called "safe ghetto"? "Yes," said Dr. Salomon. "There were selections every four weeks and everyone who was seriously ill was sent off along with anyone who had done something for which someone felt they should be 'punished.' Once my mother was in the hospital as selection time came around, but the doctor sent her out and said, 'Even if you have to crouch on your knees in pain, you must leave the hospital for a few days. The selection commission is coming through and otherwise you will be off to Auschwitz. After they leave, then you can come back in.' That was how she managed to survive."[11]

What about the other Jewish members of Dr. Salomon's family? Did they survive? Dr. Salomon sat quietly. Before his eyes there passed a parade of ghostly images, each forever caught in the freeze frame of time. Mentally he identified each, captioning photographs in an album of the dead. He saw them as they had once appeared in snapshots of picnics and other family gatherings and not as corpses stacked grotesquely at the doors of a Nazi gas chamber. In a voice suddenly grown numb, he began to recite the litany of the dead: "Sent to Auschwitz and never returned were: my mother's brother, two cousins of my mother, two nieces—the daughters of her sisters—one of them together with her husband and son. One of my mother's sisters committed suicide when she was about to be deported, as did a lady cousin of my mother."

What Dr. Salomon, and the Nazis, did *not* know was that his father was himself a half-Jew and not an Aryan! Had the Nazis known the truth, Dr. Salomon would have been clas-

sified not as a Mischling but as a Jew with three Jewish
grandparents and both he and his mother might also have been
sent to their deaths at Auschwitz. "My father was able to
keep it quiet," explains Dr. Salomon, "because he had a German name and his mother's maiden name was Albrecht. In
reality, it had been Abramsohn. They had switched to the
Christian creed and changed their name. But my father had
sent me some papers which I needed to prove that I was half-
Aryan and never told me the truth. I only heard about it later
from my brother."

Yet the irony doesn't end here. Dr. Salomon's parents had
never married, and under the illegitimacy statutes, his mother
was protecting him, as well as herself, by claiming he was
fathered by an Aryan, the very same half-Jew who was his
real father. In Dr. Salomon's situation, the Nazi illegitimacy
laws actually saved two Jewish lives.

Rolf Vogel's mother, who was Jewish (although she had
converted to Catholicism), was also deported to Theresienstadt and her son was sent to an Organization Todt labor camp
in October 1944. Vogel's father had died a month before the
start of the war. Without the protection of the Aryan spouse,
the Jewish surviving member in a mixed marriage was often
vulnerable for deportation to Theresienstadt. But Vogel believes his mother was in fact a hostage. "Had I tried to leave
the labor camp," he says, "they would have deported my
mother to Auschwitz. She guaranteed my good behavior."

In the confusing aftermath of a raid upon the labor camp
by Allied bombers in April 1945, Vogel picked up an SS guard's
cap, put it on his head, and walked away. He walked for three
days and nights before he felt he was safe. Six weeks after
the end of the war, he bicycled to Stuttgart and asked the
Americans where he could find his mother. "The American on
duty asked if my mother was a Jew," Vogel recalls. " 'Jewish
born. She's Catholic,' I told him. He said, in that case, he
couldn't give me any information. I took him by the neck and
said, "We had Hitler here. You don't know what it was like
in Germany.' He took his briefcase from under the table and

opened it. He had a list of the survivors of Theresienstadt. And there I found the name of my mother."

Arthur Miller was even more fortunate. "My mother Johanna (Chana) Weisz, was a Hungarian Jewess," he recalls. "Before they issued the ration cards, the Nazis inquired in people's houses as to the origin [nationality] of the people living there. And we were very lucky that our landlady said of my mother, 'Oh, her? She's a Roman Catholic from Hungary.' My mother still had her old ration card from the First World War. It was an identification card issued by the post office after my father had died in the war, and back then, of course, it did not have to show a big 'J.' When I was in the Luftwaffe, she was afraid to go and pick up the small amount of money—it was like a cost of living allowance—that she would have received for my serving. She never picked it up, but she could easily have done so and without any trouble. So she missed some money that way. I couldn't deduct her on my paycheck. Jewish people were not deductible on your taxes or from your monthly salary, either in the armed forces or in civilian life. My mother was supposed to be called to come to Theresienstadt, but she was just lucky. They never called her."

Heinz Elsberg's[12] father was the last Jewish journalist in Nazi Berlin. Paul Elsberg was a member of the famous Ullstein publishing family and his son, severely crippled at birth, was raised in the magnificent Ullsteinhaus on Berlin's Markgrafenstrasse. Paul Elsberg was chief economics editor of *Vossiche Zeitung* and *BZ am Mittag*, two of the most influential publications in the vast Ullstein empire. During his twenty-five-year career, he had known Walther Funk, head of the Nazi Press Bureau, when Funk was still a working journalist. And he was on good terms with Dr. Horace Greeley Hjalmar Schacht, powerful President of the Reichsbank. Because Paul Elsberg had officially left the Jewish community in 1926 when he stopped paying taxes to the Gemeinde, he did not have to wear the yellow star and he received privileged mixed marriage classification. But the most remarkable aspect of his story is that his son Heinz, a badly deformed half-Jew, was allowed to live unmolested by the Nazis. In their effort to purify the Reich by sending "incurably sick persons" to the gas chambers, the Nazis were able to test this method of instant death for its subsequent use upon the Jews.

Like his father, Heinz Elsberg is also a noted Berlin journalist. He will say very little about his life during the Nazi era other than to explain how he was not allowed to continue with his planned higher education studies in Berlin because "the professors said I am not nice [perfect] and the Führer must have only nice humans." (In 1937, Elsberg was allowed to complete his Abitur, the grueling examination that would ordinarily determine whether he would enter the University of Berlin. He passed, but was barred from the University as were all the Mischlinge.) "And so," he continued, "I lived in very small rooms during the Nazi times and I worked only in upstairs out-of-the-way positions for some editors of music who did not know I was a half-Jew."

When Paul Elsberg's sister was sent to Theresienstadt, where she perished, he decided to go into hiding. "Up until the beginning of 1945 it was all right," recalls his son, "but for the last four or five months of the war, he went away. Because he had been in such a high position before the war, and still had so many contacts within the Nazi hierarchy, he went underground as much for political reasons as for racial reasons." Paul Elsberg survived the war only to die "horribly" two years later in a Frankfurt automobile accident. Today his portrait hangs in the Berlin headquarters of Axel Springer, West Germany's postwar press lord. The Springerhaus is built upon virtually the same ground where the grand Ullsteinhaus once stood. It was only after the death of his father that Heinz Elsberg chose to become a Protestant.

There are many grim ironies in the deportation and subsequent deaths of the aged Jewish parents of the privileged mixed marriage Jews, but this is one of the most striking. Historically, when the son of Orthodox parents brought home a gentile bride, his father and mother would feel so disgraced that they would "sit shiva"—enter into the prolonged ceremonial mourning service for a dead member of the immediate family. "My son is dead," they would wail. A less drastic action would be for the parents to threaten suicide. But now, only because of that very factor of intermarriage, their son remained alive to mourn for his murdered parents.[13]

The destruction by the Nazis of the Jewish side of the families of the Mischlinge raises the question of when the Mischlinge first knew what was really happening to the Jews. Hanns Rehfeld answers it: "There is a collective lie in Germany that nobody really knew about what was happening in Auschwitz. But I remember clearly on Christmas Day of 1943, I was at a gathering of various people, most of them also from mixed marriages. We had a Christmas Party and all the details were discussed. About the gas chamber. How people were told it was only for disinfection. All those details that the rest of the world only learned about after World War II were perfectly known by all of us in that circle on that Christmas Day.

"I remember too," Rehfeld continues, "how people who were in my school grade, certain pupils, told me their brethren came home from the front on leave and told how the Jews were shot. They knew how the Jews were made to dig ditches before they were shot. If these little boys of eleven, twelve and thirteen were so well informed, I can not believe that any German who was in a public function did not know about it.

"Once in a shop where people complained about bad food supplies, I remember that somebody—I think it was the shopkeeper—said, 'Shut up or otherwise you will be sent to Auschwitz.' And everybody shut up. Everyone got very pale. They knew perfectly well what Auschwitz was.

"Taking these experiences from my childhood, perhaps with the exception of a few stupid farmers from some remote corner of Bavaria, everybody must have known something. And most of them in public life had known everything. This is contrary to what most Germans say, but I refute them. I don't believe that they didn't know it. It was impossible to be kept secret. It was meant to be kept secret. But that was impossible."

Rehfeld's comments are dramatically echoed by Charlotte

Lehmann, who says, "Nowadays very old people and contemporaries of that time all say, 'We didn't know anything.' But whoever had eyes and was prepared to open and make use of them had to know of it. We knew when the furniture wagons—the big vans—came, and on each side there was a long bank of seats and all those poor people had to step up a little ladder, sit down and put their little parcels under the seats. We saw it already in Berlin in 1941, shortly after the wearing of the yellow star had been introduced. We saw it first in the Rosenthalstrasse.

"And we heard when we were at the baker's, 'Did you know the Navaroths have committed suicide?' 'But why?' we asked. And we were told that the Nazi snoopers came and grabbed their little canary from its cage and squeezed it to death and said 'You are not worthy of having animals.' It broke their hearts so that they committed suicide. In our district there was such a terrible wave of suicides. This one jumped out of a window. That one took poison. The other went down in front of a train.

"When my father and his family had to leave their home, they were put in an apartment of four rooms together with seven other families. All these Jewish families, the Bernsteins and the Blumenfelds and the Cohns and the Abrahams, they were all together with the Steins. We had enough food, but the Steins were in a terrible situation. Through my work I would get additional ration coupons, and that meant help for the Stein family.

"We continued to meet the Stein family clandestinely, but it was always becoming more difficult. In August 1942, there was the first terrible air raid in Berlin. My mother and I went to the apartment on the Colognestrasse in Berlin-Schöneberg where the Steins and the other Jewish families had been forced to live. And in the evening, under the cover of darkness, I went upstairs and pushed the doorbell. There was only one name listed, Blumenthal, but there were many yellow stars.

"A lady with a very sad face and hungry eyes opened the

door. I said, 'Good evening, I would like to give something to Mr. or Mrs. Stein. Could I please talk with them? Or would you please give them this for me? It is just my little parcel of food.' And the lady was so shocked and afraid. 'They aren't here anymore,' she said, and she slammed the door. And my mother and I went away.

" 'They aren't here anymore.' What could that have meant at that time? We knew. It meant deportation.

"As the air raids continued, we were so desperate and depressed that my mother and I decided we would no longer go to the air raid shelter. 'Instead,' we said, 'Let's go to heaven.' And so we stayed in our apartment. Our air raid warden was required to be a Nazi as were all the lesser functionaries, and one day he said to us, 'I can not take you ladies by your hairs and drag you down to the shelter. You know it is ordered that everyone *must* go to the shelter. But if you prefer to stay in your apartment (we lived on the first floor) then please don't turn on your radio so loudly that everyone in the shelter can hear Big Ben so clearly. [Lehmann was authorized to monitor the otherwise forbidden BBC–London shortwave broadcasts only at her office.] I would even suggest that you bring along your marvelous Telefunken so that we can all share it.' "

According to Werner Goldberg, it wasn't just Nazi air raid wardens that were protective of the Mischlinge. Goldberg recalls that "one floor under us in our house there lived an SS Gruppenführer [major general], a Mr. Paulstich. He was a very nice man, but his wife was not so nice. When the Russians came in 1945, we were all in the cellar—we had all heard that the troops were coming now—and I told him to get out his papers and any other material so that we could try to help him. Instead he said to me, 'Please, Werner, don't tell my family, don't tell this to anyone, but it is impossible to help me.' 'But why?' I asked, and he said 'I can not tell you all the things I have done, but I have committed many terrible crimes. You must believe me Werner. Nobody will be able to help me.'

"Our first days under the Russians came and went. One afternoon I was in the office of the Commander of the Soviets when a message arrived: 'Please, please come home. Mr. Paulstich is taken by the Russians.' And I came right away. But we never saw him again. When I was in the archives of the crimes of the Nazis, I asked for his file. They have there the acts of this man. He was the chief of the Housing Ministry and had conducted medical tests upon people. Nobody knows where he is. I think the Russians just took him out and shot him.

"But now comes the other part. I later saw the official papers of the Nazi Party. And in the papers under my father's name there was a notice by Mr. Paulstich which said, 'He may continue to live in his home in the future.' That is the order of Paulstich—'Goldberg can stay.' He protected our entire family. All the others would lose their flats, but we had no problems in this area. After the war when I found this paper, I knew why. Mr. Paulstich had always been friendly with my father even though he knew he was a racial Jew. Mrs. Paulstich, though, would always look away whenever she saw him."

But this was not to be Paulstich's only contribution toward keeping Albert Israel Goldberg alive. Werner Goldberg tells of "a time when my father needed an urological operation and there were no Jewish doctors left in Berlin who could make such an operation. I went to the charity clinic and saw a professor there and told him of the problem. He said that he would try to find a surgeon for my father and he did, a Dr. Lewy. He was a Jewish surgeon because the Nazis would only allow a Jewish doctor to operate upon a Jew. Dr. Lewy said he would do it although he had never performed such an operation. It would have to take place at the Bavaria-Klinik für jüdische Patienten on Münchener Strasse, the last clinic in Berlin where Jews were accepted as patients.

"This was in 1942 and the round-up of Jews in Berlin for deportation had begun. During the operation, the Bavaria-

Klinik was surrounded by cars of the SS. All of the old people, the Jewish doctors, even the governors of the hospital were captured. Dr. Lewy begged the SS men, 'Please let me continue. I have to finish the operation on this patient.' But the SS refused and took the nurse and Dr. Lewy downstairs. But the doctor had hidden on him a little capsule and he swallowed it. By the time they got him downstairs, he was dead.

"I called the professor and told him what had happened. He came with his assistant and they were allowed to come in and complete the operation upon my father. Meanwhile the SS were bringing in vans and taking even the sick people away from the Klinik. But somehow the professor was able to get an ambulance to transport my father to another hospital, the Jüdische Krankenhaus on the Iranische Strasse. But when I came there to visit my father they said, 'You can not see him. He is a prisoner of the SS.'

"And in this situation I did not know what else to do. So I went to our neighbor, Mr. Paulstich. He said, 'Don't worry, I will arrange things.' From that day my father had very good care and was able to leave the hospital after seven weeks."

Goldberg's story is confirmed by his father's official medical history records, signed by Dr. G. Emanuel, of anti-syphilis serum fame, who himself lived in a privileged mixed marriage[14] (see Chapter Six). At the end of the chronology of Goldberg's ordeal appears, "Da er in Mischehe lebte, erst später wieder entlassen"—"Because he lived in a mixed marriage, therefore he was only discharged later." Once again, thanks to Paulstich, "Goldberg can stay"—alive. Had he not been in a privileged mixed marriage, Goldberg not only would have been released earlier than his recovery period, he would have been released to the SS. But as it was, in the words of Werner Goldberg, "He came home to us." Albert Goldberg was the only survivor, among both patients and staff, of the SS raid on the Bavaria-Klinik.

Werner Goldberg says that "when the Russians came in 1945, my father sewed on his yellow Star of David (which, although issued, he had not been required to wear) and waited in the cellar for the Russians to arrive. When the first of them came, my father ran to kiss him. But the Russian soldier raised his hand and slapped my father in the face. My father was shocked. The soldier said to my father 'We Russians have nothing against race like the Nazis do, but to us, the Jews are all capitalists and we don't like them either.'

"And when the Russians were gone, then came the British troops. They were looking for rooms for their military government and they took our apartment. It was not possible to argue with them. One of their generals said, 'You can not tell me that everybody who is still alive today had nothing to do with the Nazis.' And so now this flat in which we had lived for twelve years, the flat which the Nazis said we could stay in, was being taken away from us by the very people who had come to make us free. We had to leave all of our things in the flat—and we had to leave in two hours. My father was by now becoming very disturbed."

After years of having successfully saved his father by interceding with higher authorities, Werner Goldberg gave that method one more try. By now he was working for the Russians[15] so he arranged for a Soviet general to come and talk with the British. This time his luck ran out. Goldberg could not stay. The family was put out into the streets of Berlin—by the British.

Through the Russians, Goldberg was quickly able to find another flat for his family. "All we had there were some chairs," he recalls, "and my father quietly sat down in one of them. He did not stand up again. Nor did he ever again speak to anyone. He died six weeks later.

"For twelve years," Goldberg said, "my father had waited for the moment when he would again be free. He never believed that in the end he would have to pay for what the Nazis had done. During the air attacks, my father had sat in the cellar, anxious for his own life but also begging for bombs to end the Nazi regime. He knew that every falling bomb short-

ened the life span of the Thousand Year Reich. But the same
bomb that ends the regime could also be the one that kills
you. When my father died, we found a poison capsule and a
note in his pocket. Perhaps he had this capsule since the time
of his operation. We would never know."

Remarkable as it may seem, yet another Nazi helped save
one of the Goldbergs from deportation. Goldberg recalled that
his parents had belonged to the Grunewald Tennis Club since
1930 "and I joined in 1932. A member of the club had become
an Untersturmführer [second lieutenant] in the SS. He had
a Dutch name, Overhus. He telephoned me at home one evening—this was already quite late in the war—and said, 'I give
you a warning—leave Berlin for some days. There is an Aktion. I can't speak about it more but it would be sufficient if
you were to be gone five days.' "

(This may have been one of the two April 1944 actions
against the Mischlinge in which they were rounded up for deportation to the Organization Todt work camps.)

"When the first air attacks came, I had told my chief at
work to find a second location for our production. In that way,
if we were destroyed by bombs in Berlin—our plant was on
the Königstrasse—we would have another factory to work out
of. He was too busy, but I was able to find a location in Stendal
(near Rathenow) where we soon began to produce leather
clothing for the troops. It was always very important to me
to be able to prove that I was in a useful occupation and making
a useful contribution to the war effort. Since I was now already
spending two days at Stendal every week, when the call from
Untersturmführer Overhus came, it was not at all difficult for
me to leave Berlin for five days.

"But there were others who helped us survive too—like
people my father had worked with who now gave him money
'under the table.' One of these was his friend Mr. Herrmann,
a real estate man. My father went to his home once a week
and would always come back with some money. I frequently
wondered how we would continue to live. We had to pay rent

for our flat, and the first year that I worked, I only made thirty Reichsmark a month. So we had to sell a lot of our things—pictures, books, porcelains. People who had a lot of money would buy them and they were happy because they were not paying too great a price. But my father was pleased, too. He just wanted us to have some money."

On three separate occasions—the arrest and detention of Albert Goldberg in the Fabrik Aktion; his detention by the SS in the aftermath of the Bavaria-Klinik raid; and the telephoned tip-off to Werner Goldberg of an impending Aktion—the lives of father and son, a full Jew and a Mischling, had been saved by those who have been branded as war criminals. How does Goldberg reconcile this inconsistency? "Sometimes," he replied, "you don't know who your angel is. These were Nazis who would murder millions—but then one time they would get human feelings and lay their hands upon us to give us life.

"The Good German? The Bad German? No, I think the reality is somewhere in the middle."

Rolf Vogel will tell you unequivocally that "Hans Globke helped my mother." He doesn't mean that Globke aided her directly, but had the civil servants not created the Mischlinge, his mother, although she was sent to Theresienstadt, would not have been allowed to live. And of course Vogel is right. We've already seen how the fate of the Mischlinge and the survival of the mixed marriage Jews were woven together into the crazy quilt pattern of Nazi law. As a postwar journalist, Vogel interviewed Globke, then Staatssekretär to Chancellor Adenauer, and received the widely quoted Globke statement that the Nuremberg Racial Laws were designed to "protect," and thus save, "those Jews most like us."[16]

And that is exactly what did happen. Whether in Berlin, Sofia or Oslo, the mixed marriage Jews and their children received special treatment. When the yellow stars were passed out, they didn't have to wear them. When the other Jews were deported to death camps, they were still left behind.

Mischlinge! Werner Goldberg (left) and his younger brother Günther in 1930. Werner Goldberg was 11, Günther 10. After the Nazis came to power, Günther, who was darker and more Jewish looking than his brother, was frequently stopped and ordered to produce his identity papers to prove he wasn't a Jew. Both brothers became active in postwar Berlin politics. *(Photograph courtesy Werner Goldberg)*

Werner Goldberg's parents on their wedding day in 1918. Albert Goldberg was born into a Jewish family but had been baptized as a Protestant in 1900 when he was 19. His wife, the former Frieda Christ, came from a Protestant Silesian family. *(Photograph courtesy Werner Goldberg)*

"To me, he had always looked like Goethe." So said Werner Goldberg about his father, Albert Goldberg, shown here in 1938. Werner did not know that his father was a Jew until the Nazi racial laws made him trace his family tree. *(Photograph courtesy Werner Goldberg)*

A life could depend upon the subtleties of shading. This card is for a full Jew married to another full Jew. Note that the stamped letter J is closed. The J would have been stamped in blue ink. It is almost certain that the holder of this card perished in the Nazi death camps. *(Photograph courtesy Rijksinstituut voor Oorlogsdocumentatie, Amsterdam)*

This card, for a Jew in a mixed marriage, has an open J. It would have been stamped in red ink. Presumably, the holder of this card survived, although she may have later been required to present a certificate of sterilization. Phony certificates were available to the Jews for a price—from the Gestapo. *(Photograph courtesy Rijksinstituut voor Oorlogsdocumentatie, Amsterdam)*

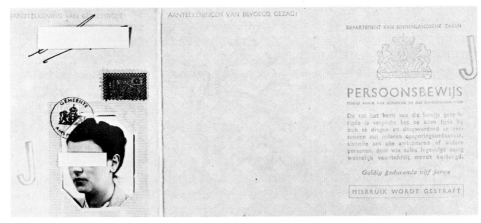

This photograph of Werner Goldberg was distributed by the Nazi Propaganda Ministry in 1939 with the caption of "The Perfect Aryan Soldier." However, the subject, Private Werner Goldberg of the Wehrmacht, wasn't an Aryan—he was a Mischling. *(Photograph courtesy Werner Goldberg)*

Hans Salomon as a member of the German armed forces, 1939. Salomon was a Mischling, but had the Nazis known that his father was not an Aryan but a part-Jew himself, they would have classified Salomon as a Jew. Fortunately, his parents weren't married, and the Nazi illegitimacy laws saved the lives of both him and his Jewish mother. *(Photograph courtesy Dr. Hans Salomon)*

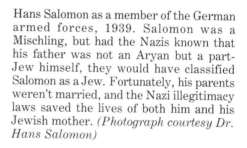

A soldier on horseback—Hans Faust in the German military, 1940. Faust was a Mischling. *(Photograph courtesy Hans Faust)*

Mario Heil de Brentani, his wife Ruth, and one of their children in March 1944. De Brentani was the editor of Field Marshal Erwin Rommel's army newspaper. His wife was a Mischling and de Brentani used his uniform to protect her from deportation. *(Photograph courtesy Ruth von Brentani)*

Hanns Rehfeld in a recent photograph. Rehfeld, a West German diplomat stationed in New York, was a Mischling. *(Photograph courtesy Hanns Rehfeld)*

Johanna Rehfeld, mother of Hanns. She saved the lives of her three Mischlinge children by having them baptized shortly before the Nuremberg Laws took effect. *(Photograph courtesy Hanns Rehfeld)*

Werner Goldberg, the son of a Jew, wearing the swastika. Goldberg was serving in the Reichsarbeitsdienst, the compulsory pre-military service. The photograph was taken in 1938. That's Goldberg's mother with him, his father was taking the photo. There are no photographs of Goldberg with his father while he is wearing the swastika. *(Photograph courtesy Werner Goldberg)*

Gertrud Salomon, the mother of Hans Salomon. Her son did everything he could to protect her, but she was still sent to Theresienstadt. Fortunately, she survived. *(Photograph courtesy Dr. Hans Salomon)*

Dr. Hans Salomon in a recent photograph. Dr. Salomon is a world famous parasitologist, and was associated with the World Health Organization (WHO). Photograph copyright by Photo-Grammes, Berlin. *(Photograph courtesy Dr. Hans Salomon)*

Arthur Miller (Müller) and his mother. She was a Jew. After the war, they emigrated to Flint, Michigan. *(Photograph courtesy Arthur Miller)*

Heinz Elsberg today. His father was the last Jewish journalist in Berlin, and a member of the famous Ullstein publishing family. Photograph copyright Nicola Galliner, Berlin. *(Photograph courtesy Heinz Elsberg)*

Rabbi Martin Riesenburger of East Berlin. During the war, the Nazis allowed him to bury the Berlin Jewish dead in religious ceremonies at a Jewish cemetery. His wife was a Christian. Photograph copyright Puck Pressedienst, Berlin. *(Photograph courtesy Klara Riesenburger)*

Klaus Peter Scholz in the German army during the winter of 1939–1940. Scholz was a Mischling who after the war chose to become a practicing Jew. *(Photograph courtesy Klaus Peter Scholz)*

ns Faust and his mother in 1927. Al-
ugh she was a Jew, she was able to have
son freed from a Nazi concentration
p where he had been interned along
other members of the German Com-
ist Party (KPD) in 1933. *(Photograph
rtesy Hans Faust)*

A very dapper Hans Faust strikes a pose of distinction in this postwar (1947) portrait. *(Photograph courtesy Hans Faust)*

Werner Goldberg in 1979, his last year as a member of the Senate of Berlin. Photograph copyright Pressebilderdienst Kindermann, Berlin. *(Photograph courtesy Warner Goldberg)*

Ongeldig. The identity card for a Dutch "Invaluable" Jew—a member of the select and protected Blue Knights. The ever-protective Dutch authorities took care to cover his features before giving the author the photograph, but they neglected to cover his name. *(Photograph courtesy Rijksinstituut voor Oorlogsdocumentatie, Amsterdam)*

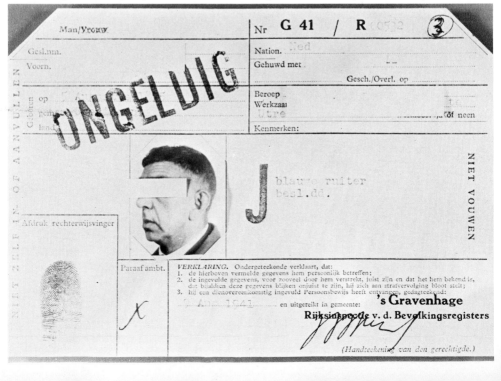

They were the special cases. In the interview, Globke denied he was ever a Nazi, insisting that the bureaucrats who wrote the Nazi laws had never joined the Party. But that is a lie: Stuckart was a member of the Party's Old Guard and was even an honorary member of the SS. Lösener, too, was a longtime Party member. The furor over the interview helped cost Globke his job with Adenauer.

Arthur Miller viewed it from another perspective: "Of course, you couldn't openly profess Judaism, but you could save your parent." In his case all it often required was tossing off an obligatory and barely audible "Heil Hitler." An accommodation. A small price to pay for one's survival. Just how great a bargain it was becomes evident when Miller tells of "several of my mother's cousins, in some cases their husbands and children as well," who were "deported to extermination camps, where they perished."

Hanns Rehfeld and Ruth von Brentani made identical assessments of their experiences as Mischlinge: "We were not heroes." Indeed, Ruth von Brentani claims they were just "ordinary people caught up in extraordinary circumstances."

Often those circumstances led to desperation. Some of the mixed marriage Jews, all of whom had long since cut their ties to the organized Jewish community, still turned to that group for help. Although he was a baptized Protestant (but a Jew in the eyes of the Nazis), Werner Goldberg's father appealed to Heinrich Stahl, president of the Berlin Jüdische Gemeinde, for financial help and assistance in finding a job. (Before the Nazis came to power, Albert Goldberg had been a director of the Commerz-und-Disconto Bank of Berlin.) Allegedly, Goldberg's pleas fell upon deaf ears. But we can certainly excuse Stahl for having other matters on his mind. In 1942 he was deported and sent with the rest of the members of the Gemeinde to the East. He died in Theresienstadt later that year.

"In the entire human organism, there are nowhere two peoples who attract and detest each other more than the Jews and the Germans."

MOSES HESS (1812–1875)
Pioneer Zionist, early associate
of Marx and Engels, originator
of the term "Nationalsozialismus"
(National Socialism).[1]

Chapter Four

The Mischling Who Smelled
Like a Jew

WHEN HANNS REHFELD'S 86-year-old grandmother responded to the knock on her door by committing suicide rather than face deportation to Theresienstadt, one might expect that the Nazis would have buried her in a mass grave. But they didn't. In one of the most macabre manifestations of the twisted Nazi mentality, she and the thirty-three other Berlin Jews who died in 1944, most of them suicides like herself, were given full religious burials at the historic Jewish cemetery in the Berlin suburb of Weissensee. Throughout World War II, it remained the only fully functioning Jewish cemetery in Berlin. Indeed, it may have been the last in the entire Reich.

"The Nazis did not have the facilities to burn Jewish corpses in Berlin and they couldn't just leave them lying around," says Klara Riesenburger,[2] the widow of Martin Riesenburger, the Jew the Nazis allowed to live in order that he could bury the Jewish dead. "Since there was no killing factory in Berlin, most of the Jews who died here were the elderly or suicide victims. So the Nazis let them have the final dignity of a Jewish ceremonial burial. The year with the most dead was 1942. That year my husband buried 811 people.[3] By the last year, 1945, he only had two burials."

After World War II, the main character in this Kafkaesque tale, Martin Riesenburger, became the Landesrabbiner (National Rabbi) of the German Democratic Republic (GDR, or East Germany). Rabbi Riesenburger died in 1965. His widow, a Christian who converted to Judaism after the war, lives in

East Berlin. Their story should have been that of a typical non-privileged mixed marriage, for the couple had no children. Instead, it illustrates one of the more unusual reasons why a Jew was given special treatment because he was needed by the Nazis.

With the exception of one of her statements, that she was made to wear the yellow Star of David even though she was not a Jew but the Aryan partner in a mixed marriage, Mrs. Riesenburger's story has held up under severe double checking. Although her recollection of wearing the star is doubtful, it may have greater significance when viewed from the standpoint of her very strong conscious identification with the Jews. Similarly, Dr. Peter Kirchner, president of East Germany's Jewish Community, maintains that his parents were forced to hide him in the underground despite his being raised—and not just attempting to "pass" as—a Christian Mischling. Perhaps for both Mrs. Riesenburger and Dr. Kirchner, the implied lack of heroism in their stories of survival has led them to color their recollections.

"Before the war," begins Mrs. Riesenburger,[4] "my husband worked in the Jewish old people's home on Grosse Hamburger Strasse [later to become a Nazi prison for Jews] and was in charge of the cemetery at Weissensee. He was arrested in 1938, but when the Nazis learned that he worked at the cemetery and looked after the burials, they freed him. Later, when the last rabbis in Berlin had been sent to concentration camps, because my husband was a preacher [among German Jewry a legitimate title for a layman who helps conduct services], he was given the order to take charge of burying the Jewish dead."

Although he was once again arrested during the war (perhaps in the Fabrik Aktion), no efforts were made to deport Riesenburger presumably because of his mixed marriage status and his usefulness. Although he was a layman, Riesenburger ranked highest in the religious hierarchy among those Jews still remaining in Nazi Germany during the last three years of the war.

Mrs. Riesenburger says the Gestapo closely supervised and watched the burials. "When the Jewish members, those who carried the corpses to their graves, came for the burials, Mr. Riesenburger warned them that the Nazis were on the grounds, listening and watching." (This has a historical precedent: in 1712, Berlin sent policemen to attend Jewish synagogue services and report back on what they saw and heard.)[5] She remembers, "There were three young people who tended the flowers on the graves and worked at the cemetery with my husband. They too were saved. One was a young girl who now lives in Israel, and of the young men, one went to America. I don't know where the other is."

Occasionally, a particularly courageous Christian could be seen in attendance at a Jewish funeral in Weissensee. Such was the case when Arnold Berliner, founder and editor of the influential journal *Die Naturwissenschaften (The Natural Sciences)* committed suicide in 1942 rather than face certain deportation. Max von Laue, winner of the 1914 Nobel Prize for Physics, defender of Einstein and onetime president of the Deutsche Physikalische Gesellschaft (German Physical Society), was one of the few non-Jewish mourners at Berliner's burial.

Although other Jewish cemeteries had been vandalized, the cemetery at Weissensee and its graves were never molested by the Nazis. In fact, Weissensee became a sanctuary for the Jews, where they could walk about and get fresh air without harrassment.[6] The only damage to the cemetery and the tombs came from the Allied bombings. In 1944, 4,000 graves and the Great Mourning Hall in the center of the cemetery were destroyed in an air raid. The records of the nearly 114,000 burials in the cemetery since 1880, including those of some of the most important names in German Jewry between World Wars, had to be reconstructed. It is ironic that the Nazis didn't destroy Weissensee, but Allied bombs almost did.

"My husband also conducted secret religious services at the cemetery," said Mrs. Riesenburger. "These were probably the only Jewish religious services conducted in wartime Berlin.

In the evening, the building used for the prayers for the dead was locked up and my husband and the others prayed inside, in the dark. Once they even had matzoh during Passover. A few times they secretly made and brought in challah (a traditional loaf of bread) for the Sabbath. They even had butter to put on it. All of this was of course forbidden, but they took the great risk anyway. They were always very careful, especially during the Jewish High Holy Days. The Nazis kept close track of when those holidays would be observed and increased their supervision at those times.

"Allied bombs probably saved our lives. On 3 February 1945, the flat where we lived in Berlin-Kreuzberg was destroyed in an air raid. We lost all our belongings. My husband's priceless library, everything, was in flames. All that we could save fit into a rucksack which we took turns carrying on our backs. Then we went to the cemetery and we lived there, in the office, until the end of the war. On the first of May, the day after Hitler's suicide and only one week before the surrender of Germany, some Jews who lived on Neue Königstrasse, not too far from where our flat had been [and also the same street on which the family of Dr. Peter Kirchner lived], were rounded up and transported to the Goebbels-Bunker in Berlin-Friedrichshain, where they were murdered. We might have been among them. If the Nazis had been victorious and had not been defeated by the Soviet Army, all of the remaining Jews who were still working would certainly have been killed."

"And on 21 April," recalled Mrs. Riesenburger, "we thought death had finally caught up to us. Some SS men came through the gates of the cemetery carrying guns and we were certain they had come to kill us. But when they found out that the Soviet Army was so near, they removed their uniforms, dropped their weapons, and ran away. For two days we heard the sounds of war coming closer. On Monday, 23 April, Soviet troops reached the cemetery. After twelve years, we were free.

(Last minute massacres by SS commandos were common

in Berlin. The surviving conspirators in the 20 July 1944 assassination plot against Hitler, including Admiral Wilhelm Canaris of the Abwehr and resistance leader Dietrich Bonhoeffer, were murdered during the dying gasps of the Third Reich—some as late as 23 April.)

"The Soviet Army helped us right from the beginning, or we would have starved. Toward the end of the war, the Nazis did not give us many food rations. Perhaps it was because we now had so few Jews to bury. Among the first Soviet soldiers who arrived there were some who were Jews and they brought us cans of meat. One day a Soviet soldier came and fetched my husband. I was very afraid but the soldier said, 'Don't worry, your husband will return.' He was invited for dinner. The first person my husband had to bury when we were free was a Russian soldier, Michael Bodjana. He was only twenty-eight and had been killed in action. He was buried on 13 May.[7]

"My husband posted notices on the trees of Berlin that he would be holding Jewish services and that any remaining Jews—those who had been freed from concentration camps and were returning to Berlin, or the so-called 'illegal Jews' who had been in hiding under false names—could come and pray. He was also able to make this announcement on the radio. Then he conducted Sabbath services at the cemetery on 12 May. This was the first open Jewish service since the war. In July he began to conduct services in the small synagogue at the Jewish Hospital on Iranische Strasse [where Werner Goldberg's father had been held as a prisoner of the SS]. And on 29 July he performed the wedding of two people who had met, and somehow survived, in Auschwitz. It was the first Jewish ceremonial wedding in Berlin since 1938."

The confusing aspect of Mrs. Riesenburger's story surfaces in her contention that "when we lived in Berlin-Kreuzberg, my husband was not allowed to use any public transportation. He always had to walk to the cemetery. I worked at Siemens, the electrical factory. It was forced labor. Later, I had to clean the streets. As the wife of a Jew, I had to wear the star [sic].

Because I had to go to work, I could use the public transport, but I could not sit down. I had to stand. In the factory I was called terrible names like Judenschwein [Jewish pig]. When my husband used to go to the cemetery, all of the neighbors looked out of their windows and there was a man going to work wearing the yellow star."

(Because the childless Riesenburgers did not have privileged mixed marriage status, he would have been required to wear the star.) Apparently, the Riesenburger's apartment was not in a Jewish ghetto. Otherwise, such a sight would hardly be a cause for neighborly concern.

One of North America's most respected rabbis, W. Gunther Plaut, the distinguished senior scholar of Toronto's Holy Blossom Temple, claimed in his 1981 autobiography, *Unfinished Business*, that Martin Riesenburger, whom Plaut met at Weissensee in 1962, was not a real rabbi.[8] Plaut describes Rabbi Riesenburger as wearing the Order of Stalin, when in reality it was the East German-awarded Patriotic Order of Merit, a bronze and silver medallion which carries with it an annual stipend of 750 East German marks. Wilhelm Pieck, the first president of the German Democratic Republic, conferred a silver Mogen David (the Star of David) upon Rabbi Riesenburger, which the rabbi wore with his robe much as a bishop wears a cross.

Jews have held several key posts in the East German government, a fact not widely reported in the East or West. Albert Norden, a powerful member of the Politbüro until his death in 1982, was the son of a rabbi. Klaus Gysi, Minister of State for Church Affairs, was a Mischling—his father was a Jew. Gysi was chief editor of *Aufbau* (the postwar Soviet sector literary monthly, not the New York-based exile publication for which Hannah Arendt wrote) from 1945 to 1948, and published the first new work by Bertolt Brecht to appear in Germany in a decade.[10]

The dwindling Jewish community of East Germany has been without a rabbi since Martin Riesenburger's death. A Hungarian rabbi pays regular visits to the tiny East Berlin congregation which has only 300 active (and mainly elderly) members. Officially there is no anti-Semitism in East Germany, but there are also virtually no Jews. The headquarters of the Jüdische Gemeinde of the GDR have been reconstructed in the ruins of the great synagogue on Oranienburger Strasse in Mitte-East Berlin. There is a world-famous photograph of the ornately turreted synagogue dome ablaze on Kristallnacht. Now trees grow wildly from the hollow eyes of its skull.

Dr. Peter Kirchner, a forty-eight-year-old neurosurgeon, is president of the East German Jewish community.[11] He was a Mischling who, although raised as a Christian during the war, afterward chose to become a Jew. Dr. Kirchner is among a handful of Mischlinge to have followed that course, as most have remained in the Christian faith. Bernhard Vaks, who retired in 1982 as director of religious affairs for the Gemeinde, was also a Mischling—his father was a Jew. By trade an orthopedic shoemaker, Vaks administered the cemetery at Weissensee as well as the Jewish community's kosher meat market, which employs no Jews and whose best customers are the Muslim personnel of the Arab diplomatic community.

Dr. Kirchner's claim that he was in hiding during the war is difficult to understand and accept. His family's copy of the 1939 so-called "Peoples and Professions" questionnaire clearly shows Dr. Kirchner's Mischling status.[12] Dated 1938, the questionnaire was scheduled for distribution that year, but Hitler's Anschluss of Austria put both the form and the ultimate fate of the Jews on the back burner for a year. This document, conveniently distributed throughout the Jewish community by the Reichsvereinigung of Dr. Leo Baeck, was used by the Nazis to learn who considered themselves Jews. It is also the source for the variously interpreted 1939 census figures of Germany's Mischlinge population. Dr. Kirchner's wife would have been classified as a Mischling of the Second Degree—she had one Jewish grandparent. Their marriage would have been forbidden under the Nazi rules.

"I have a Jewish mother," explains Dr. Kirchner, "and a

Christian father. I was born in a Jewish hospital. And I was beschnitten [circumcised]. If my parents had not done this, I would not have been obliged to wear the star." Ironically, Dr. Kirchner first came into consideration for the Jüdische Gemeinde position because he was the only surgeon in East Berlin who knew the procedure for performing Jewish ritual circumcisions.

Dr. Kirchner claims to have attended Jewish schools. Others who have seen his school report card confided that it clearly shows his having received Christenlehre (Christian teaching) in the Jewish schools in 1942.[13] Mischlinge children raised in the Christian religion were given Christian instruction until the Jewish schools were closed in June 1942. Dr. Kirchner explains that "I had some neighbors on my street who lived in mixed marriages. The children in these families did not have to wear the star. They were not allowed to attend higher schools, but the fact that one partner of the family was Christian and that the child was raised as a Christian was a protection for the other partner who was a Jew in that he or she was not sent to a death camp."

Did many people do this to survive? "There were some who tried," was Dr. Kirchner's reply.

But sometimes the decision of a Mischling child to choose Christianity over Judaism led to postwar tragedy. The story of Charlotte Lehmann[14] is a good example. "My father was a Jew," said the woman who throughout the war worked in the office of German Foreign Minister Joachim von Ribbentrop, "and my mother was a Christian, a housekeeper for a Jewish family. And I was born out of wedlock. I wasn't christened. My father and my mother could not marry because of the difference in their faiths. The family of my father was shocked. The family of my mother was shocked. And, in between, there stood I.

"My father and my mother said, 'Well, let her decide for herself what religion she chooses to belong to.' And when I was twelve years old, there came the crucial time. My father said to my mother, 'I am now engaged to a Jewish friend. She is an opera singer and we are going to be married.' And my mother asked, 'But what about Lotte?' My father told her, 'Perhaps it might be easier for you if we take Lotte. We will adopt her as our child. That might be the best thing for you. Maybe you will have the chance to get married to someone.'

"And so my mother asked me. Now it was up to me to decide whether to go to the family of my father or to remain with my mother—alone. My father had always taken good care of my mother. We were not in need. Nor did we suffer from discrimination. I was a bright and sometimes snappy child, so I said to my father, 'Would you still think of adopting me if I were Number Zero in my class at school and if I had legs shaped like a zero too? Would you still want me then? No, I think not. I will remain with my mother.' And on my thirteenth birthday I was baptized in the church of my mother."

Because there was no official stigma associated with illegitimacy under the Nazis, Charlotte Lehmann was never under suspicion about her ancestry, although her facial appearance is decidedly what the vicious caricatures in *Der Stürmer* disdained as being "Jewish." There was no reason for her to worry about tracing the family tree for Nazi snoopers. Only one side, the name of her mother, had been filled in on her birth certificate, and her mother was clearly Aryan. When Charlotte Lehmann was asked in April 1940 to come to work at the Foreign Ministry, she was still somewhat hesitant. She told the head of the press section at the Foreign Office on Berlin's Wilhelmstrasse "quite frankly what was the case, and he said, 'Let me take care of it. Your birth certificate is all right and you needn't worry at all.' "

Charlotte Lehmann's first job at the Foreign Office was to listen to foreign radio news and comments and translate them. Later she became the press conference stenographer for the spokesman of the Wilhelmstrasse, the notorious anti-Semite, Dr. Paul Karl Schmidt. He is still active today, writing under the pseudonym of Paul Carrell.

After the war, Charlotte Lehmann eventually joined the foreign service of West Germany and in November 1964 accepted a posting to the West German consulate in New York. It is the same office where Hanns Rehfeld now serves as Consul in charge of Politics, Press and Protocol. Since the end of the war, Lehmann had searched in vain for the name of her father, Ludwig Stein, among lists of victims and survivors of the Holocaust. She had no idea that her father had been aided by a Wehrmacht officer and spent the war safely in the Swiss embassy in Budapest, as told in Chapter Two. Lehmann's mother died in 1962 in a Bonn traffic accident.

"One day during lunch hour," recalled Lehmann, "I walked into the department where all the files were kept to get some back data on a life insurance case I had been working on. But instead of the restitution compensation file, my hand gripped the records of the social security department. And just for fun I thought, all right, let's have a look. Maybe I will see one of my school friends who might still be alive.

"I looked. Ludwig Stein. Born 16 May 1885 in a little town in the Austrian-Hungarian section. It must be he! It is his name and birthday and his place of birth. And he is here in New York! I had only a registration card with no address or telephone number so I got the Manhattan telephone book. There was nothing. Then I looked in the Queens book. Nothing. All the telephone books of the five boroughs of New York, and still nothing.

"I asked someone, 'Everybody has a telephone here in America, don't they?' And of course they told me no. So I looked at the file and there was written 1407 Linden Avenue, Brooklyn. I had no idea how far away it might be, but I took the subway there. I was quite amazed—I had only been in New York for a week, but I found it. It was an apartment block. I read the many, many names on the mailboxes. Here it is: Stein—ninth floor. I pushed the button for the apartment and then for the elevator.

"I couldn't get to the ninth floor fast enough. And there a lady opened the door and asked, 'Well, who do you want to speak to?'

" 'I want to see Mr. Stein,' I told her. 'You've pushed the wrong button,' she said. 'This is apartment A. Mrs. Stein lives there—in apartment B.' 'Yes,' I said, 'and Mr. Stein?' 'He passed away a few weeks ago,' she replied. My father had died on the first of September, the very day when I was asked by the Foreign Office whether I would like to go to New York as a cultural attaché. I was stunned when I heard this. It was all I could do to ask the woman, 'And Mrs. Stein?'

" 'Well, she's very lonely,' said the woman, 'but you may ring her bell and perhaps she will be glad to have a visitor. Who are you anyway?' she inquired. I said I was a friend and thanked her. Then I pushed the button. 'Who is it?' asked the voice from within. 'Well, this is Lotte Lehmann, your friend from Berlin.' Very hesitantly, she opened the door. When she recognized me, she said, 'I wouldn't have trusted you. I don't open the door to anyone. I still have terror and fear at every knock at the door. But I opened the door because I recognized in yours the sound of his voice.' "[15]

After a joyous reunion, Lehmann learned the details of her father's and stepmother's escape from Nazi Germany. When she asked Mrs. Stein why they had never applied for West German restitution monies, she learned her father's viewpoint on the issue. He had said, "Thanks to a German Wehrmacht officer, we have survived. From the murderers I don't take any money. And from the innocent especially not. No, we have a good existence. We are healthy and have kept our sanity in spite of all the madness of history. We have kept our clear minds and we have kept our healthy bodies. We have won the war."

The following Sunday, Charlotte's half brother Herbert, whom she had not seen since 1941, also came to the Steins' apartment. Herbert told Charlotte that his mother had been "going mad" since their father passed away. "Now," Herbert assured Charlotte, "it is time for you to throw away your German passport. You belong to us. Here is your family. Forget about the German consulate. Forget about Germany."

But to Lehmann, that meant forgetting about her mother.

"Every weekend you will come to our mother," Herbert was saying. "What a relief it is for me to know that you are in New York." Then he told Charlotte how he could no longer stand hearing his mother lament about the past and about the death of their father each and every day.

"But I was very happy," Lehmann remembers. "On Friday evenings I went to Mrs. Stein and she lit the Sabbath candles and we ate gefilte fish. I would stay with her until Monday morning, going straight to the consulate from her apartment. And I had said, 'No, I can't do that. Give up my German passport and apply in the United States as an immigrant? I can't do that.' And Herbert and his mother Valerie would always say, 'But you belong to us.'

"One day I asked Mrs. Stein what had happened to the rest of her family. And now I learned the reason why she was so hysterical. She told me, 'I am the only survivor of seven sisters and brothers. They have gassed them all like rats.' It was so terrible for her. And all day she would mutter, 'God curse this damned Germany which has ruined our lives.'

"I could understand her feelings," Lehmann recalls. "We got along very well together every weekend, but I must confess that it was difficult to listen to all her complaints from morning until night and to always hear, 'God curse this damned Germany . . .' And so it went until the beginning of April. I told her I would be there again next Friday but I would have to leave on Sunday morning that weekend. A colleague of mine from the Foreign Office linguistics department in Bonn had been assigned as an interpreter to a United Nations conference and she would be staying with me during her visit. Sunday afternoon the Munich Bach Choir would be at Carnegie Hall with Karl Richter, and I had bought tickets for the performance of Bach's St. Matthew Passion.

"And then Mrs. Stein said to me, 'Yes. Well, St. Matthew Passion. Haven't you had enough from this type?' You know who was meant by 'this type'—Christians. And she said . . . she was so desperate . . . 'Well, we are Jews, and we have studied the Bible looking for the answer to why all this was possible. And we have studied the New Testament thoroughly too.' Then she recited to me by heart the following passage from St. John: 'He entered in His own realm and His own wouldn't receive Him. But to all who did receive Him, to those who have yielded Him their allegiance, He gave the right to become the children of God.'

"Her eyes blazing, she pointed at me and demanded, 'And what have you *done* with that right as the children of God? What have you done during all the 2,000 years? And now your damned Christ, your damned Germany . . .' I sat paralyzed as she continued, 'And now comes a musical company from your damned Germany and you have nothing else to do than to run to them.' Then she threw me out.

"I talked with Herbert afterwards. He told me that under these conditions it is not possible to see his mother as long as she is so sick. But Herbert understands. He also told me, 'My wife, my children, we are happy to know you and there is no reproach or resentment against you. There are no problems between us, but as long as mother is alive, we must avoid anything that might hurt her feelings. That is our Fifth Commandment. And it may be that if we meet again it might hurt her feelings.' "

That was the last time Charlotte Lehmann heard from Herbert Stein. It was April 1965.

Shortly before her retirement from the German foreign service in 1978, Lehmann was posted to Montréal where she served as Vice Consul for Cultural Affairs. She had but one request to make of the North American journalist who interviewed her in 1982: Would he send her a plastic grocery shopping bag from the Montréal-based Steinberg stores—one bearing the printed legend "Yes, Steinberg is on your side."

Like Dr. Peter Kirchner, Cristal Senda[16] was raised as a Christian Mischling. Today she's a devout Orthodox Jew, a member of San Francisco's Congregation Sherith Israel. A nurse, she is active in the efforts of the Bay Area Jewish community in organizing support for the cause of the Falashas, the oppressed black Jews of Ethiopia.

Her family's name was Dummasch and they lived in Tilsit, East Prussia (now Sovetsk, U.S.S.R.). Her father was a Jew, her mother was "second generation—her father had been a Jew." Senda is quick to explain that "this intermarriage business wasn't anything new. It started way back in the 1800s. But most of my family, including my father, had converted to Christianity around the time of World War I."

Senda, like her three sisters and her brother, was baptized at birth. Thus, when the Nuremberg Laws were promulgated, "we weren't bothered. We were treated just like all other Germans from the border." (Lithuania was on the other side of the Memel River.) But Senda's conscience bothered her when she learned of the plight of some of the still-Jewish members of her family living in Berlin-Moabit. "They were only third cousins," she says, "my father's cousin and his daughters. And when I told my sister that I was concerned about what was happening to them, she told me to have nothing to do with them. 'Why are you going back to that old religion?' she asked. 'We have it all erased now.' "

Ignoring the advice and pleadings of her family, once a week Senda made a grueling eleven-hour train ride from Tilsit to Berlin just to bring food to her Jewish cousins. First she would go to the waterfront to buy smoked whitefish, "then I would pack it into a suitcase and take the train. It was a long ride, we went through the Polish Corridor all night, but we never had to show our papers or anything. I would get off at the Friedrichstrasse Bahnhof and have breakfast at the Excelsior Hotel. You could get a very decent meal there for only a few food coupons and I would always have something left to bring to my cousins. Sometimes I would also take them candles which they could use for lighting on the Sabbath. At other times I would bring them bread and rolls. Sometimes even butter, for them to eat in place of challah. Whatever I could carry, I brought to them, especially the things I knew they were unable to get on their own. Once, because I could find no other smoked fish, I had to bring them eels. I knew that they were observant of *kashruth* [the Jewish dietary laws] and they were not supposed to eat eels, but they did. When you are hungry, you will even eat a horse. I know—because I once did.

"One day in March 1942," says Senda, "I came to Berlin with a whole suitcase filled with food. I was very cheerful until I turned the corner of the street where my cousins lived. Then I saw that their things were strewn all over the street. I didn't have to ask anybody what had happened, I knew they had been deported. I never saw them again."

When she returned to Tilsit, Senda told her family for the first time that she "felt like a Jew." The schism in her family which that statement precipitated affects her as emotionally today as it did forty-one years ago. One of her sisters now lives in Port Credit, Ontario. She regularly "berates" Senda for "becoming involved in this Jewish business." But Senda "prays night and day that someday my sister will return to her senses." Her brother, who still lives in Germany, "denies being Jewish," according to Senda. "Instead he says we are Germans. But every week he receives the *Jewish Forward*, the Yiddish-language newspaper, although all he can read of it is the English-language insert."

Senda believes her family "stayed with their own, although they wanted to be different." She emigrated to the United States in 1950. Her husband, who was a Catholic, converted to Judaism. Senda did not formally do so. "I've always been a Jew," she explains.

Klaus Peter Scholz,[17] now of Montréal, felt the same way. Born in Hamburg, his mother was a Jew, his father a Protestant. He and his older sister Eva Maria were baptized at birth. His parents divorced when he was ten and the children lived with their mother.

Like Werner Goldberg, Dr. Hans Salomon, and many other male Mischlinge, Scholz entered the Reichsarbeitsdienst in 1938 and a half-year later, "around the time of Kristallnacht," he went into the Wehrmacht. He left when the Mischlinge were forced out. Scholz says his mother "told me to go into the army and not to emigrate because she thought it could help us." She was wrong. Because of her lack of official status as a divorced Jewish partner in a mixed marriage, she had no protection. She was sent to Theresienstadt, as were the mothers of Rolf Vogel and Dr. Salomon. And like them, she survived.

The Wehrmacht provided as safe a haven for Scholz as it had for Hans Faust and Werner Goldberg. Scholz recalls that when the order came through to give the Mischlinge "n.z.v." discharges, "the officers of the Hamburg Traditional Regiment to which I belonged tried to help me. They made two requests to keep me, but both were turned down. They were afraid I would have trouble if I went back, so they offered to try a third time. But I told them, 'Don't play into God's hands. If it is meant to be like this, I will go back.' "

Shortly before Scholz went into the Wehrmacht, his father, a prominent lawyer, had insisted that his son be publicly confirmed as a Protestant. "I said that he had never taken care of my religious beliefs before," remembers Scholz, "so why should it matter now? My father said I must do this because it was important for him and his career. I told my father that I had always felt more Jewish than anything else. At first my father was furious. Then he offered to give me a gold watch if I would go through with the ceremony. 'Are you trying to buy me?' I asked. But I needed the watch so I went along with it. My mother was not allowed to witness my confirmation. She had to sit in an upstairs room of the church."

The fears that the officers of Scholz's Wehrmacht battalion expressed for his future were well founded. Once Scholz left the army, things were indeed tough for him. When he returned to Hamburg he couldn't find work. And just like Werner Goldberg's experience in Berlin, everyone was asking Scholz, "Why are you not in the army?" So Scholz turned to his father for help. After all, he had done his part and gone through with the public confirmation ceremony.

"My father gave me a month's worth of support money," remembers Scholz, "and told me to find a job. And of course

I tried but couldn't. When I came back the next month to ask for more money, my father threw me out. In front of an office full of clients he told me to 'Get out of here, you Jew. I don't want anything to do with you until your mother lies under the green lawn.' He was a famous divorce lawyer you know. And meanwhile at home, all that I was hearing from my mother was, 'I expected this. I knew all along that the army wouldn't save me. How awful all this is for me as a Jew.' But what about me? What about my plight?

"Soon I was sent with some other half-Jews to work at the plant of Rudolph Otto Meyer. They were manufacturers of heating and air conditioning systems. They had installed the units in the Vatican in the 1920s and they were quite world famous for this. The company was now being run by the Wittenburg family. The owner's wife was Jewish—they took great care to keep this quiet—and so they tried to help as many half-Jews as they could by hiring them. But one of my co-workers was a Gestapo spy who claimed, among other things, that I 'smelled like a Jew.' And so I was denounced, in the usual manner, by a postcard sent by an informer to the Gestapo office."

What follows is, at best, an incredible chain of events. The Gestapo decided to deport Scholz to a concentration camp. He was told to report to a Gestapo collection center where deportees were detained pending transport to the camp. On his last night of freedom, he said good-bye to his sister. She also was about to leave Hamburg, but for a much different reason. As Scholz explained, "She had committed Rassenschande [the Nazi sin of race mixing]. She was pregnant by an Aryan." (Technically, she hadn't broken any Nazi law. As already established, it was perfectly legal for a Mischling of the First Degree to have extramarital sex with a Jew or an Aryan, and presumably her Aryan lover had remembered to look at her papers first. It was marriage that was forbidden, unless special consent could be arranged. But both Scholz and his sister thought she had committed a serious infraction, and with their mother deported to Theresienstadt and Scholz about to be deported on the basis of a denunciation, leaving town seemed like a good idea.)

Scholz told his sister the location of the Gestapo prison in Hamburg where he was to be held until his deportation. Only a few days before—this was in July 1943—Hamburg had been devastated in a series of massive Allied "fire-storm" bombing raids which left over 50,000 civilians dead. Eva Maria Scholz's lover, the man responsible for her pregnancy, was on active service as a marine procurement officer in the Italian-Yugoslavian theater of war. Concerned whether his loved ones had survived the desolation of Hamburg, he requested and was granted a short period of home leave. He arrived in Hamburg just as Eva Maria was about to depart. She was able to tell him what had happened to her brother and, more important, she pinpointed the Gestapo location at which he was being held. Eva Maria's friend knew someone at the Gestapo office from their days as law students. He hurried to the prison and after a five-hour meeting, succeeded in having Scholz set free—and just in time, for the transport was already being loaded with human cargo destined for a concentration camp. Eva Maria did leave Hamburg for a safe hideaway in the country, where she had her baby. She remained there for the duration of the war, after which she returned to Hamburg and married her lover.

Meanwhile Scholz had found another job. He was hired, at 77 Pfennig an hour, to salvage steel beams from buildings in the bombed-out sections of Hamburg. "Sometimes we found bodies too," he remembers. "No one else was allowed into these areas by the authorities. We were hired by a man named Ziencke, a former gas station operator, who was now getting rich by hiring half-Jews for starvation wages through his Gestapo contacts." Scholz was sent home from that job in February 1945. He heard that he was going to be shipped to a concentration camp that was being set up near the port of Hamburg. That night, the area near the port was heavily bombed by the Allies.

Scholz's mother was the only one of her family to survive the Holocaust. She was a member of the Samuel family, an old Hamburg family that dated back to the 1700s. Scholz says she was never the same after Theresienstadt. "It destroyed her mind." She died in 1971.

In 1957 Scholz emigrated to Canada. His first job there was working in the warehouse of a manufacturer of kitchenware for 77 cents an hour—the same amount in cents that he had received in Pfennig fourteen years before. But this time there was a difference. He stayed with the company and when he retired several years ago, he did so as a director of the firm.

"All my life I wanted to belong somewhere," he says. "When I came to Canada, people said, 'Oh! you're from Germany? Do you belong to the German Club?' I would tell them I was half-Jewish and they would say, 'Oh! but you're only *half*-Jewish.' I went to see Rabbi Harry Joshua Stern at Temple Emanu-El[18] [the large Montréal Reform congregation] in 1958 and told him my problem. Because my mother was a Jew, I was already considered a Jew. But I still made it official. I had to belong somewhere. I think everybody has to."

"There is no way a Jew can become a Gentile . . . he can convert or marry out of his faith, but he is a converted Jew. Being Jewish is more than embracing the faith, it's a matter of parentage. Even in Israel, if your mother is Jewish and your father Gentile, you are considered a Jew."[1]

ANN LANDERS,
Syndicated columnist[1]

Chapter Five

The Mysterious Dr. Mailander

ONCE THE FATE of the Mischlinge became a topic of the Wannsee Conference delegates, the Nazi Party sought a solution that would insure the disappearance of this Third Race. Although sterilization was discussed and virtually agreed upon, rumors of the imminent deportation of the Mischlinge of the First Degree were running rampant by September 1942. Ministerialrat Bernhard Lösener, the bureaucrat who defined the Jews and the Mischlinge in 1935 and had been cast in the role of Defender of the Mischlinge ever since, wrote to Reichsführer SS Himmler in an effort to save "his" Mischlinge. In his letter, Lösener stressed the loyalty of the Mischlinge of the First Degree and asked that the matter be submitted to Hitler for resolution, much as had been done with the question of the mixed marriage Jews. Apparently this step was never taken, but the resulting indecision was the same. On numerous occasions, the Nazis had proposed drastic new regulations to subject the Mischlinge to segregation, sterilization and, now, even deportation. In effect, nothing much ever did come of it.

But things wouldn't have been true to form if there weren't some exceptions. An undetermined number of Mischlinge of the First Degree were sent to their deaths as a result of the Lublin Aktion of November 1942, but these were the only Mischlinge to be killed in the entire destruction process. They met their deaths because they had the misfortune to find themselves among a group of 2,000 Jewish inmates of German concentration camps being transferred, to make the German camps Jew-free, to the killing centers of Auschwitz and Lublin.[2] These Mischlinge had been arrested and confined for various infractions. Almost certainly, many among them had been denounced for acting like full Jews, and they now found themselves sharing the same fate as their Jewish relatives.

When Mischlinge were sent to Organization Todt[3] labor camps in 1944, they were sent as replacements for Germans whose bodies could better serve the Fatherland on the war fronts. Some mixed marriage Jews, and even their Aryan spouses (like Emil Lappe, husband of Ruth von Brentani's sister) were also sent to work camps around that time. Whether the theory that an enforced separation would help unravel the threads that held the mixed marriages together was uppermost in the minds of the Nazis at this time is unclear. It is more likely that the mixed marriage Jews were finally seen as being useful—a potential source of manpower to maintain roads, dig ditches and perform other vital behind-the-front-lines tasks. The Nazis thought most of the mixed marriage Jews were making their living as "black marketeers," and were highly expendable. So while the mixed marriages technically and legally remained intact, in some cases the spouses were, for a time, physically separated.

The Nazis had already decided to dispose of some of their most embarrassing cases of mixed marriage by deporting the Jewish partner (usually a widow) to Theresienstadt. Among this latter group was Ida Schneidhuber,[4] the Jewish widow of August Schneidhuber, one-time SA (Sturmabteilung) Obergruppenführer (the Nazi Party storm trooper equivalent of an SS lieutenant general) of Munich. Born Ida Wasserman, her continued presence in Munich long after the murder of her husband in the 1934 "Night of the Long Knives" bloodbath was considered a tarnishment of the Nazi top brass. The Theresienstadt daybook records her arrival, along with a notation that she was to be considered "privileged." Under "Kinder" (children) is the entry "Mischlinge 1."

SA Obergruppenführer Schneidhuber, a major in the anti-Semitic Freikorps, the group responsible for the 1922 assassination of Germany's Jewish Foreign Minister Walter Rathenau, was not murdered because he happened to be married to a Jew. Schneidhuber was ranked among the seven top officers of the SA and he was one of the four Obergruppenführers—which included Ernst Röhm—liquidated in the bloody Hitler-ordered purge.

And what could the Nazis do with Baron Karl von Hirsch,[5] scion of the Jewish philanthropists who underwrote much of the emigration by German Jews to Canada in the early part of the century? Balancing the fact that both of his parents were Jews (although they had baptized him as a Christian almost at his birth) against his contribution in building the Baghdad Railway, the decision was made to send him to Theresienstadt with "privileges." Apparently, these were maintained until the liberation of the camp in 1945. Meyer Levin, the novelist and playwright, was one of the first Americans to enter the so-called "privileged ghetto." He reported that the "better" German Jews in Theresienstadt had survived through feeling superior to the "verminous Eastern Jews" who had been exterminated in the slave camps and the crematoria.

The remaining restrictions placed upon the Mischlinge by the Nazis were mild in comparison with the fate that had befallen the Jews. In September 1944, Hitler decreed that Mischlinge of the First Degree in the bureaucracy were no longer entitled to receive service medals or honors, but the Mischlinge were not removed from their posts. The Nazi bureaucracy simply could not cope with the total penetration of their Frankenstein's Monster, the Mischlinge, into the German nation. They were continually faced with the problem of the Mischlinge in sports, the Mischlinge in the economy, the Mischlinge as members of organizations. There were Mischlinge almost everywhere. Because the Mischlinge Problem overwhelmed the Nazis, the Mischlinge survived.

For example, take the Mischlinge in sports. Helene Mayer[7] is considered to have been the greatest woman fencer of all time. She won a Gold Medal for Germany in the 1928 Olympics and attended school in the United States after 1932. Although her father was a Jew, she was called back to Germany by Dr. Joseph Goebbels to compete for the Fatherland in the 1936 Berlin "Aryan" Olympics. Mayer won a Silver Medal for Germany in the competition, greeted the Führer with a "Heil Hitler," and returned to the United States and her studies. Mayer, like Werner Goldberg, was typically Aryan in appearance with blue eyes and blond hair. Jürgen Landeck said of her, "Hitler and Goebbels would have liked to look like Helene Mayer. By comparison, they looked like a couple of Jews."[8] (Her portrait appears on a 1968 West German postage stamp.) One of two full Jews who played for Nazi Germany in the "Aryan" Olympics did win a Gold Medal for the Reich. He was Rudolf Ball and the sport was ice hockey.[9]

If you look at the photographs of the 1936 Berlin Olympics, you will note a distinguished looking gentleman, usually in formal dress and top hat, standing next to Hitler. This was the man they called "Excellenz," Theodor Lewald, and he was the official German Commissioner for the 1936 Olympic Games. His mother was Aryan, but his father was of full Jewish descent. This makes Lewald's role as a principal architect of the "Aryan-only" structure of the Berlin Olympics somewhat hypocritical. Lewald survived the war unmolested and died in 1947 of medical complications resulting from his advanced age.[10]

Reinhold Georg Quaatz[11] was one of the most prominent Mischlinge in the German economy. First classified as a non-Aryan in 1933, he was forced to resign from the board of directors of the Dresdner Bank, today the second largest bank in West Germany. Quaatz was a close friend and ardent supporter of the political ambitions of powerful press lord Alfred Hugenberg, one-time Hitler rival and chairman of the right-wing German-National People's Party (Deutschnationale

Volkspartei or DNVP) as well as leader of the "Green Shirts." Hugenberg was later Minister of National Economy, Food and Agriculture in the Hitler cabinet.

Emil Maurice,[12] the first commander of the SS, and one of the leaders of the murder spree which claimed the life of August Schneidhuber, was a Mischling of the Second Degree, according to historian Walter Hagen. Maurice was once Hitler's chauffeur and, with Rudolf Hess, took notes from Hitler's dictation of *Mein Kampf* at Landsberg Prison—in the room provided by yet another notorious Mischling, Count Anton Arco-Valley (see Chapter Eight.)

One suspects that Hagen would have been in a good position to know the truth about Maurice's ancestry, as he has since been identified (by historian Raul Hilberg) as actually being SS-Sturmbannführer (major) Wilhelm Höttl of the Intelligence Service. Hagen/Höttl was originally called as a defense witness in the Eichmann trial, but part of his testimony wound up being used by the prosecution. Hannah Arendt has quoted Eichmann as saying, "There were Jews even among ordinary SS men," but was Eichmann still following the Nazi Party's equation of Mischlinge with Jews? If, as Hilberg claims, Mischlinge could not join the SS, one must wonder how any Jews possibly could? Or did Eichmann's definition of Jews also include Mischlinge of the Second Degree? The SS was hardly an equal opportunity employer.

Lt. Colonel Theodor Düsterberg[13] was a strong candidate for the German presidency in the 1932 election—that is until Goebbels learned that Düsterberg's grandfather, an army doctor who had served with distinction during the 1813 war of liberation, had been not just a Jew, but president of a synagogue in Paderborn to boot. The revelation helped cost Düsterberg the election; he received under seven percent of the vote. Hitler, also a presidential candidate, took over 36 percent, more than one-third of the total vote, but still lost to war hero Generalfeldmarschall von Hindenburg.

Düsterberg was the second commander of Stahlhelm (steel-helmet), the veterans' organization of the DNVP. His predecessor, Franz Seldte, became Hitler's Minister of Labor. Once Düsterberg legally became a Mischling of the Second Degree, it virtually guaranteed that he would be allowed to live out his life without fear of arrest or deportation. He died in 1963 at the age of 88.

By contrast, Georg Gottheiner[14] was fully Jewish by descent. A former member of the Reichstag and an official in the Ministry of the Interior, he was recalled to government service by Franz von Papen. Gottheiner was placed in charge of the Politsche Abteilung, the organization responsible for the Nazi-sponsored putsch against the Social-Democratic Braun government of Prussia.

Another Jewish confidant of von Papen was Heinrich Kaufmann-Asser.[15] He served as ministerial director and chief of press relations of the Reich government in late 1932. After Hitler became chancellor, he appointed Kaufmann-Asser as the Nazi envoy to Argentina. He was subsequently recalled and fully pensioned.

Perhaps the most bizarre story is that of the Hungarian Jew, Ignace Trebitsch-Lincoln.[16] This one-time head of a Protestant Mission to convert the Jews of Canada was elected to the British House of Commons in 1910. Later he spent three years in prison on a charge of falsification of documents and was accused of the 1925 murder of a London barkeeper. However it was in his role as press spokesman for the abortive Kapp putsch of March 1920 that he first earned the gratitude of Hitler for having tipped him to the failure of the monarchist revolt against the fledgling Weimar Republic. Trebitsch-Lincoln eventually emigrated to China where he took the name of Chao-Kung and became a priest in a Buddhist temple. When he died in Shanghai in 1943, he was given a full obituary in the *Völkischer Beobachter*, the official Nazi Party newspaper.

Albert Speer, only weeks before his death in 1981, provided a list of additional names of Mischlinge in the Nazi economy.

In one of the last letters written by Speer, the former Hitler intimate and wartime Minister of Armaments said that "In my own department, there were other so-called Mischlinge who were retained at their posts, such as, for example, the president of Mercedes-Benz, Happel, and his manager, Werner; Meyer of MAN [the Nuremberg-based heavy equipment manufacturer] and others."[17] Rolf Vogel later substantiated the names on Speer's list.

Charlotte Lehmann[18] believes that "The Wilhelmstrasse, the Foreign Office, was quite a decent ministry. They had a special file for dubious or delicate family connections. And when there was a risk of control by the Nazis, they took away the files and replaced them by fakes. They paid much attention there to the privileged mixed marriages. For example, when there was a famous artist who was married to a Jewish woman they said, 'No, forget about it. We need him for a presentation.' There were some—famous actors like Paul Wigner and famous musicians—that they didn't touch. Because these people had such great renown abroad, they just didn't dare risk it."

Lehmann vehemently asserts that "Richard Strauss too was among this group. His wife was Jewish. It was so well hidden, and the Strauss's themselves were interested that nobody knew about it." They must have done a good job of hiding it, as research has been unable to corroborate Lehmann's claim. Strauss, however, was fired by the Nazis from his position as head of the Reichsmusikkammer, the officially sanctioned organization of German musicians, because the Gestapo intercepted a letter written by the composer to his onetime collaborator Stefan Zweig in which Strauss personally disavowed any feelings of anti-Semitism.

A 1981 British biographical dictionary states, "Strauss's Jewish daughter-in-law and his two half-Jewish grandsons came under his protection . . . and in order to secure their immunity Strauss was forced to abide by detestable political actions in order to save them—which he did."[19] But wasn't his daughter-in-law in a privileged mixed marriage? Would the Nazis have dared deport her and risk outraging world opinion over the fate of one Jew, who just happened to be married to the son of Richard Strauss? His grandsons were certainly Mischlinge, so one must wonder just what was needed to "secure their immunity" much less to "save them." Strauss is still considered Nazi-tainted by Israel. In 1982, the government renewed its ban on his music being played over Israeli radio stations.

The story of German actor Joachim G. Gottschalk, who committed suicide because he feared disclosure of his wife's Jewish antecedents, was filmed in the Soviet sector of Berlin in 1947 under the title of *Ehe im Schatten (Marriage in the Shadows)*. This film about mixed marriages greatly touched postwar German audiences. Berlin reviewers cited many instances of people who became so emotionally affected from viewing the film that they broke down in tears and had to leave the theater before the movie ended.[20]

Another famous mixed marriage that also ended in tragedy was that of Jochen Klepper, a Berlin evangelical clergyman and popular hymn writer, who was married to a Jew. Klepper's wife, of course, received an exemption, but the Nazis firmly drew the line when it came to Renate, Mrs. Klepper's full Jewish daughter by a previous marriage. On the eve of their last turndown by Nazi authorities, and with Renate's deportation imminent, Jochen Klepper, his wife and her daughter killed themselves. Klepper's sister Hildegarde still lives in Berlin.[21]

That a Protestant clergyman would be married to a Jew was not at all unusual in an era which saw many clergymen deported as racial Jews. The sight of such a clergyman wearing den gelben Stern (the yellow star) over his pastoral robes was not uncommon at Theresienstadt. This was the time when the Jewish "preacher" of a synagogue (Martin Riesenburger) could have a gentile wife.

At least one Nazi obsession—that the Mischlinge would continue to make their presence known in all facets of German life—appears vindicated. The Mischlinge interviewed for this book hold a variety of professional positions in contemporary German society. A majority—Rolf Vogel, Heinz Elsberg, Hans Faust and Werner Goldberg—are journalists. Goldberg was a section head at Sender Freies Berlin (SFB, or Radio Free Berlin) and is editor of *Die Mahnung*, the organ of the BVN—Bund der Verfolgten des Naziregimes (League of Victims of Political Persecution Under the Nazis). Goldberg was a member of the Senate of Berlin, the West Berlin central parliament, from 1958 until 1979. He is active in theater, film and television production. His younger brother Günther served as mayor of the Berlin suburb of Wilmersdorf, where Arthur Miller lives. Charlotte Lehmann and Hanns Rehfeld are respectively former and present members of the diplomatic corps. The East German Jewish Community is and has been led by Dr. Peter Kirchner and Bernhard Vaks. Another prominent Mischling, West German federal parliamentarian Heinz Korry, fell victim to a politically motivated assassination in May 1981.

How closely do the Christian Mischlinge maintain their links to Judaism? Hans Faust occasionally attends synagogue services and is active in the worldwide Hebrew Christian Alliance movement. Heinz Elsberg is Berlin correspondent for a German Jewish newspaper. Virtually all of the Mischlinge have some object in their homes, be it a ceremonial menorah or a long playing album of High Holiday prayers chanted by a cantor, which reflects their Jewish heritage.

Rolf Vogel, author of several best-selling nonfiction works, is editor and publisher of *Deutschland-berichte* (literally: *Germany Report*), a highly regarded monthly publication which brings news of Israel and Jewish affairs to Germans. He is also a major lobbyist for Israel and Israeli interests in Bonn. (He made the deal to equip the West German army with Israeli-made Uzi submachine guns.) In 1954, Vogel became the first postwar German journalist to visit Israel. He was West German Chancellor Konrad Adenauer's official observer at the trial of Adolf Eichmann.

Vogel became a footnote in history through his role as the

emissary who first carried word to Israel of the impending historic journey to Jerusalem by Egyptian President Anwar al-Sadat. Vogel interviewed Franz Josef Strauss, former West German Minister of Defense, upon his return from a visit to Cairo in May 1977. Strauss asked Vogel to "please tell our friends in Israel that Mr. Sadat will come to Jerusalem."

Within days, Vogel was in Jerusalem meeting with key members of the Likud coalition (which had defeated the Labor Party on May 17 in national parliamentary elections): Moshe Dayan (who left Labor to become Foreign Minister), Ezer Weizman, Simcha Ehrlich, Zalman Shuval and Yosef Burg (Minister of the Interior under Prime Ministers Begin and Shamir). The mothers of both Vogel and Burg were at Theresienstadt. Vogel's mother survived. Burg's didn't.

Heinz Elsberg worked in the famous Büro Grüber, where the Protestant clergyman Propst Heinrich Grüber aided many baptized Jews in escaping deportation until he was sent to Dachau for his efforts. Paul Elsberg, Heinz's father, had a friend in the banking house of Jacquier und Securius, whose offices were in the same building as the Büro Grüber. Through this connection, Heinz met the courageous Grüber and soon began to work for him. The Büro Grüber, known to many only by its location "An der Stechbahn," became a beacon of hope for the persecuted. Grüber eventually expanded his operation to help all Jewish victims of the Nazis. This caused his arrest, but Grüber survived Dachau and testified against Adolf Eichmann in Jerusalem in 1961. Grüber was the only German (and except for Judge Michael Musmanno of the United States the only non-Jewish) witness for the prosecution.

Hans Faust was sentenced to jail late in 1944 for Judenbeguenstigung, the crime of aiding and abetting Jews. If one recalls the Seyss-Inquart report to Martin Bormann about the loyalty of the Mischlinge, then perhaps that Nazi fear had a firm basis in reality. Faust's anti-fascist credentials are impeccable. He joined the Kommunistische Partei Deutschlands (KPD, the Weimar era German Communist Party) in 1931, and was first arrested for "disparaging the [Nazi] government" in July 1933. Although his mother was Jewish (Faust was not baptized into the Christian faith until 1951), she was able to file a petition of grace which resulted in his being released from KZ (concentration camp) Börgermoor in Emsland during the 1933 Christmas Amnesty. His mother died the following year.

Because his parents had been divorced since 1920, Faust's father, Heinrich Friedrich Wilhelm Faust, a Roman Catholic, was able to work as an engineer in the Luftwaffe Ministry—under Göring and Erhard Milch—until his death in an automobile accident in December 1939. During the Holocaust, several of Faust's mother's cousins and, in some cases, their children as well, perished in Nazi death camps.

Although one hears it often said that the "Jews served on the U-boats," apparently neither Jews nor Mischlinge played an active part in Hitler's Navy. This refutes the published recollections of German Grand Admiral Erich Raeder as well as subsequent statements made by one of the leading historians of the Nazi era. (Some of the "illegal" Jews hiding underground in Berlin were called "U-boats," which also adds to the confusion.)

The contradictions stem from the self-serving statements in Raeder's postwar memoirs regarding his intercession with Hitler to provide freedom from molestation for "a number of Jewish people known to me." Given what we already know, there's not much reason to doubt his word. Much less credible is Raeder's assertion that "as far as Jews in the Navy were concerned, I took their part personally and was almost completely successful. Two Jewish officers were forced out of the service on the basis of the Nuremberg anti-Semitic Laws; we saw to it that they obtained good positions in civil life. When the war broke out, they were immediately recalled with their full naval rank, and justified our action by performing excellent and wholehearted service. In another case, I managed to persuade Hitler and [Rudolf] Hess to permit the excellent officer concerned to stay in the service."

Raeder continues, "It is an indication of the high state of unity and morale in the Navy that in every case where an officer's position was endangered because of his non-Aryan descent, his superiors took up the fight personally for him, seeing to it that he received the same treatment and promotion, even for top positions, as other officers . . . And without exception every naval officer of Jewish blood performed capable and devoted service during the war."[22]

Professor Peter C. Hoffmann of McGill University in Montréal, the noted historian of the 20 July plot against Hitler, agreed with Raeder's story.[23] He pointed out that the appendix of Raeder's book lists the names of Jewish naval officers removed from service after the implementation of the Nuremberg Laws. Says Professor Hoffmann, "The list is so ludicrously short, most Jews must have been allowed to stay. Perhaps no one was even removed, but a list was submitted to meet official demands."

But Professor Klaus-Jurgen Müller of the Bundeswehr-Hochschule in Hamburg was skeptical. Considered the leading authority on the German military, Müller was aware of the Mischlinge having served in the Wehrmacht and in the Luftwaffe, but had not found any records indicating their service in the Navy.[24]

The final word, however, came from the sole survivor of the Jewish naval officers ousted after the Nuremberg Laws. Kapitän zur See a.D. Hans Heinrich Lebram (his rank is that of naval captain), now living in retirement in the Baltic Seaport of Kiel, says Raeder is wrong.[25] And he should know. He was one of the "two Jewish officers" referred to by Raeder as having been "immediately recalled with their full naval rank." According to Lebram, that never happened.

Even stranger is the tale of Otto Mailander. The 18 January 1980 issue of the *San Jose* (California) *Mercury* carried a story worth quoting: "The odyssey of a German-born American who helped build the V-2 rocket during World War II and then escaped to work on the U.S. space program ended today when his ashes were scattered over the Sierra. Dr. Otto Mailander, who fled advancing Russian troops in 1945 with famed rocket engineer Wernher von Braun died Tuesday. . . . Mailander was born in Germany, the son of the American consul in Breslau who was appointed by President Grover Cleveland."

The article goes on to say that Mailander, "von Braun and hundreds of other scientists were working on space missiles when World War II began. Some of the leading scientists, including von Braun, were briefly jailed when they at first refused to cooperate with the Nazis. Mailander was one of almost a dozen scientists of Jewish heritage who escaped the gas chambers because of their work on rockets."

The obituary then states that Mailander (who would appear to have been a Mischling) "was among more than 100 scientists who managed to smuggle 28 V-2 rockets and all the plans for several types of missiles out of Germany. They walked 145 miles, hiding under bridges as Russians searching for them crossed overhead, to surrender to the Americans. Mailander made a leather strap to hold von Braun's arm, which had been broken while loading the rockets onto trucks. Mailander, who spoke fluent English, served briefly as German interpreter for General George S. Patton. . . . He [Mailander] worked for the National Aeronautics and Space Administration [NASA] at Cape Canaveral . . . from 1945 until his retirement." The *Los Angeles Times* carried the story three days later. Eventually it reached Detroit and the obituary pages of the *Jewish News*.[26]

Every one of these newspapers had fallen victim to a bizarre hoax. For "Dr." Otto Mailander was neither "of Jewish descent" nor a scientist. He had been living in the United States since World War I. What gave his story an element of truth was an obscure reference in the June 1941 *Contemporary Jewish Record* summary of news from Germany. It read, "A report on 19 March revealed that several German Jewish scientists were released from concentration camps in connection with war work." The V-2 team began their work at Peenemünde about that time. Could Mailander have been among them? Would a Jew, especially a man of science, have chosen to work for the enemy sworn to destroy him—creating instruments of mass destruction designed to kill the innocent— rather than face his own death? Albert Speer thought it quite likely. In his opinion, "It is certain that it would have been possible for von Braun to take in some Jewish scientists for the development of the V-2."[27]

Wernher von Braun's brother Magnus disagrees.[28] "If there was a Jew in our group, I certainly would have known it," said the former Chrysler Corporation engineering executive. (Wernher died in 1977). He too had seen the Mailander obituary. Speaking from his Arizona retirement home, with the barest trace of a German accent evident in his southwestern rancher-like twang, von Braun took the newspaper story apart piece by piece. "I never knew of an Otto Mailander before I saw the obituary," he insisted, "and besides, it was I who made the leather bandage for my brother's arm. And that isn't even the way he broke it."

Soon enough, others confirmed von Braun's story. NASA archivist Lee D. Saegesser wrote that he had "searched the materials in the History Office Archives but . . . found no mention of Dr. Mailander. I am enclosing a list of some of the Germans (V-2 scientists) who came to the U.S. after World War II. His name is not on this list." Saegesser added that someone at the National Air and Space Museum at the Smithsonian Institution remembers receiving a newspaper clipping on Dr. Mailander.[29]

According to the Office of the Historian of the United States Department of State, "No person by the name of Mailander appears in either the Register of the Department of State during the years 1884–1889 or in the list of consular officers who served in Breslau, Germany."[30]

Mailander, however, is what can be called a "Jewish surname." It shows up frequently in the area around Fürth, near Nuremberg, once the center of a prewar thriving Jewish community. But there is no record of an Otto Mailander in the surviving archives of the community. This in spite of a claim made by Mailander's widow, a respected former educator, that late in his life "Otto would suddenly lapse into Hebrew prayers. He said he had learned them from his grandfather."[31]

Ultimately, Mitchell Sharpe of the Alabama Space and Rocket Center in Huntsville, supplied the full list of names of the members of the von Braun group that had surrendered to the American Army in the Austrian Tyrol.[32] The list was drawn up by the Army on 2 August 1945 while they were overseeing what by then was being called "Project Paperclip." (It was originally known as "Project Overcast.")[33] The first surname to appear under the initial "M" is Michel.

So who then was "Dr." Otto Mailander? Incredibly enough, he was just a lonely and homesick German housebuilder who happened to be working in Cocoa Beach at the same time as the members of the von Braun team were developing America's pioneer space probes for NASA. Because that stretch of Eastern Florida is hardly crowded with German-speaking natives, the equally-as-lonely members of the von Braun team were delighted to while away the hours in various Cocoa Beach watering holes conversing in German with Mailander. The upshot of all this was that Mailander stole their collective identities. Dissatisfied with his real place in life, he created a composite portrait based upon his conversations and parlayed it to the point where he wound up lecturing on the space program before not only groups of California school children, but even the employees of Ames Laboratories, a leading defense contractor. At one point, recalls someone who sponsored one of his appearances, Mailander brought along a "guest scientist," who was presumed to be another member of the group of twelve Jewish V-2 scientists.

Where could Mailander have heard about Jewish V-2 scientists? Almost certainly it would have been from one of his fellow Cocoa Beach nocturnal conversationalists. Could Mailander have actually talked to one of the Jewish scientists?

Magnus von Braun doesn't see how it could have been possible. He wondered why someone on the V-2 team would tell a stranger they were of Jewish descent but never have told von Braun. The last words of Magnus von Braun on the subject were "Let sleeping Mailanders lie—or is it let lying Mailanders sleep?"[34]

Otto Mailander's daughter, Dolly Faust, of Boulder Springs, Wisconsin, was more succinct. "My father was the world's biggest bullshitter," she said, quickly adding, "Besides, we are not Jews. We are Germans."[35]

Presumably by now we have learned exactly what that means.

"I decide who is a Jew."

KARL LUEGER,
Burgomaster of Vienna (in the
pre-Hitler era).
(Often also attributed
to Hermann Göring)[1]

Chapter Six

The Wife of Colette

IN FRANCE, THERE WERE no Mischlinge. There the exemptions given to Jews differ greatly from those in Nazi Germany—not only in the sheer number of those covered, but on the basis for which the exemption was granted. Here, the key clause was not Article Seven of the Reich Citizenship Law, but Article Eight of the French *Statut des juifs*. This provided exemptions to Jews for "exceptional literary, scientific or artistic services" they rendered unto France. In many aspects, it grants rights akin to those enjoyed by the select group of privileged mixed marriage Jews in the Reich, but still falls somewhat short of bestowing full Honorary Aryan status.[2]

The Vichy government of Marshal Henri Philippe Pétain promulgated the *Statut des juifs* on 3 October 1940, less than three months after Pétain became "chief of state" of the Nazi puppet government of Occupied France. The Statut was far more stringent than a German ordinance issued the previous week which had also defined the Jews, but more along the lines established in the Reich by the Nuremberg Laws and its subsequent Commentaries. The Nazis had again defined Jewishness by religious practice, but the Vichy law used race as the determining factor. To the Germans, three grandparents who had observed Jewish religious practices constituted proof of an individual's Jewishness. The much more strict Vichy definition was two grandparents "of the Jewish race" in those cases where the spouse was also Jewish.

Xavier Vallat, the first Vichy commissioner general for

Jewish affairs, and a rabid anti-Semite, was responsible for the drafting of the Statut. Vallat denied the existence of any race other than Jews (as in the German Mischlinge category), and so there was no separate classification in the Statut for half-Jews. Nor were there any Nuremberg-style laws regarding intermarriage. To Vallat, a Jew was a Jew no matter what belief he now professed. As he once told a reporter, "A baptized person or the son of a baptized person is a Jew . . . a transmission agent of Jewish tradition." Only in cases where two or less Jewish grandparents were involved (e.g. a mixed marriage) did baptism make a difference and, even then, only if it was performed before 25 June 1940—well before the promulgation of the law. That exemption probably comes closest to granting a status roughly equivalent to the German Mischling of the First Degree classification. For Vallat, genuine assimilation meant an abandonment of Jewish culture so complete that it would have been erased from memory.

Not only were the French laws more restrictive, but the opportunities for exemption were fewer. Article Eight was eventually joined by a series of exemptions for Jewish war veterans, the immediate families of Jews who died fighting for France, and most important of all, those French Jews of "notable prestige and accomplishment,"—France's Jewish National Treasures—who for a variety of reasons were felt to be useful enough for Vichy to retain them in their important posts, which they had been forced to relinquish by the anti-Jewish laws. A group of twenty-one professors was among the first to receive this exemption. One of them was Dr. Robert Debré of the College of Medicine in Paris. A noted bacteriologist and specialist in children's medicine, he would become France's postwar representative to UNICEF and, in 1959, president of the National Academy of Medicine.

He was also the father of Michel Debré, who was to become President Charles de Gaulle's Minister of Justice and then serve as premier from 1959 to 1962. Later Michel Debré would hold every important portfolio in the French cabinet: Finance and Economy, Foreign Affairs and Defense. At 72, he is still a member of the French National Assembly and the European Parliament. Both Debrés received the Croix de Guerre (the medal for bravery in combat) and the French Medal of the Resistance.

A thorough but fruitless search of the files of the *Journal Officiel de la République Francaise* (the Vichy publication of record for laws and decrees) in the cavernous periodical room of the respected Bibliothèque Nationale in Paris failed to locate any trace of an exemption issued to Professor Debré.

Virtually the same thing had happened to Columbia University Professor Robert O. Paxton, the historian who co-authored (with Professor Michael R. Marrus) *Vichy France and the Jews*. "Like you," said Paxton, "I spent rather a lot of time trying to find the decree of exemption from the *Statut des juifs* for Dr. Robert Debré without success. At one point, I thought I might ask Michel Debré about it, and then decided against that approach. You might want to take that route," suggested Paxton.[3]

But that path had already been followed and produced an astonishing reply. Michel Debré vehemently denied that his father received "an exemption on the part of the Nazi government."[4] Technically he is correct, if one splits hairs, because the decree of exemption was issued by the Nazi puppet Vichy government. But important new evidence proves the existence of a much more complex relationship between Professor Debré and the Nazis than is even hinted at by the Vichy exemption. Presumably, Michel Debré must have knowledge of the existence of this new evidence for his own reputation is clearly tainted by it. Thus one must ask whether Michel Debré deliberately lied? Or was he perhaps making too fine a distinction between puppet and master? Regardless, how else can one explain the virtual disappearance from the public archives of Professor Debré's Vichy exemption? Surely only someone at the highest government level could have wielded enough influence to suppress such a potentially incriminating document.

Now it was time for Serge Klarsfeld to come to the rescue. Klarsfeld and his gentile wife Beate have frequently acted as the conscience of European Jewry. It was Beate Klarsfeld who first tracked down Klaus Barbie, the Nazi "Butcher of Lyon," in his Bolivian lair in 1971, a full twelve years before his deportation to France to eventually stand trial for his wartime crimes against humanity. And it was also Beate who publicly slapped the face of then West German Chancellor Kurt Georg Kiesinger in a courageous act of protest that sharply reminded a world, which had promised never to forget, that Germany was being led by a former Nazi Party functionary.[5]

It was no surprise that Nazi-hunter Serge Klarsfeld could produce a copy of a 1943 Vichy police document: A report on the visit of an Inspector Soustre with Professor Robert Debré. Following the liberation of Paris by the Allies, this document too was "liberated" from the secret files of the Vichy police.[6] Otherwise it might also have met the same fate as did Professor Debré's decree in the Bibliothèque Nationale. Often the only remaining evidence of collaboration can be found in Nazi and Vichy internal reports, notes and memos of meetings—the only documentation to have survived the massive postwar official cover-up.

One can be reasonably certain that Inspector Soustre's questions were answered honestly and without any fabrication by Professor Debré. It would have ill suited Debré under these circumstances to lie about delicate matters which could so easily be checked and double-checked by the Vichy police. The indictment against Professor Debré is damning because it is delivered in his own words. In effect, it becomes his confession. It is a self-inflicted *J'accuse*.

The Vichy exemptions were granted prior to the German regulations of June 1942 instructing Jews in the Occupied Zone of France to wear the yellow Star of David. The Nazis are never referred to as such in the report, they are called "the Occupying Authorities."

The reason for the investigation is clearly stated on the report: "Professor Debré comes to the Academy of Medicine without wearing his star; he pretends to be exempt." Certainly a Jew could die for far less—and most who wore the star did. But the message in the investigation is clear: Debré was under the protection of the Nazis. And who in Vichy would dare risk incurring the wrath of the Nazis for harming, of all people, a Jew?

Debré is identified as being "of French nationality," having been born in Sedan, site of the decisive battle of the 1870 Franco-Prussian War, to Simon Debré and his wife Marianne. Professor Debré is said to be the "bearer of identity card No. 978.706 issued by the Prefecture of Police on 2 May 1941. It carries the notation 'JUIF' [Jew]."

On 31 May 1943, less than one month before Klaus Barbie arrested and allegedly tortured and murdered Jean Moulin, the leader of the French Resistance, Inspector Soustre called at the Paris residence of Professor Debré. There, "under questioning," Debré said that "he was a Jew and that he didn't wear the Star because he had been released from all the regulations under the *Statut des juifs* by the decree of 5 January 1941, issued by the Vichy Council of Ministers. It is by virtue of this decree, signed by Marshal Pétain, that the Secretary of State for National Education [Jérome Carcopino] issued an order on 11 July 1941 reinstating Professor Debré in his capacity at the Academy of Medicine. It was retroactive to 20 December 1940."

The report continues to quote Debré: "According to what he says, these facts would be known by the Occupying Authorities, who would always make exceptions for him. Recently, his telephone having been disconnected following a denunciation, the Occupying Authorities had it replaced for him immediately." There is no misunderstanding exactly what Debré means here. Obviously, the denunciation would have been made to the Vichy police who then pulled the plug on Debré's phone. But he was able to go over their heads to the

Germans to get it reconnected. A denunciation to the police would have meant deportation for any other Jew. Clearly, Debré had friends in high places. Collaborationist Jews like Debré fared better under the occupation than not only most French Jews, but even better than Resistance leaders like Jean Moulin.

Soustre's report says that Debré "claims to be the doctor of the children of some German citizens in France and has also looked after the personnel of the Japanese embassy." (Japan, of course, being a partner of Nazi Germany in the Fascist Axis.) "Professor Debré adds that he visited the German offices on several occasions without wearing the star. The German administrators, knowing on the other hand his outstanding character, never considered him to be a Jew according to the definition given in the decree of 5 January 1941. At the time when wearing the star was [made] compulsory, a request was made (Debré did not say who made it) to the Prefecture of Police and he received word that his was a special case by virtue of this same decree.

"At the medical association, Professor Debré is not listed among the Israelite [a commonly used French term for Jews] doctors. His situation is considered completely separate."

The report then provides background information on Mrs. Debré ("an Aryan without any occupation") and the couple's three children. The eldest, "Michel, born 15 January 1912" is described as "married, two children, government attorney at the State Administrative offices at Vichy." This is clearly at odds with the information in Michel Debré's official biography, which claims that he was a member of the French Resistance in 1940. (He must have been lonely, for the movement never took root until the February 1943 conscription of Frenchmen for labor service in Germany.)[7] Michel Debré also says he served with the French army from 1939 to 1944. He mentions nothing about being in government service in Vichy. Soustre's report does not mention that Michel Debré was baptized as a Roman Catholic—perhaps this occurred after commissioner general Vallat's 25 June 1940 cutoff date.

In conclusion the report states, "The Jew doctor Debré is released from the bans instituted by the law of 3 October 1940 by the decrees of 5 January 1941. The decree is not signed by Marshal Pétain as he [Debré] pretends it to be, but by Jérome Carcopino, who was secretary of state for national education and youth. Although he claims that the Occupying Authorities do not consider him to be a Jew, Professor Debré is nevertheless registered at the Prefecture of Police and doesn't possess any dispensation from wearing the star.

"The decrees related to the ban of the law of 3 October 1940 can not clear him from the application of the German laws—and given the high professional profile of the Professor Debré, we have limited ourselves to the task of this investigation as we have been asked without underlining any infraction."

During the 1946 treason trial of Xavier Vallat, one of the few who testified in his favor was a Jewish doctor, Gaston Nora. Debré is on record as stating that when he and Nora visited Vallat during the Vichy era, "Vallat politely received them."[8]

The contradictions between Vichy era documentation and postwar recollections are also evident in the official biography of another de Gaulle intimate, the noted economist Jacques Rueff. He was one of the few of his profession ever to be elected a member of the Académie Francaise, taking the seat vacated by the death of the poet Jean Cocteau. Rueff, who died in 1978, was chiefly responsible for the financial reforms that put France on the road to economic recovery after the establishment of the Fifth Republic by President de Gaulle in 1958. Rueff's biographical entry in the 1969 *Current Biography* covers three pages[9] and lists his honors and accomplishments, including the fact that he is "an honorary vice-governor of the Bank of France." What it does not say is how Rueff was given that honorarium by the Vichy government of Marshal Pétain.

The early portion of his biographical sketch states that Rueff became assistant governor of the Bank of France in 1939. It goes on to say that "when the Germans occupied France in May 1940 Rueff resigned from his position with the Bank of

France, and during most of the Occupation he lived in the South of France with his wife's family." No mention is made of the exemption granted Rueff from the *Statut des juifs* by Marshal Pétain on 22 January 1941. But unlike the decree for Professor Robert Debré, Rueff's exemption can still be found in the public archives, on pages 377–378 of the 24 January 1941 *Journal Officiel*.

The format of the exemption deserves a closer look. The first portion contains a statement to Pétain by Yves Bouthillier, minister of state for France, extolling Rueff's services to the state and requesting Pétain to allow Rueff to return to his position as a member of the government finance inspection service. Pétain then grants the necessary permission and issues an exemption to the 3 October 1940 law for Rueff.

Next comes a curious notice by Bouthillier. First, the resignation of Rueff as vice-governor of the Bank of France is accepted. But, in what appears to be an elaborate sham, Rueff is immediately appointed as the bank's honorary vice-governor—the post he was still holding twenty-eight years later. A replacement is named for Rueff's old post as vice-governor and the charade ends there, followed only by a brief official notice of Rueff's reinstatement to the government finance inspection service. It is all wrapped up in a tidy bundle. There are no loose ends.

A year before they invaded France, the Nazis published a book titled *Juden in Frankreich (Jews in France)*.[10] Compiled by Heinz Ballensiefen and purporting to list the Jews who "control" France, it is not unlike the two books published in the United States during the 1930s by indicted (but not convicted) Nazi propagandist Elizabeth Dilling. *Juden* was virtually a hit list of prominent French Jews, all of whom the Nazis promised to remove if and when France came under their control. Jacques Rueff's name appears there twice. On page 77, in a chapter on Jews in the Daladier government (Édouard Daladier became premier in 1938), "the Jews Baumgart and Jacques Rueff" are listed as teaching economics in the Free School of Political Science—a post *Current Biography* says Rueff left in 1934.

The second listing for Rueff is on page 102, in the section headed "Jews in Transportation." Rueff is among those Jews listed as committee officers of the Societé des Chemins de Fer (René Mayer, later to be the second Jewish Premier of France, also served on the committee). Rueff's identification as director of the Mouvement Général des Fonds in the Treasury is again out of date, Rueff having served in that post in 1936-37. (His assistant there was Maurice Couve de Murville, premier of France at the time of the *Current Biography* publication.)

But Rueff is hardly alone in having been fingered by the Nazis as a target for removal and then receiving an official exemption when their Vichy puppets began to make good on the promise. A search through the *Journal Officiel* turned up these additional exemptions:

Raymond Berr, the mining engineer; his exemption was granted by Pétain on 15 April 1941. "The Jew Raymond Berr," is, like Rueff, given double billing by the Nazis in *Juden in Frankreich*.

General of the Army Darius-Paul Bloch was exempted by Pétain on 10 December 1940. He is the "General Bloch (Jude)" on Ballensiefen's hit list. General Bloch's brother Marcel changed his name after the war to Marcel Dassault, and the General followed suit and became General Darius-Paul Dassault. Marcel Dassault is the aviation magnate who produced the Mystére and Mirage aircraft, favorites of Israeli Air Force pilots, and in the process became the richest man in France.

According to Marcel Dassault's biographer, Pierre Assouline,[11] General Bloch refused to take advantange of his exemption and declined the opportunity to become an Honorary Aryan in an anti-Semitic state. Instead, he lived clandestinely in Nice at the home of Professor Henry Chrétien, the inventor of the CinémaScope process and future winner of a 1954 "Oscar." From this position of safety, he was able to discreetly carry out missions for the Resistance. After the liberation of

Paris, General Bloch was named Grand Chancellor of the Legion of Honor and served as Military Governor of Paris.

Certainly those Jews like Dr. Robert Debré, Jacques Rueff and General Bloch who received exemptions from the Vichy puppet government were not penalized for this by postwar French governments. Nor did the specter of a Vichy exemption serve to preclude their subsequent highly visible public participation in the social and political milieu of the Fifth Republic. As we have seen, Dr. Debré and General Bloch received high official honors for their efforts in aiding the Resistance. Had both men not received Vichy exemptions originally, they would not have been at liberty to make themselves so useful when the right moment came.

How much of a double standard is involved? One of General Bloch's brothers, René, a surgeon, perished at Auschwitz. And Marcel was sent to a concentration camp. But General Bloch? A villa in Nice is hardly the equivalent of internment in a Nazi prison camp. Jacques Rueff must have felt much the same way.

After the war, Marcel converted to Catholicism—as, it has been alleged, did former premier Léon Blum upon his release from Buchenwald. By coincidence, the families of both General Bloch and Dr. Debré were considered to be among the most prominent of Strasbourg Jews before the turn of the century. General Darius-Paul Dassault died in 1969.

Not listed in *Juden in Frankreich* but nevertheless still receiving exemptions from Pétain were: Chief of Artillery Pierre-Salomon-Israel Brisac, on 10 December 1940 (the same day as General Bloch); Armand Mayer and Pierre Lion, both mining engineers and both on 7 February 1941; Marcel-Félix Garsin, agricultural engineer—on 21 January 1941; and of course, the twenty-one professors who included Louis Halphen and Robert Debré. The latter's Article Eight exemption for "exceptional services" was one of only two such petitions made on behalf of Jews by the great classicist and then Rector of the Academy of Paris, Vichy Education Minister Jérome Carcopino.[12]

Emmanuel Berl made the *Juden in Frankreich* list three times, where the "Jew Emanuel [sic] Berl" is identified along with the names of those publications for which he wrote. Berl, who died in 1976, is described oddly enough in the *Columbia Dictionary of Modern European Literature* as being "always conscious of anti-Semitism."[13] That same biographical sketch says that "because of his advocacy of the Munich Peace Pact, Berl had to be hidden during the German occupation." Perhaps, but hidden from whom? It is known that Berl drafted some of Marshal Pétain's speeches after Pétain took office.[14] Berl always insisted he was more French than Jewish, which may be the state of consciousness that the *Columbia Dictionary* refers to. He also believed that France should refuse citizenship to all Jews save those who renounced Zionism and the "Yiddish way of life."[15] However, Berl apparently never received a formal Vichy exemption.

Other notable French Jews alleged to have received exemptions include the publisher Pierre Bènés and prominent businessman Léon Joanovici.[16]

Sometimes only high-level intervention by the Nazis could save a Jew's life. Such was the case with the novelist Colette. Although Colette wasn't a Jew, her third husband, Maurice Goudeket, was. And it was his good fortune to be married to someone as important as Colette at the time of the occupation. A major Gestapo roundup of French Jews on 12 December 1941 had netted Goudeket, who was interned at a camp in Compiègne until February 1942. A letter of 13 February from Colette to a friend says only, "Maurice, who's been 'away' since 12 December, has just been given back to me."[17]

In his autobiography,[18] Goudeket wrote, "All this while [his internment], Colette never relaxed her efforts to have me freed. There was no step which she was not prepared to take, no humiliation which she would not face. She saw collaborators and Germans. Who shall blame her? I hope I should have done as much."

But even with Goudeket free, Colette continued to see Germans. Her name, along with that of the widow of philosopher and Nobel Prize winner Henri Bergson (here spelled Teutonically as "Bergsohn"), is found on a typed list of topics to be discussed at a meeting between an unnamed Nazi official and SS-Hauptsturmführer (SS captain) Theodor Dannecker. On the basis of internal evidence, the meeting was held sometime immediately after 7 June 1942, the day the Star decree took effect. A copy of the agenda, retained by one of the participants, has pen lines drawn through those topics discussed at the meeting. The category under which the names of Colette and Madame Bergson appear: "Exemptions from wearing the Star for mixed marriage Jews whose spouses are important in French 'culture and in politics' " has been marked in a manner to indicate that the subject was broached.

And apparently it was. On 18 June, SS-Sturmbannführer (SS major) Herbert Hagen (Adolf Eichmann's traveling companion on a 1937 visit to Palestine) prepared a typed report on a high-level meeting held 16 June to discuss the granting of the exemptions. It would appear that Hagen may have been the other key participant in the Dannecker meeting.[19]

The first name on the Hagen list is that of Bergson's widow. (Here, the name is spelled correctly.) It is followed by "the wife of the writer de Jouvenelle [sic] if it is shown that she is indeed a Jew." This puzzling reference *may* have been to Colette, as her second husband, whom she had divorced in 1924, was the onetime editor-in-chief of *Le Matin*, Henry de Jouvenel. Perhaps Colette thought her chances might be improved if she petitioned the Nazis under de Jouvenel's name, although he had died in 1935. Shortly before Goudeket's arrest, Colette had completed what was to be her last full-length novel, *Julie de Carneilhan*, in which the heroine's initials reverse those of "Colette de Jouvenel." Could this interesting play on names still have been on Colette's mind when she approached the Germans, particularly as the novel closely follows some of the events of her second marriage? If so, it apparently confused the Nazis sufficiently to the point where they wondered why Colette might consider herself a Jew.

However, it is much more likely that this reference is to Marcelle Prat, the first wife of journalist Bertrand de Jouvenel, whose activities and political leanings would have stood him in great favor with the group meeting on 16 June. The noted Israeli historian Zeev Sternhell recently accused de Jouvenel of having been fascist, anti-Semitic and a Nazi before the war. In October 1983, a French court condemned Sternhell's book *Ni Droite, ni Gauche. l'Ideologie Fasciste en France (Not Right, nor Left. Fascist Ideology in France)* on the basis of his accusations against de Jouvenel.[20] If a request for an exemption was made for his wife, it would indicate that de Jouvenel had entrée to the Nazi hierarchy, and would substantiate Sternhell's claim.

However, Colette's former husband, Henry de Jouvenel, was Bertrand's father by his earlier marriage to Claire Boas, a Jew. This meant Bertrand was Colette's stepson. How close were they? Colette seduced Bertrand when he was sixteen and she was forty-seven. As the son of a Jewish mother, Bertrand ordinarily would have been considered to be a Jew, as there was no separate classification for Mischlinge in France.

If indeed Bertrand de Jouvenel had enough high-level contacts to make an exemption request, could not Colette have approached him to act as her intermediary with the Nazis on behalf of Goudeket? Neither Goudeket nor de Jouvenel in their published memoirs chose to acknowledge that this may have happened. Perhaps it would have been embarrassing for Goudeket to admit publicly that Colette sought to aid her third husband, a Jew, through the alleged Nazi connections of her one-time lover, the half-Jewish son of her second husband.

The third name on the list is definitely Colette's—only this time, curiously, it is an exemption request for "the wife of the writer Caulette [sic]." Colette was also known to be a lesbian, but if the Nazis didn't know enough about her to determine whether "she is indeed a Jew," how much could they have known about her private life? Interestingly, Gertrude Stein, the American expatriate writer, also a known lesbian *and* a

Jew as well, lived in France throughout the war and was never molested by the Nazis. More likely, "wife" was just a smirking Nazi comment on their perception of the Goudeket-Colette marriage. Whatever the logic, one of Colette's pleas must have worked, for Goudeket was never again jailed. Hagen granted "temporary" exemptions to those on the list on 13 July 1942.[21] Colette continued to be published in Paris during the Nazi occupation, but so were works by Elsa Triolet, the friend of Louis Aragon. Triolet not only was a communist, she was also a Jew and a Russian. And if indeed Colette did make several radio broadcasts for the Pétain government's Radio Nationale, does her action pale beside that of Simone de Beauvoir, who produced cultural programs for the network?[22]

Another name on the Hagen list was that of the Jewish wife of Fernand de Brinon, Vichy's representative in Paris. The Nazis were embarrassed when a group of anti-Vichy protestors in Zürich drew world attention to her Jewish origins. If Pétain wanted to suggest names to Hagen for exemptions, Ambassador de Brinon would have been the intermediary, and the humiliated Ambassador had to ask the Nazis for an exemption for his wife. Mme. de Brinon (née Frank) received her exemption in person from Major Hagen. One wonders whether Hagen, the former journalist, took advantage of the opportunity to hand-deliver Colette's as well?

Marshal Pétain personally interceded on behalf of three of his friends: the Comtesse d'Aramon, the Marquise de Chasseloup-Laubat, and the latter's sister, Madame Pierre Girot de Langlade. As befitting these ladies' station in French society, the petitions were granted. Even Premier Pierre Laval intervened on behalf of a Paul Boron, and Admiral François Darlan once declared in a cabinet meeting that "the good old French Jews have a right to every protection we can give them. I have some, by the way, in my own family."

Subsequent exemptions were also issued to six Jews who worked for the anti-Jewish police of Louis Darquier de Pellepoix (who replaced Vallat as commissioner general for Jewish affairs in June 1942), and to one Jew who worked for SS Major

General Walter Schellenberg's secret service,[23] the Sicher-
heitsdienst (SD).

A protégé of Reinhard Heydrich, the first chief of the SD,
Schellenberg was known to have employed Jews as agents of
his foreign intelligence service. The SD was the intelligence
arm of the SS (Schutzstaffeln). Formed in 1932, it soon became
the principal intelligence and counterintelligence service of
Nazi Germany, rivaled only by the Wehrmacht's Abwehr. The
SD was Amt (Section) VI of the SS. There were seven Amts
of the Reichssicherheitshauptampt (RSHA), the Central Security Department of the Reich. The RSHA was the main
administrative arm of the Reichsführer SS, Heinrich Himmler.
The dreaded Gestapo (Geheime Staatspolizei—secret state
police) the very heart of the SS, was known as AMT IV. "Cicero," the valet-spy in the British Embassy in Ankara, was
an SD operative, as was originally Klaus Barbie. When Admiral Wilhelm Canaris was ousted as chief of the Abwehr in
February 1944, Schellenberg was appointed to preside over
the new centralized German intelligence service, the Militär-
isches Amt (Military Bureau).[24]

A parallel situation of Jews working for the Nazis led to
the creation in the Netherlands of a privileged group of Jews
known as the "Blaue Reiter" ("Blue Knights").[25] Ironically,
they were namesakes of the German abstract art school
founded by Vasily Kandinsky, Franz Marc and Paul Klee. The
proponents of Aryan art considered these artists "degenerate,"
but those who felt that way were usually those minor Nazi
functionaries who were not given access to the piles of European art loot. First to receive the "Blue Knight" designation
was a German-Jewish art historian. His task was to advise
Nazi art collectors like Hermann Göring which of the paintings
(almost invariably stolen from deported Jews) were deemed
worthy of display (presumably for only the purest and most
aesthetic of reasons) on the walls of Göring's Karinhall hunting
lodge. The hypocrisy on both sides is rarely so transparent
as it is in this symbiotic Nazi-Jewish relationship.

The "Blue Knights" were exempt from wearing the yellow

Star of David, and lest they should suffer even temporary embarrassment if arrested, the Nazis needed only to check their identity cards in the central record office index. The cards were boldly stamped "Ongeldig" (it means "Invaluable") in huge blue letters. That left no question of their official status. Originally there were but twenty-seven of these "invaluable" Jews in the whole of the Netherlands. Six of them were known to have been Dutch Nazis. A thorough German stenographer named Frau Slottke, who apparently spent most of her time in the Netherlands typing elaborate tables of exempt Jewish groups, prepared a 1943 memo which confirms that six of a group of twelve Dutch Nazi Party Jews in an exempt group were free from wearing the star and also lived in mixed marriages. These Jews were members of the synagogue-burning NSB, led by Anton Mussert, a man the Germans frequently called "a Jewish lackey." Max Blokzijl, the Goebbels of the NSB, was a quarter-Jew, as was the leader of the NSB's Education Department.[26]

As the potential market for useful Jews grew, the number of "invaluables" kept by the Nazis eventually swelled to forty-nine. Again, thanks to Frau Slottke and her lists,[27] we know that, of these, forty lived in mixed marriages; the other nine had full Jewish spouses. The ranks of the "Blue Knights" now included one Jewish woman whose husband was serving with the SS at the front, five individuals with sons fighting for the Fatherland, three married members of the world famous Concertgebouw-Orchester, a German Olympic champion of 1896 (this would have to be either Alfred or Gustav Felix Flatow, the only German Jews to win Gold or Silver Medals, both in gymnastics, that year),[28] the wife of a leading Dutch economist and the son-in-law of a former librarian of the Royal Library at the Hague. Almost all survived the war.

At least three other "Blue Knights" also served as art experts for the Nazis. The identity card for "invaluable" Professor Johannes Joseph Cohen of the Rijks-Universiteitte, Utrecht, is one of the few still in existence. Before making a photostat available to the author, the still-protective Dutch authorities took great care to partially obscure Cohen's features on the photograph.[29]

Three of the "Blue Knights" were even allowed to emigrate. They were the Hungarian-born, internationally renowned violinist and composer Carl Flesch and his wife, the Dutch-born former Berta Josephus-Jitta, and the art dealer Friedländer, a Göring favorite. All three left Holland for Switzerland, Flesch dying there in 1944.[30]

Although he wasn't a "Blue Knight," another Amsterdam art dealer, Benjamin Katz, had tipped off Göring about the Jacques Goudstikker collection of Renaissance pictures and Eastern art in 1940. For this, in the words of a Göring aide, "we paid him a very good commission." Estimated to be worth several million dollars, the Goudstikker collection included the Vermeer called "Christ and the Woman Taken in Adultery." Göring paid almost two million guilders for the Vermeer and even tossed in several paintings from his own collection. After the war, the Vermeer was revealed as a fake created by the Dutch master forger Van Meegeren. Göring personally arranged for Katz to receive a visa to Switzerland and to take his funds, presumably including the Göring commission, with him.[31]

Apparently Göring was somewhat more lenient than other top Nazis when it came to granting special exemptions to useful Jews. Both he and his wife Emmy "never had any doubt" that his second-in-command, Field Marshal Erhard Milch (see Chapter Eight), was a half-Jew,[32] and Göring often aided Jewish friends of Emmy. Werner Goldberg's speculation that Göring played a key role in obtaining the release of the mixed marriage Jews arrested in the Fabrik Aktion appears well founded. After the failure of the 1923 Munich beer hall Putsch, Göring had been given shelter by two Jewish women, Frau Ilse Ballin and her sister, who also tended to his wounds. Göring arranged for both sisters to emigrate to Argentina in 1939. They too were allowed to take their money with them.[33]

Leo Blech, the conductor of the Berlin State Opera, was another Jew protected by Göring. Blech eventually emigrated to Stockholm.[34] Whether Göring was also personally involved in the Alfred Mombert affair is not known, but the poet and onetime member of the Stefan George circle (a literary movement which used the swastika as a völkisch symbol) was freed from a concentration camp where he had become ill, and was allowed to emigrate to Switzerland.[35] Journalist Sigrid Schultz [36] says Göring "helped a number of very rich Jews, the banker Goldschmidt, for instance, in order to please the actress he was courting."[37]

Historian Leonard Mosley, Göring's biographer, credits his subject with having said, "I'll decide who is and who is not a Jew." This is interesting in view of the fact that Göring's godfather, Dr. Hermann Ritter von Epenstein (Göring is named after him), was a Jew. Göring's mother, Fanny, eventually became von Epenstein's lover. The father of von Epenstein was a Jewish doctor at the court of King Frederick Wilhelm IV of Prussia.[38] Although he converted to Catholicism, the family name appears in the same official lists as other titled German families of Jewish blood. As a child in school, Göring was once made to wear a sign around his neck reading "Mein Pate Ist Ein Jude" ("My godfather is a Jew.") It is chillingly similar to the "Jew-boy" taunting young Richard Wagner received because of his Jewish stepfather.

But perhaps the most useful Jew the Nazis ever found was Dr. G. Emanuel, a Berlin neurologist.[39] Dr. Emanuel developed and produced an anti-syphilis serum for the use of the SS, whose ranks were notoriously plagued by the disease. The official SS manual even refers to Dr. Emanuel's serum by his name, probably the only Jewish name in the manual—but why shouldn't it? He wrote the instructions for its use. The Nazis, greatly pleased by all this, rewarded Dr. Emanuel with privileged mixed marriage status, even though he and his Aryan wife were childless.

It is widely known that medical experiments upon the already doomed Jewish concentration camp inmates were often initiated whenever someone in the Nazi hierarchy received a request to test a new drug, especially a serum, upon humans.[40] When it came to a serum as vitally important to the Nazis as that developed by Dr. Emanuel, it becomes difficult to imagine that the testing procedure would have been any different.

Requests for such medical experiments were often made to Himmler directly, as he was virtually in charge of the entire program. If indeed Himmler as Reichsführer SS did not first suggest the possibility of human experimentation with the Emanuel anti-syphilis serum before its use by SS men, the thought would have occurred to someone on his staff.

Thus we can be virtually positive that Jews were used as human guinea pigs to test Dr. Emanuel's discovery—first by being injected with bacterial cultures of syphilis, and then by being given the antidote. Himmler certainly would not have allowed the serum to be used upon his men otherwise, nor would Dr. Emanuel have been so handsomely rewarded for a medical advance that would ordinarily have taken years of use to prove its effectiveness.

"We have to kill the Jew within ourselves."

RAHEL VARNHAGEN (1771–1833),
German writer, friend
of Heine.[1]

Chapter Seven

Some of Our Best Wives Are Jews

FOR A MOMENT, Waldemar Baron von Oppenheim was skeptical. The Abwehr, Germany's super-secret intelligence agency, inviting *him* to become a spy? The Baron told his recruiter that, put simply, he did not think that he, with his Jewish ancestry, should become involved in spying for the Nazis. But his contact reassured him that the Abwehr had many people like the Baron among its operatives, "including some who are full-blooded Jews."[2]

And so, in June 1941, the scion of one of the most powerful German-Jewish banking families became Abwehr secret agent Number A.2408, operating under the not too highly imaginative code name of "Baron." He hid his instructions, reduced to postage stamp size, under the back cover of the treasured heavy gold watch he had inherited from Grandfather Oppenheim.

Waldemar von Oppenheim joined the NSDFB, the Nazi Party banking group, in July 1932, seven months before Hitler came to power. By marriage, he was related to the formidable Wallenberg banking family of Sweden. Raoul Wallenberg, who was to that family what the Baron was to the Oppenheims, chose to direct his considerable talents to aid the victims, and not the oppressors, of World War II.

Although evidence would indicate that the Baron was probably a Mischling of the Second Degree, nevertheless he was under the personal protection of Admiral Wilhelm Canaris, then director of the Abwehr. When the Baron ran afoul of the

Gestapo, the Abwehr intervened on his behalf. Oppenheim's reports to the Abwehr were usually rated as "valuable," if not "excellent." When Himmler and Schellenberg (Canaris's successor as spy chief) were secretly plotting peace behind Hitler's back in early 1945, Oppenheim was the man they approached to act as their intermediary.

In his memoirs, former Chancellor and later Ambassador to Turkey Franz von Papen[3] (himself related by marriage to the Warburg family of German-Jewish bankers) claimed that he often aided "Jews who had been maltreated." As proof of his good deeds, von Papen offers "a letter of thanks from a Herr Feldheim, who lived in my own home town, and whom I had managed to free from a concentration camp." Claims of this nature are often found in the postwar memoirs of those Nazis who survived judgment at Nuremberg.

But von Papen's diplomatic assignment in Turkey helped make possible the unfolding of a bizarre drama in which one of the principal characters was a Hungarian Jew in the employ of the Abwehr. Admiral Canaris, who hired this operative, was implicated in the 20 July 1944 assassination plot against Hitler and was among the last prisoners to be executed by the Nazis in the waning days of the war. But the Abwehr (some even say Gestapo) agent, Andor Bandi Gross, is still alive. The espionage affair, widely known as "Operation Cicero," is too well known to repeat here. It became the subject of a bestselling book by L. C. Moyzisch as well as a first-rate movie, *Five Fingers*, starring the late James Mason.

Bandi Gross was a pseudonym for Andrew Gyorgy. He worked for the Germans, the Jews and the Hungarians, and reputedly cheated them all. Yet Adolf Eichmann chose him to accompany Joel Brand, a Hungarian Jew, to Turkey in 1944 in the complex plan to exchange the lives of Hungarian Jews for Allied goods. For each truck delivered to Germany, one hundred Jews would be saved from the ovens. Ten thousand trucks would have meant one million lives and the closing of Auschwitz. But the plan was scuttled by the Allies.

The fact that Eichmann personally selected Gyorgy for this assignment lends credence to the claim that Gyorgy was indeed the Gestapo man he was rumored to be. Although he had been converted to Catholicism as a child, Gyorgy always called himself a Jew. Carrying a Hungarian diplomatic passport, Gyorgy, a black marketeer in hard currencies, was a frequent traveler throughout the Reich. As a result of his participation in the Operation Cicero affair, he served a prison sentence in Turkey after the war. He had been charged with espionage activity and the distribution of counterfeit money. After his release in 1953, he traveled to Israel to claim a debt of $100,000 he said the Israeli Government owed him. He was threatened with legal charges as an alleged Nazi collaborator, but was eventually paid an undisclosed sum. He now lives in Europe under yet another assumed name.[4]

Gyorgy was not the only Jew in the employ of the Gestapo. Georg Kareski, a German Jewish banker with close ties to the Nazis (see Chapter Nine), was used to launder funds paid another German Jew sent to England to spy for the Gestapo. Journalist Robert Gessner told of yet another case, "a young Jew from Upper Silesia [who] has made no secret of the fact that he was the chief Nazi spy concerned with the activities of Jewish organizations and the movements of Jewish foreign correspondents. Everybody knew him. He was pointed out in the cafés on the Kurfürstendamm, at a synagogue service, at meetings of Zionists, at the Jewish theater, and at every place Jews generally gathered."[5]

Jews occasionally show up working for even the most rabid of Nazi anti-Semites. Hitler intimate Ernst ("Putzi") Hanfstängl, who himself is widely believed to have received Honorary Aryan status, tells of a Jewish "principal assistant" to Alfred Rosenberg, race theoretician and editor in chief of the *Völkischer Beobachter*. (This was the official newspaper of the Nazis, and Hanfstängl had put up part of the money for them to buy it.)

Said Hanfstängl, "I used to see him [Rosenberg] most

mornings sitting in a dingy café at the corner of the Brien-
nerstrasse and the Augustenstrasse with a Hungarian Jew
named Holoschi . . . the man called himself Hollander in Germany and was another of those Jewish anti-Semites." Rosenberg was also said to have been an intimate friend of another
Jew, Steffi Bernhard—her father was Georg Bernhard, the
famous editor of the *Vossische Zeitung*. Again quoting Hanfstängl, "Rosenberg was distinctly Jewish in appearance, although he would have been the first to protest furiously if
anyone had questioned his ancestry."[6] Rosenberg was tried
at Nuremberg and hanged as a war criminal in 1946. The surname of Robert Ley, head of the Labor Front, is easily
changed to "Lewy" with the addition of just one letter, but
there is absolutely no proof to substantiate any allegations of
Jewish ancestry of either Rosenberg or Ley.

Rumors have placed some of the already-exempted Jews in
mixed marriages among the ranks of the Jewish Police, the
internal ghetto enforcement groups which functioned under
the strict control of the Nazis at the time of the deportations.
However, most of the Jewish Police were eventually deported
along with those Jews who served in the Judenrats. Even
Jews working for the anti-Jewish police forces (like that of
Louis Darquier de Pellepoix in France) first had to receive
individual special exemptions in order to continue functioning
without fear of eventual deportation along with their victims.

Functioning on an even lower level were the infamous Jewish street spies, particularly those in Berlin. During the last
years of the Reich, these Jews were used by the Gestapo to
prey upon and turn in other Jews, especially the so-called
"illegal Jews," who were evading arrest and deportation by
hiding in the streets and U-Bahn stations of the city. The Gestapo also used these Jewish spies to finger those non-exempt
Jews who were partaking of such forbidden pleasures as attending the theater without wearing their yellow Stars. As
Jews without exemptions were prohibited from attending
theater performances anyway, this would have resulted in a

serious double offense for any Jew unlucky enough to be caught there, and indeed some were. For a Jew to be caught *anywhere* without wearing the Star was bad enough.

The street spies have always claimed they only worked for the Nazis under duress or to protect a member of their family from deportation. But some were said to have "betrayed their own family as well—for money." Meyer Levin tells of a "certain half-Jew who had roamed the streets in a Gestapo car as an expert in identifying Jews by their looks; the Germans had paid him a few hundred dollars a head."[7]

By turning in their always-increasing quota of "illegals," the Jewish street spies could stave off their own deportation, although frequently it would only provide a temporary respite. The advantage to the Gestapo in employing Jews as street spies was obvious: as Jews, they could recognize other Jews who might easily have passed unnoticed through the Gestapo net. The Jews quickly learned who among them was a traitor, but often it was a lesson learned too late. One who did succeed at this deadly game of trading off "illegals" for her own life was Stella Kübler, who along with her husband (she is said to have married a Rolk Isaakson, who apparently did not survive), became the most notorious and feared of all the street spies. Forty years later, her name could still evoke momentary fear in Berlin Jews. A recently published book says Kübler is dead.[8] Many, however, doubt it. Journalist Hans Faust says only, "My God, I hope so." When Faust was jailed in December 1944 for "aiding and abetting Jews," a street spy, perhaps even Stella Kübler, betrayed him. Only Faust's status as a Mischling kept the Nazis from killing him.[9]

Of course, there were also Jewish traitors, and at least one was executed by the anti-Nazi underground. Certainly, being Jews made their crime of collaboration doubly heinous.[10]

As we've seen, the usefulness of individual Jews to the Nazis took many forms. Quite often, what the Jew brought into the bargain was not just money but a specialized knowledge, whether of art or of an anti-syphilis vaccine valuable enough to the Nazis to warrant a bureaucratic exemption. In many of these cases, the already thin line between cooperation and collaboration was crossed more often than a bridge across the Rhine. Often, the usefulness of a Jew was handsomely rewarded, the most sought after prize being "Honorary Aryan" status. (This bizarre procedure found a modern counterpart when Queen Elizabeth II of England was recently given "Honorary Man" status so that she could take coffee with the Princes of the patriarchal House of Saud.) Perhaps the most famous of the Honorary Aryans were the Warburgs.

Max Warburg[11] was a member of the internationally renowned Hamburg merchant banking dynasty. After Germany's defeat in World War I, his efforts helped to scale down the Versailles-imposed German reparations and eventually abolish them. That, of course, was also one of Hitler's goals. Max's brothers, Paul (a member of the first United States Federal Reserve Board) and Felix, were partners in New York's Kuhn, Loeb & Company. Max received his Honorary Aryanship (a status both his brothers were alleged to have assiduously coveted in the United States and only received when Paul's son married the daughter of publisher Condé Nast) in reward for "his services on behalf of the economic structure of the Third Reich." This life-saving device was personally bestowed upon Warburg by Hitler. (Warburg was known to have been under the protection of Reichsbank President Dr. Schacht, the "friend" of Paul Elsberg.) That prompted James Gerard, the pre-World War I United States Ambassador to Germany, to tell a *New York Times* reporter in Berlin that "so long as they are rich, they can be useful."

Rumors that Hitler had been secretly aided by Jewish bankers began to surface in the 1930s. Mike Gold, the left-wing Jewish-American writer, claimed that "some of Hitler's most important secret conferences were held in the home of a Jewish banker."[12] Although Gold could have meant Baron von Oppenheim of Cologne, recent revelations of the role played by a member of the prominent Warburg banking family in obtaining crucial early support for Hitler by American banks and oil companies, point to a member of that dynasty. The most noted modern member of the Warburg clan, the venerable Sir Siegmund Warburg of the British banking house, was rumored to have been a member of Dr. Max Naumann's ultra-Rightist Verband nationaldeutscher Juden (Association of National German Jews) prior to his emigration from Germany. Shortly before his death in October 1982, Sir Siegmund vehemently denied the allegation. His name is not found in the surviving fragmentary V.n.J. records. For more on the V.n.J. see Chapter Nine.

Eric and James Warburg, of the American branch of the family, personally convinced President Franklin D. Roosevelt that the tales of Jewish persecution under the Nazis were greatly exaggerated—an explanation Roosevelt was all too eager to accept. Thus, the American Warburgs carried out the same objective as the V.n.J.'s Hans Priwin and the Berlin Jewish banker Oscar Wasserman. At the time of the abortive worldwide Jewish boycott of German-made goods, Priwin, a member of the V.n.J.'s executive committee, appealed in a transatlantic radio broadcast for a cessation of anti-German feeling. He told Americans that reports of atrocities against the Jews, the raison d'être for the boycott, were "despicably false." Wasserman meanwhile cabled the New York Stock Exchange to "use all of your influence that the spreading of such false rumors of atrocities may be discontinued."[13]

Throughout this time, the American Warburgs[14] continued to travel to Europe on the North German Lloyd line and to oppose the boycott because "its destructive effort falls squarely on many Jewish manufacturers and merchants." No doubt Max Warburg was one of the first names that came to their collective mind. Nor was all this lost upon hatemongers like Father Charles E. Coughlin of Detroit. At the start of a new season of his nationally broadcast anti-Semitic radio diatribes, Father Coughlin somehow managed to exclude the Warburgs from his usual litany of "Jew Bankers."

With all this going for him, it should come as no surprise to learn that Max Warburg survived the Nazis, succumbing to the ravages of old age in 1946. Unlike almost all of the other recipients of Honorary Aryan status, Warburg died in exile.

Professor Otto H. Warburg, winner of the 1931 Nobel Prize in Medicine, was allowed to continue his research on cancer cells unmolested by the Nazis.[15] Certainly, his Honorary Aryan status helped. Although raised as a Protestant, Dr. Warburg's name appears on the majority of the multitude of listings of Jewish winners of the Nobel Prizes.[16] (One wonders if there are any such lists for, say, the Presbyterian recipients of the awards?) Did the Nazis ever suspect that Professor Warburg could easily have chosen to emigrate? He was being mentioned for the general science chair at Hebrew University in Jerusalem well into 1934. Warburg had earlier established a chair of botany at the university. However, the ultra-right-wing German Citizens of the Mosaic Persuasion[17] decided to prove their patriotism to the Reich by cutting off their annual contribution to the Warburg endowment. Presumably, the Honorary Aryan decree straightened everything out. Professor Warburg remained at his post as Director of the Kaiser Wilhelm Institute for Cell Physiology in Berlin-Dahlem until 1951. He died in 1970.

Professor Warburg was a longtime member of the Kaiser-Wilhelm Gesellschaft (KWG: the Kaiser Wilhelm Society), the organization which administered the various Kaiser Wilhelm research institutions. During World War I, the Kaiser Wilhelm Institute for Physical Chemistry and Electrochemistry was directed by Fritz Haber, a Jew who won the 1918 Nobel Prize for Chemistry. Under Haber's supervision, the Kaiser Wilhelm Institute for Physical Chemistry and Electrochemistry was the only associate facility of the KWG to convert to the German war effort. It was in his laboratory at the Institute that Haber developed mustard nerve gas—the deadly use of which by the Germans came close to making Haber a war criminal in the eyes of the Allies. Haber's other wartime research led to the German production of nitrates for war munitions.

Under the Nazis, the Kaiser Wilhelm scientific institutes became models for Nazi research. Otto Hahn, who received the 1944 Nobel Prize for Chemistry for his 1938 breakthrough discovery of nuclear fission, was among the many German scientists heavily involved in atomic research at the Kaiser Wilhelm Institute for Chemistry. The Kaiser Wilhelm Institute for Physics, built in Berlin-Dahlem in 1937 by a combination of Nazi government and Rockefeller funds, was at the forefront of the "Aryan Physics" movement. Why then should we suppose that it would have been any different at the Kaiser Wilhelm Institute for Cell Physiology?

Professor Warburg's most significant work was in the area of the metabolism of tumors. He is considered the first to have proved conclusively that cancer cells can grow without oxygen and can be damaged by radiation.

However Professor Warburg was not the only Jewish Nobel Prize winning scientist that the Nazis allowed to continue working. Gustav Hertz shared the 1925 Nobel Prize in Physics with James Franck, another German Jew. They were honored for their discovery of the laws governing the impact of an electron on an atom. Their research is widely credited with having helped formulate modern atomic theory. Without Hertz and Franck, there might have never been an atomic bomb.

Gustav Hertz was professor of experimental physics at Berlin's Technische Hochschule (Institute of Technology). He was the nephew of Heinrich Rudolph Hertz, the German physicist who first demonstrated the existence of electric or electromagnetic waves. The fathers of both men were Jews.[18] Although Gustav Hertz is said to have later converted to Christianity (perhaps because of his Mischling status), most sources flatly state he was a Jew.[19]

Certainly, Professor Hertz was classified as a Jew in early 1935 before the promulgation of the Nuremberg Laws, whether he had converted or not. Told that only Aryan professors would be allowed to give examinations at the Technische Hochschule, Hertz resigned from the faculty with the intent of emigrating to the Netherlands to work for the Phillips Company. This was only shortly after Professor Warburg had been handed his opportunity to emigrate—the general science chair at Jerusalem's Hebrew University.

Fate, or perhaps it was the Nuremberg Laws, intervened in Hertz's case. When the Siemens Company of Berlin, then, as now, a leader in the German electrical industry, offered him the directorship of their research facilities. Hertz accepted, and held that post until the collapse of Nazi Germany in 1945.

Once Hertz's Mischling status was legally established by the Nuremberg Laws, he was made an honorary professor at the Technische Hochschule, and he continued to sit in on some examinations. Although Hertz had become a Mischling, he was still not an Aryan. The entire charade is highly reminiscent of the ploy later used by Vichy France to make Jacques Rueff an honorary vice-governor of the Bank of France (see Chapter Six).

Hertz was never disturbed by the Nazis during his tenure at Siemens. His first wife died in 1941 and he remarried two years later. Presumably he was one of only a handful (at best) of Jews to be married in 1943 Nazi Germany. Most were being murdered.

Of the twenty then-and-future German Nobel Prize winning scientists forced out of their university posts by the Nazis, Professor Hertz was the only one who did not emigrate.[20] After Hitler's fall, Hertz went east with the Russians. In 1947, he was reported to be working on atomic research for the U.S.S.R. Ironically, virtually every one of the other nineteen exiled Nobel scientists ultimately played a role in the Manhattan Project, the successful American effort to develop an atomic bomb before the Nazis. Hertz spent his last years in East Germany and died there in 1975.

As a key industry in the Nazi war effort, the Siemens Company regularly employed Jewish slave labor. Using typical Nazi euphemisms, Oswald Pohl, the virtual administrator of the concentration camps, advised Reichsführer SS Himmler in 1942 that "employable Jews who are migrating to the East will have to interrupt their journey and work in war industry."[21] Postponing death in an extermination camp by working in Nazi war industry would only bring a temporary respite. A labor shortage, created in part by the forced removal of the Jews from the work force, was ironically going to be filled by Jews already condemned to death, but still forced to give more of their lives to help the Nazi war effort. Among those Jews sent to Siemens as slave laborers was Herbert Baum, a leader of the Jewish anti-Nazi resistance. Baum and the members of his group were executed by the Nazis. He is memorialized at Weissensee, where the cemetery's main road bears his name.

Klara Riesenburger has claimed that she worked at Siemens as a slave laborer, although she may have been sent there near the end of the war (even though she was the Aryan spouse in a mixed marriage) simply because no more Jews were left to supply forced labor. Both Ruth von Brentani and Rolf Vogel[22] have said that some mixed marriage spouses were sent to Organisation Todt camps for the same reason. That might explain why, in the confusion of the waning months of the war, so many of the mixed marriage Jews (like Paul Elsberg), and even some Mischlinge, went into hiding.

The key words to keep in mind when thinking of the Siemens Company during this period are "war industry." Certainly the Nazis were not using slave labor to produce longer-burning light bulbs for German consumers. A report from Reich Armament Minister Dr. Albert Speer's labor expert refers to a success "at Siemens . . . with the Jewesses doing electromechanical installations."[23] Professor Hertz, as director of the Siemens Research Laboratory, had to be aware of the use of Jewish slave labor in the Siemens factory, if indeed he did not actually condone the practice.

A damning indictment against the Siemens culpability in the destruction process comes from Charlotte Lehmann.[24] After her father's marriage to Valerie Stein, Lehmann's mother sent her to a girl's school in Berlin-Schöneberg. It was located in the Bayerischen Platz-Kurfürstendamm area, a district where many of Berlin's wealthiest Jewish families lived. One of Lehmann's closest Jewish friends and classmates there was Ursula Davidsohn, daughter of a prominent Berlin attorney, considered to be the leading German specialist in family rights and family law. Ursula had emigrated to England before the war, but her father stayed behind. He loved Germany—he would not believe that the Nazi madness would continue. Ursula had the money to get him out of Germany and begged him to leave. He refused. Like Hanns Rehfeld's grandmother, when he heard the final knock at the door, he committed suicide. He too was buried at Weissensee by Martin Riesenburger.

In England, Ursula met and married Dr. Fritz Beer, the voice of the "London Calling Europe" program broadcast by BBC-shortwave into Nazi Germany. That was the program Lehmann and her mother listened to in violation of strict Nazi rules. Had the Lehmann's air raid warden reported them to the authorities, both women would have faced the death penalty.

During a chance meeting in postwar London at the farewell party for a departing West German ambassador, Lehmann asked Ursula Davidsohn about the fate of her sister Hetty, a medical doctor who had received her training in Heidelberg. After the war, Ursula had tried to find Hetty. She traced her to Siemens, where she located Hetty's former supervisor, who was the source of this information.

Davidsohn told Lehmann that Hetty had been brought to Siemens as a slave laborer, but when the company learned of her medical background, she was made medical supervisor of a contingent of 300 Jewish slave labor workers—former inmates of German concentration camps. It was Dr. Hetty Davidsohn's job to keep the Jews healthy enough so that they could work a strenuous twelve-hour shift at full productivity for the Nazis. In addition to her medical duties, Hetty was also required to put in a full day's labor. Once the Nazis felt they had sapped every last bit of strength out of these Jews, they would ship them to the gas chambers at Auschwitz. Then a fresh crop of Jews would be brought to Siemens.

This procedure repeated itself every six months. Hetty's supervisor would protect her by telling her not to come in for her shift on the afternoon that the deportations would occur. And twice Hetty stayed away. When she knew that this tragedy was set to unfold before her eyes a third time, she could not bring herself to again be used as a tool of the Nazis. When her supervisor warned her not to report for work, she told him, "No, this time I will be going with them." When the Nazis came for the group the next day, Hetty went with the workers.

As the pathetic human convoys filled with fewer and fewer Jews came and went through the gates of the Siemens Company, one Jew always remained behind: Professor Dr. Gustav Hertz, Nobel Prize winner, and director of the Siemens Research Laboratory.

Of course Professor Hertz wasn't the only Mischling participating in the destruction process. Some who received Honorary Aryan status were so eager to express their gratitude that they joined wholeheartedly in destroying the Jews. Ministerialrat Leo Killy of the Reich Chancellery was a Mischling of the Second Degree, his wife was a Mischling of the First Degree. Killy had joined the Nazi Party and entered the Reich Chancellery while keeping his family origins a secret. When the first racial decrees were issued, Killy offered to resign but was asked to stay on. His superior spoke to Hitler, who agreed to Killy's continuing service. Then, on Christmas Eve in 1936, while the Killy family was sitting around their Christmas tree opening gifts, a courier arrived with the ultimate in Nazi Christmas presents: a "liberation" for Killy and his children.[25] They had been transformed into Germans. Again, it is worth remembering the often overlooked Article Seven of the Nuremberg Laws ordinance which created the Mischlinge race: "The Führer and Reich Chancellor may grant exemptions from the stipulations of implementary ordinances."

By 1942, this procedure had become so widely abused that even Hitler was becoming alarmed and authorities were advised of his desire to cut down the number of applicants.[26] An official report states that the applications had been handled too "softly." Hitler no longer thought that only the blameless conduct of a Mischling was sufficient ground for his "liberation." The Mischling now was required to show signs of "positive merit," a sterling example of which might be if, unaware of his ancestry, he had fought for the Nazi party uninterruptedly and for many years prior to 1933. But nothing much came of this, for to do so would have been a tacit admission that the Führer had been wrong in granting so many "liberations" up to this time, including the 340 given to full Jews. And besides, in the seven years since the proclamation of the act, most of the "liberations," especially those for soldiers, had already been received and acted upon.

It wasn't much different outside of Germany. The viciously anti-Semitic (they were known for their bestial torturing and murdering of Jews) homegrown Croatian Fascist party, the Ustashe, were described by Nora Levin in *The Holocaust* as being "fanatics bent on the destruction of the Jews."[27] But nearly all of the members of the fascist ruling clique in Croatia, including Ante Pavelic, the head of the government and leader of the Ustashe (he was also the probable assassin of former Yugoslavian King Alexander), were married to Jewish women.[28] For the main part, the Croatian exemptions for Jews dutifully followed the German example. Honorary Aryanship was granted to all Jews who made contributions (usually their property) to "the Croat cause." According to a Nazi internal memorandum, the number of these Croatian Honorary Aryans increased steadily from month to month. As late as December,

1944, the Ustashe headquarters dispatched one of these Honorary Aryans, a Jew named Alexander Klein,[29] as a procurement official to Hungary and Italy. By the end of the war, only three categories of Jews remained alive in Croatia: Honorary Aryans, Jews in mixed marriages and the Mischlinge, the same groups that could not be erased in the Reich itself. Most of the 1650 survivors among the Jews of Zagreb were members of these groups.

"Obedience is in their blood. Both the Jews and the Germans only have one existence, and that is to be obedient to laws."

HANS-JOACHIM SCHOEPS[1]

Chapter Eight

The Aryanized Field Marshal

DID ANY JEWS FIGHT in the Spanish Civil War of 1936-39? One quickly thinks of the American volunteers—of which 30 percent were Jews[2]—in the Abraham Lincoln Battalion or those, along with some Canadians, in the Mackenzie-Papineau Battalion. (The latter "Macpaps" were organized by Sam Carr,[3] a Ukrainian-born Jew whose family narrowly escaped death at the hands of followers of Simon Petlyura in a pogrom, and who was later jailed by Canada as a recruiter of Soviet spies.) Fighting for the Spanish Republic against the Fascist Nationalistic Forces of Francisco Franco was always the exclusive franchise of the Left. But a number of Italian Fascist Jews were among the first non-Spanish combat troops to fight on the side of the Spanish Fascists, often alongside German troops. They arrived about the same time as the Loyalist International Brigades, creating the often bizarre sight of rightist Jew fighting leftist Jew on the soil of Holy Catholic Spain.

These Jewish Fascists were full Jews. But they were also loyal Fascists "from the tops of our heads to the tips of our toes."[4] Many were veterans of the fight for Fascist ideals, having taken part in the successful Italian "pacification" of the Sanusi[5] in Libya and the invasion and conquest of Ethiopia in 1935. The claim of Ethiopian Emperor Haile Selassie to be the "Lion of Judah" went unrecognized by these Jews. In fact, some of the "natives" they so easily murdered with modern weaponry may have been loyal Falashas, the black Jews of Ethiopia.

171

The Jews who fought for Fascist Italy were first to receive exemptions when the Italians began their anti-Semitic campaign. Although one Holocaust expert claims that only 3,000 Jews were exempted in Italy, the statute exempting "former members of the Fascist Party together with their parents and grandparents, their wives and children and grandchildren" certainly indicates otherwise.[6]

The involvement of Jews in the Italian Fascist movement began with the early struggles in Fiume, long before the 1922 March on Rome. Mussolini's best known Finance Minister in the 1930s, Guido Jung, was a Jew. Another Jew, Jole Foa, was the high-profile secretary of Roberto Farinacci, the leader of Italy's anti-Semitic movement. It was Farinacci who wrote the infamous *Il regime fascista* article "proving" that hatred of the Jews was fundamental to Christian doctrine. Other prominent Italian Jewish Fascists were Mussolini's biographer, Marghereti G. Sarfatti, Ivo Levy, and three individuals commonly identified only by their surnames: Goldman, Volpi and Uccelli. "Volpi" presumably could be the onetime Finance Minister Count Giuseppe Volpi, who began his career at the Banca Commerciale, which was directed by a Signor Toeplitz, himself a Polish Jew. The Italian waters are particularly murky in this area.[7]

To a degree, there was a parallel of early involvement by Jews in the Nazi Party during the crucial period between the founding of the party in 1920 and the abortive Munich beer hall Putsch of 1923. Some of the first members of the Nazi Party were full Jews. Since party membership at this time was small, it is likely that they may even have come into direct contact with Adolf Hitler. The only reference to these individuals as Jews appears in party records at the time of their expulsion. They are identified as: Oskar Neumann, Hermann Samuel, a "Baron Irizu," and Michael Hornistein. The name of Neumann surfaces again almost twenty years later in Slovokia, where he, or someone with that same name, not only received an exemption from the Slovokian Gestapo, but also carried out covert assignments for them. As regards the Baron, since his surname is difficult to decipher on the records, "Irizu" is offered as an attempt at reconstruction.[8]

Four years before the Munich beer hall Putsch, a half-Jew, Count Anton Arco-Valley, assassinated Kurt Eisner, the German-Jewish revolutionary who organized the 1918 Munich uprising which overthrew the monarchy. After the failure of Hitler's coup, the Count gracefully gave his cell in Landsberg Prison to Hitler so that he could dictate *Mein Kampf* to Emil Maurice and Rudolf Hess in relative comfort.[9]

Far more important than the actual involvement of Jews as members of the Nazi Party was the role they played in the formulation of Nazi ideology. The very term "anti-Semitism" was coined by Wilhelm Marr, son of the great Jewish actor, Heinrich Marr of Hamburg, when the younger Marr organized his Bund der Antisemiten (The League of anti-Semites) in 1879. Marr also virtually created the separate racial classification for Jews in his pamphlet *Der Sieg des Judentums über das Germanentum (The Victory of Judaism over German Civilization)*. Marr designated the Jews as inferior human beings and gave prejudice against them a scientific pseudo-biological basis. He even offered "proof" to show that the Jews were aiming at world mastery. Richard Wagner became one of Marr's first disciples.[10]

The concept of the "Jewish Menace" was first expounded by a Jew, Arthur Trebitsch. Like Marr's theories, it too became a virtual cornerstone of Nazi anti-Semitic propaganda. Trebitsch's brother Siegfried was George Bernard Shaw's German translator, and later fled the Nazis. But Arthur Trebitsch feared a different enemy: he believed he was being persecuted by the Jews.

Trebitsch was for a time the Führer of the Austrian National Socialist movement. After he quarreled with his disciples, they attached themselves to the rising star of another young Austrian, Adolf Hitler. It was Trebitsch who first arrived at the conclusion that Germany had lost World War I because of

Jewish machinations. That theory was quickly noted and filed for future reference by Hitler, then hard at work developing his own scenario to explain how the Jewish "stab in the back" had caused Germany's humiliating defeat.

Shortly after the end of World War I, Arthur Trebitsch and Oswald Spengler—each independent of the other—began to predict the ultimate decline of the West. The basic differences between their philosophies of gloom was that Trebitsch could see salvation coming from those individuals who, like himself, had "recovered from their Jewishness." He also was filled with hope for those he called "the half-Aryans and three-quarter-Aryans." By these words, Trebitsch paved the way for the creation of the Mischlinge.

Another popular Trebitsch theory held that the Catholic Church, giving up its own plans for sole domination, had agreed to join World Jewry in a common assault upon the Nordic Protestants. Victory was to be followed by a division of the spoils between the Rome-Zion axis, the Jews getting Northern Germany. Just how great a debt Hitler owed Trebitsch for sowing the seeds of his ultimate success becomes evident from an observation made shortly before Trebitsch's death in 1927. It was said of Trebitsch that "the intensity of his faith in his Aryan mission . . . moved listeners, especially women and youths, to tears and to ecstasy."[11]

Julius Wiesner, the botanist and rector of the University of Vienna, was a baptized Jew. Houston Stewart Chamberlain, Richard Wagner's son-in-law, dedicated his venom-filled *The Foundations of the Nineteenth Century* to Wiesner.[12] Chamberlain was both a favorite of Arthur Trebitsch (who praised his philosophy for having made "the transition from Kant to Trebitsch") and Nazi racial theory ideologues like Alfred Rosenberg, author of the Chamberlain-influenced *The Myth of the Twentieth Century*.

Even Richard Wagner himself figures into the speculation. Wagner is often thought to have been a half-Jew. His stepfather, the actor Ludwig Geyer, was a Jew, and adherents of this theory claim knowledge of the existence of a sexual relationship between Geyer and Wagner's mother prior to the birth of the composer.[13] Notorious for his own anti-Semitism, Wagner is remembered too for having his "good Jew." Hermann Levi, son of a rabbi, was personally selected by Wagner to conduct the premier performance of *Parsifal* at Bayreuth in 1882.

There was also a string of Jews who purged themselves of their unwanted heritage by producing a work of racial hatred and then taking their own lives. Otto Weininger,[14] considered by Spengler to be one of the three saints produced by Judaism, published his *Sex and Character* and then committed suicide at twenty-three in the room where Beethoven had died. Self-destructive fantasies were also played out by Walter Calé, Max Steiner and Nietzsche's friend Paul Rée, who threw himself into an Alpine glacier.[15]

Another victim of this epidemic of suicides among self-hating German Jews was Benedict Friedländer. He left a sizeable fortune in his will to a man he never met—Eugen Dühring, "The Philosopher of Jew Hatred." When news of the bequest reached him, Dühring was astounded but took the money.[16]

One of Hitler's favorite propaganda weapons was the spurious *Protocols of the Elders of Zion*, which purported to be a documentation of the secret Jewish ruling cabal and its plans for world domination. It was also one of history's cruelest hoaxes. Henry Ford used it as the germ of his *The International Jew*, a widely circulated four-volume series of anti-Semitic diatribes written for Ford by former Detroit newspaperman W. J. Cameron.[17] The articles originally appeared in Ford's *Dearborn Independent* and Cameron successfully enhanced the credibility of the *Protocols* by placing them in a contemporary setting. That, and the Ford imprimatur, was all it took, for the *Protocols* were even introduced onto the floor of the United States Congress.[18] In more recent times, the *Protocols* have found a new sponsor in the persons of several radical Arab leaders. But at least one Jew, Jakob Brafman,[19] a journalist, helped create this terrible myth. And the Russian ambassador who first brought the forgery before the eager eyes of the Tsar was himself a half-Jew.

The Propaganda Ministry of Dr. Joseph Goebbels was particularly fond of circulating books by German author Arnolt Bronnen. Yet Bronnen was a Jew. Born Arnold Bronner, he exchanged the "d" in Arnold for the Germanic "t," and replaced the "r" in his family name with an "n." But even that wasn't enough. A supporter of the Nazis since 1927, he was appointed by Goebbels to a high position in the Nazi radio network. To get around the question of his racial origin, he persuaded his mother to take an oath before a notary "confessing" that she had committed adultery and that he was the result. Thus, he could not possibly be the son of her husband, the Jewish teacher Ferdinand Bronner. The Nazis were satisfied.[20] Another of Goebbel's favorite Jewish authors was Rudolf Borchardt, the German translator of Swinburne. He was born in Königsberg (now Kaliningrad, U.S.S.R.), the capital of East Prussia (where Werner Goldberg's father and Hannah Arendt were also born), to a Jewish family that had been Protestant for generations. Borchardt's own word on that matter was sufficient for the Nazis.[21]

For Arnolt Bronnen, and in the cases of Charlotte Lehmann and Dr. Hans Salomon, illegitimacy, or claim to that state, was one of several Nazi theories which eventually worked to the advantage of both full Jews and half-Jews. Under this loophole in the Nazi racial laws, it was possible for a mother to save the life of her Jewish child simply by swearing that she did not know the identity of the child's father. (Remember, it was not *her* job to check the papers of her male sexual partners.) The Nazis would "presume" (the same word used in 1983 by the American Reform rabbinate to make children of mixed marriages into Jews) that a full Jew was not the father of the child, otherwise the mother would not be ashamed to reveal his identity. The Nazis would then give the child the full legal standing and protection of Mischlinge of the First

Degree status. And even if a Jewish male were to admit paternity in such a case, the German courts would rule against him. After all, if he were a Jew, it would stand to reason that he must also be a liar, wanting only to steal a half-German child for the Jews.

This procedure was not as incredibly naïve on the part of the Nazis as it sounds. Although the first to take advantage of it apparently were those Jews who wanted to officially clear themselves of any Jewish stigma so they could work for the Nazis, it would be foolish to think that only a few full Jews used it to save their children's lives. And why shouldn't they? It may have been the only course open to them. Certainly, it must have been especially traumatic for the more religious Jews among this group to have to falsely swear they were guilty of promiscuous behavior in order to save their child.

Many believe that Field Marshal Erhard Milch, second-in-command to Hermann Göring as Commander of the Luftwaffe, was a half-Jew whose mother swore that he was illegitimate (as had the mother of Arnolt Bronnen) to cover up this fact. Milch, who was tried at Nuremberg as a war criminal, had begun his career peacefully enough as managing director of Lufthansa.[22] But rumors began to circulate about Milch in 1933, together with a dossier of photographs of tombstones in the Breslau Jewish cemetery with the name Milch engraved upon them. Besides being an old German-Jewish family name, "milch" is also the German word for milk. Even its English version is not uncommon as an American-Jewish surname, as for example, Harvey Milk, the San Francisco city supervisor and gay rights activist who was murdered by a disgruntled policeman in 1978.

Dr. Peter Kirchner,[23] president of East Germany's Jewish Community, claims Milch's Jewish origin was "generally known among the older generation. He was from a mixed family and Göring made him an Honorary Aryan." In fact, some documents exist which make Kirchner's assertion highly credible. Milch's diary for 1 November 1933, reads, "Göring has spoken with Hitler, [Minister of War Werner] von Blomberg and [Rudolf] Hess about my parentage. Everything is in order."[24] The documents consist of a four-page letter from Milch's mother stating that he was illegitimate, and a two-page document signed by Anton Milch, the Field Marshal's father-of-record, acknowledging the fact. Another man is named as Milch's true father, and he is an Aryan. Although the document does not cast any shadow over the Aryan ancestry of Anton Milch, it effectively removes Field Marshal Milch from any connection with such a widely known Jewish family name.

At his Nuremberg trial, Göring informed the American prosecution team that he had asked Dr. Wilhelm Stuckart of the Interior Ministry to alter Milch's birth certificate "in accordance with certain facts that had been established." Later, this was confirmed by Göring's then other State Secretary, Paul Körner. This early exercise in the art of racial modification must have come in useful for Stuckart. Two years later, he would help create a whole new race for others like Milch, those Jews who were "most like us."

A highly respected encyclopedia of the Third Reich[25] flatly states that Milch's mother was a Jew, and that the true purpose of the "affidavit" she submitted was to disclose that the Field Marshal was actually the illegitimate son of his father (Anton Milch) and thus not her own child. According to his biographer, Göring always thought Milch was a half-Jew, and obviously, so did Milch's one-time friend, Lt. General Ernst Udet, Director of the Office of Air Armament.[26] Udet's 1941 suicide note, written on his wall and addressed to Göring, asked why the Reich Marshal had surrendered him "to the Jews." Almost certainly he meant Milch. But why the plural? Who else in the Nazi hierarchy could he possibly have had in mind?

To Arthur Miller,[27] the word that Milch "may even be one of us" meant a signal of hope that all the Mischlinge would be spared. However, Professor Klaus J. Herrmann[28] thinks the entire illegitimacy story was a smokescreen. He believes that "the answer lies much further back than Milch's paternity. It clearly is not a question of his father-of-record's religion. I never thought for a moment that he was a Jew. He was an officer in the German Navy during World War I, serving as a pharmacologist. I have never heard of anyone in that position who was Jewish." Regardless, historian Robert E. Conot believes that story. In his 1983 book, *Justice at Nuremberg*, Conot says Milch's father had been a Jewish pharmacist. But Conot does not speculate on whether Anton Milch may have been baptized in order to serve as an officer in the navy.

Certainly there are other theories. Dr. Waltraud Rehfeld[29] is president of the Bund der Verfolgten des Naziregimes, or BVN. Dr. Rehfeld, a Christian, is the widow of Helmut Rehfeld, a Mischling who was denounced and sent to Buchenwald for taking down a picture of Hitler from his office wall. Had a full Aryan committed the same offense, the punishment would not have been as severe. But had a Jew done the same thing, he would have died. Helmut's brother Herbert was also sent to Buchenwald following a denouncement. The story of their younger brother Hanns is told in Chapter Three.

Dr. Rehfeld knows "a relation of Field Marshal Milch, a Professor Milch. He emigrated to London before the war. I don't know if he was a cousin, but he was certainly a relative. When I met him after the war, he told me that Field Marshal Milch was either a full Jew or half-Jewish. He belonged to this family and I know that the man I met was a Jew."

During Milch's trial at Nuremberg (where, presumably, he was the only part-Jew to sit behind the prisoner's docket), an accusation surfaced in the German press that a relative of Milch in the Netherlands once wrote the Field Marshal seeking help for him and his family to emigrate. He allegedly received a reply warning that if he dared to write even one more personal letter to Milch, the entire family would be sent to a concentration camp. And shortly afterward, they were. The article was headlined "The Aryanized Field Marshal."[30]

Then there was Jonas Wolk. He was an Eastern European Jew, one of the Ostjuden, who resented the treatment he perceived himself as receiving from those German Jews who always felt vastly superior to their Eastern European brethren. Wolk wanted to teach them a lesson, so he began to write for Julius Streicher's notorious Jew-baiting publication, *Der Stürmer* (literally "The Attacker," as a shock trooper who storms an enemy position in a military offensive). Of Wolk, it is said that while Streicher never shook his hand, he always received good payment for his articles, which he wrote under the nom de plume of Heinz Brand. Wolk's specialty was researching Hebrew writings and concocting gruesome tales of Jewish atrocities committed upon the "goyim" during the Middle Ages: well poisonings, ritual murders and the like. The circulation of *Der Stürmer* was always up when Wolk's tales appeared. (The May 1934 issue was called the "ritual murder number.") It is thought that Wolk's wife, who was not Jewish, carried on an affair with the sexually obsessed Streicher, which makes the whole handshake story somewhat superfluous. Wolk was reported to have left Germany around 1939. Nothing has been heard of him since.[31]

Perhaps the strangest of the many allusions to the Jewish origin of members of the Nazi inner circle are those perversely fascinating tales about the Führer himself. One month before the outbreak of World War II, Adolf's nephew, Patrick Hitler, penned a by-lined article for the 5 August 1939 issue of *Paris-Soir*. He recounted the details of how "Mon Oncle Adolf" had summoned him to Berlin in 1930 and tearfully begged Patrick never to make anything public about his past. Cried Uncle Adolf, "The day they know about this—I would rather put a bullet in my head"[32]—"this" being the fact that Adolf himself was a Mischling of the Second Degree.

Patrick Hitler took his show on the road. He made a successful world lecture tour, enthralling audiences in auditoriums like Toronto's Massey Hall by spilling even more secrets from the Hitler family closet. Ironically, his credibility was greatly enhanced by one of the world's most unlikely sources. Hans Frank, the vicious Nazi Governor General of Poland (he was hanged by the Allies after the war), stated in an interview that Hitler always feared that Patrick would one day go public with his revelations. Even with this ambiguous endorsement, most Holocaust experts—like Concordia's Professor Herrmann—tend to dismiss the claims about both Hitler and Reinhard Heydrich.

Heydrich, known as "The Hangman," is the subject of an often quoted essay in a postwar German history book published by a mainstream German publisher.[33] According to the article, Heydrich was selected to lead the campaign to exterminate the Jews because "Hitler and Himmler knew that Heydrich had Jewish blood in his veins and therefore chose him for this task." To back up their claim, the editors offer the following quote from Himmler: "He [Heydrich] still could be used for another wonderful purpose, namely for the fight against the Jews. Intellectually, he had overcome the Jew within himself and gone over to the other side. He was convinced that the Jewish part of his blood was damnable, he hated this blood which had played such an awful trick on him. The Führer really couldn't have chosen a better man than Heydrich for his battle against the Jews. Towards Jews he had no pity and no mercy."

Hannah Arendt in *Eichmann in Jerusalem* flatly states, "It was generally known that Heydrich and Milch were half-Jews."[34] She believes that during the nine days it took for Heydrich to die from wounds inflicted by Czech patriots, he repented of "not murder but that he had betrayed his own people." Curiously, Hans Frank was the only other major Nazi war criminal to repent in the face of death.[35]

Perhaps this bizarre speculation only reflects the Nazi obsession with racial genealogy. Yet it is widespread enough to make one wonder whom the Nuremberg Racial Laws were really designed to protect? Put crudely, just how many Jews were there in the Nazi woodpile?

By 1823, half of Berlin's Jews had converted to Christianity.[36] The Nuremberg Laws were enacted a little over a century later. Some of those Berlin Jews could easily have been the grandparents of high-ranking members of the Nazi Party hierarchy.

In the early part of the twentieth century, one leading German rabbi lived long enough to see seven of his grandchildren convert.[37] In the words of Heinrich Heine, for a Jew in nineteenth-century Germany, a baptismal certificate was "the admission ticket to European civilization."[38] With it in hand, a baptized Jew could attend university, serve in the military, and most important of all, have access to the coveted professions and public offices that were closed to Jews. This mass migration of Jews toward Christianity was paralleled in England by the Sephardic families. Among the most celebrated examples of nineteenth century European conversions are Heine, Karl Marx, Benjamin Disraeli, Anton Rubinstein, the journalist Maximilian Harden (originally Witkowski, virtually the same surname as Hans Faust's grandmother) and Friedrich Julius Stahl, the spiritual father of the Prussian Junkers. One can easily recall with a shudder the words of artist Max Liebermann: "This thing with anti-Semitism will only become something when Jews finally do it themselves."[39]

"And then they come, eighty million worthy Germans and each one has his decent Jews. Of course, the others are vermin, but this one is an 'A-One' Jew."

HEINRICH HIMMLER
in a speech delivered at Posen
4 October 1943

"A directive from the Reichsführer SS, Heinrich Himmler, in 1943 plainly stated that all European Jews would be murdered without exception . . . [it] was completely countermanded soon after it was conceived and handed down."

WILLIAM STYRON
This Quiet Dust and Other Writings

Chapter Nine

Down With Us!

IT WOULD BE FOOLISH to believe that only baptized Jews or half-Jews helped create the momentum which eventually claimed six million Jewish lives, although historically, some of the most vicious anti-Semites were Jews who had converted to Christianity. Martin Luther was greatly influenced by the spurious anti-Christian polemics attributed to the Jews but actually written by Anthony Margaritha, a convert. During the Spanish Inquisition, one of the most feared of all torturers of Jews was the brutal Jerome de Sante Fe, originally Rabbi Joshua of Lorca. Some of the worst damage in the years immediately preceding the Holocaust was undoubtedly self-inflicted, and this chapter looks at a few of the people whom Max Liebermann may have had in mind. With friends like these, what need did the Jews have for outside enemies?

For starters, there was Dr. Max Naumann, a full Jew, and his V.n.J.—Verband nationaldeutscher Juden (Association of National German Jews).[1] While some of the most colorful accusations against Dr. Naumann and the V.n.J. now are recognized as being nothing more than the whole cloth from which legends are created, Dr. Naumann's legacy remains as damning as ever.

Dr. Naumann, a Berlin lawyer and former captain in the Bavarian army, founded the V.n.J. in 1920. At the peak of its influence the organization boasted of having 3,500 members throughout Germany. It was Dr. Naumann who first publicly called for the expulsion of the Eastern European Jews from

Germany. This was but one of many helpful suggestions first made by Jews which the Nazis would later apply to every Jew. By describing the Ostjuden (Eastern Jews) as "pitiful creatures . . . of a not quite human level,"[2] Dr. Naumann hoped to demonstrate that the National German Jew was spiritually and even racially (!) different from the wretched Jewish masses in the East. His attitude toward the Ostjuden problem was technically on a par with that of the right-wing anti-Semites. Indeed, the V.n.J. had once gone so far as to publicly acknowledge "the truth of some anti-Semitic charges" made in the rightist press.

Dr. Naumann referred to the Ostjuden as "economic parasites." That's another of those useful terms which the Nazis would eventually gleefully adopt and use in propaganda against all Jews. However, Dr. Naumann does not deserve sole credit for having been the first Jew to affix this opprobrious label onto his co-religionists. Writing about the Diaspora, Aharon David Gordon, the ideological father of the Palestinian Jewish Worker's movement, said, "the Jews were characterized by parasitism and were a fundamentally useless people." Another Jew, Abraham Schwadron, criticized the "parasitic rootlessness" of the Diaspora Jews, and even the renowned Rabbi Dr. Judah L. Magnes got in a lick. In his 1910 Passover sermon at New York's Temple Emanuel, Rabbi Magnes took note of the "parasitic nature" of Judaism.[3] How very thoughtful of all these Jews to have made life so much easier for Nazi speechwriters!

Like their counterparts on the German right, the V.n.J. perceived Eastern European immigration as a distinct threat to the German nation. The ultra-German Jews of the V.n.J. considered these new immigrants with their orthodox religious practices, kaftans, sidelocks and Yiddish pronunciation to be an embarrassment. A contemporary observer in Berlin recalled that the National-German Jews "recoiled from any contact with them . . . they were in fact disgusted. They felt they had nothing in common with the bearded Hebrews of Poland;

Vom nationaldeutschen Juden

Von
Dr. Max Naumann

The manifesto of Dr. Max Naumann's V.n.J.—the Association of National-German Jews. This 24-page pamphlet was published in 1920. Twelve years later, Dr. Naumann endorsed Adolf Hitler in his campaign for the Reichstag. *(Collection of the author)*

their earlocks struck them as funny and they did not hesitate to laugh." To Dr. Naumann and his followers, these immigrants were the final obstacle which prevented assimilated German Jews like the members of the V.n.J. from receiving total acceptance from their countrymen.

These were the same Polish Jews about whom American author Grace Humphrey (author of *Women in American History* and *Heroes of Liberty*) wrote in 1931: "If one of these Jews sat down by me in the street-car I would move or stand up; what with the dirt, the smell, the fear that something would crawl over onto me, I couldn't ride with them, but cringed and drew away as I never do from negroes [sic]. There's something sinister about them."[4]

In a bizarre precursor of the fate to soon befall all German Jews, the V.n.J. in 1923 claimed that most Eastern European Jewish workers in Germany were Communists and endorsed the Bavarian government's plan to expel these Jews. The Jewish Telegraphic Agency, the news-gathering service for English-language Jewish newspapers, headlined their correspondent's dispatch "National-German Jews Have No Objection to Expulsion of Jews from Bavaria." Some thirty foreign Jewish families were expelled, with twelve other families only escaping deportation through legal appeals. Seven years later, the V.n.J. advocated the boycott of a Jewish theatrical performance in Berlin with the argument that the kaftans worn by the actors would only serve to reinforce already existing negative Jewish stereotypes. In case anyone missed the point, the V.n.J. published photographs depicting Eastern European Jews in a number of degrading poses. It was a worthy imitation of *Der Stürmer*.

But Dr. Naumann did not want only the Eastern European Jews to be expelled from his version of a perfect—Ostjudenrein—Germany. In 1921, the V.n.J. proposed that German Zionists either migrate to Palestine or accept alien status in Germany. It was Dr. Naumann who first branded Zionism as a "racist ideology," predating the infamous November 1975

United Nations resolution which equated Zionism with racism. Once again, a Jew said it first![5] Later, in a 1931 series of articles written for predominantly gentile readers, Dr. Naumann portrayed German Zionists as "racial fanatics"—as if Nazis were anything but! Interestingly enough, one of the Zionists prominently attacked by Dr. Naumann (in the September 1930 edition of the V.n.J.'s newspaper) was Georg Kareski, whom we shall encounter again very soon.

Other Naumann-led campaigns of the V.n.J. opposed "Jewish parochial schools" and the establishment in Berlin of a Hebrew-language theater, which Naumann saw as representing "Jewish nationalist propaganda efforts." But of all the V.n.J.'s unholy crusades, one of the strangest had to be Naumann's call for adoption of a "German God."

Dr. Naumann argued that the God of Israel no longer existed for the National-German Jew, who now should place his religious faith in a "German God." Holidays to honor this new deity would no longer have to follow the Jewish calendar. The next step was to advocate the observance of Sunday as the new Jewish Sabbath in place of the traditional Saturday.[6] To Naumann, this would eliminate yet another difference between German and Jew.

Of course, the ultimate goal called for Jews to celebrate Christmas, a move which Dr. Naumann saw as being a "positive reaffirmation of one's National-German identity." As early as November 1924, the V.n.J.'s news organ was carrying ads from a designer of Christmas advertising.

Those "last vestiges of Jewish tribal feelings"[7] which served to emphasize the separate historical nature of the Jewish people were anathema to the V.n.J. But all this doesn't even come close to Naumann's major claim to infamy: under his direction, the V.n.J. became the only Jewish organization in Germany to endorse a Nazi-led national revolution.

In August 1932, as a crucial election for control of the Reichstag approached, Dr. Naumann personally endorsed Adolf Hitler's National Socialist Party as being the only po-

Mitteilungsblatt
des Verbandes nationaldeutscher Juden e. V.

Das Mitteilungsblatt erscheint vorläufig in zwangloser Folge und geht allen Mitgliedern des Verbandes kostenlos zu.
Die Geschäftsstelle des Verbandes befindet sich: Berlin W. 35. Blumeshof 9. (Lützow 3069)
Bankkonto: E. & Ingobine, Berlin W., Iägerstraße. · Postscheckkonto: Berlin Nr. 111 231

| Jahrgang 1921 | September | Nr. 1 |

Das Programm der nationaldeutschen Juden.

Man verlangt von uns ein „klares Programm."

Programme schmieden heißt Worte aneinanderreihen und Worte sind gefährlich, denn das bestgewählte Wort gibt Anlaß zu Mißverständnissen für den Freund, zu Verdrehungen für den Feind.

Was wir wollen, haben wir ausgesprochen in unserer Zeitung, in der Flugschrift „Brennende Fragen", in unserem Aufruf. Aber der Deutsche verlangt nun einmal ein „Programm", ein handliches Stück Papier, auf dem die Gesinnungen und Absichten sauber und übersichtlich nach Ziffern geordnet sind. Wohlan, wir wollen sprechen wie Walter von Stolzing, als er den Eingesühl der regelgetreuen Spießer besiegt. „Für Dich, Geliebte, sei's getan." Und die Geliebte, um die wir es tun, ist unsere deutsche Heimat, der wir dienen wollen mit Leib und Seele.

Der Sänger setzt. Fanget an!

Unser Programm lautet — — — — — — drängen.

Wir wollen die Grundlage schaffen für gemeinsame Arbeit nationaldeutscher Juden und nationaldeutscher Nichtjuden zum Wiederaufbau des armen, zerschlagenen Vaterlandes.

Daß diese Grundlage heute noch fehlt, kann niemand leugnen. Das deutsche Volk ist zerrissen in zwei Bevölkerungsgruppen. Die Nichtjuden, die Juden. Wie es dazu kam und ob es so kommen mußte, wollen wir heute nicht untersuchen. Die Tatsache besteht und selbst ein Blinder muß sie wahrnehmen, er kann sie mit Händen greifen.

Unter den Juden wie unter den Nichtjuden sind Nationaldeutsche, sind solche, denen Deutschland im Herzen über alles geht, die nicht anders als deutsch empfinden und denken können. Aber sie können zusammen nicht kommen, das Wasser ist allzu tief. Wir müssen erst die Brücke von Ufer zu Ufer schlagen.

Wer gemeinsam mit einem anderen arbeiten will, muß Verständnis für das Wesen des anderen haben. Das gilt für ganze Gruppen wie für den einzelnen Menschen. Die nationaldeutschen Nichtjuden müssen Einblick gewinnen in das wahre Wesen der Juden, die nationaldeutschen Juden in das der Nichtjuden. Heute weiß keiner von dem anderen mehr, [...] was ihm in landläufigen Schlagworte sagen, was ihm in früher Jugend als Vorurteil eingeimpft wurde. Juden [...] glauben sich zu kennen, aber sie kennen sich nicht. [...] und kennen lernen.

[...] meint: Jude sei Jude, einer wie der andere. [...] daß diese Meinung ein Vorurteil ist. Daß [...] aber das Verhältnis zum Deutschtum ausschließlich bestimmt wird durch das Gefühl und daß dieses Gefühl bei Juden genau so verschiedenartig ist, wie bei Nichtjuden. Daß auf dem Boden dieser Gefühlsverschiedenheit der nationaldeutsche Jude mit dem nationaldeutschen Nichtjuden Schulter an Schulter steht und von dem Juden, der nicht nationaldeutsch fühlt, durch eine unüberbrückbare Kluft getrennt ist.

Der Jude meint, jeder Nichtjude sei im Grunde seines Herzens „Antisemit", und er stellt sich vor, jeder Antisemit sei wie der andere. Auch er muß lernen, daß diese Meinung ein Vorurteil ist, auch er muß Verständnis gewinnen für die Seele des nichtjüdischen Deutschen. Er muß lernen, daß nicht jeder „Antisemit" ein rettungsloser Dummkopf oder ein vorteilsüchtiger Geschäftsmann ist, daß die Menschen, die sich selbst Antisemiten nennen, von einander so verschieden sind, wie es Menschen nur sein können. Wohl gibt es „Gesinnungs-Antisemiten", mit denen kein vernünftiges Wort zu reden ist, weil der Judenhaß ihnen zur Zwangsvorstellung wurde und ihr Gefühl im Banne hält. Wohl gibt es „Geschäfts-Antisemiten", für die der Judenhaß nur ein Mittel zum Zweck ist, die ohne Bedenken in's andere Lager übergehen, wenn dort der größere Vorteil winkt. Aber der deutsche Jude muß lernen, daß diese beiden Gruppen nur einen winzigen Bruchteil derer darstellen, die sich selbst für Gegner der Juden halten. Daß unter dem weitaus überwiegenden Rest sehr ehrliche, vornehme und kluge Menschen sind, die nur darum die Gesamtheit der Juden für widerwärtig und schädlich halten, weil sie in Vorurteile verstrickt sind, weil sie Einzelerscheinungen verallgemeinern, weil sie die Juden nicht kennen.

Wie bringen wir die beiden Gruppen zusammen, die im Gefühl für das Deutschtum zu einander gehören? Wie überbrücken wir das tiefe Wasser?

Indem wir nicht blindlings auf jeden wahren und vermeintlichen „Antisemiten" gleichmäßig losschlagen, indem wir unterscheiden lernen, wen wir in berechtigter Notwehr bekämpfen müssen und wen wir mit Wort und Tat davon überzeugen können, daß seine Meinung über die Juden nur ein Vorurteil ist. Der Antisemitismus als Gruppenerscheinung kann nicht bekämpft, er muß abgebaut werden. Jeder „anständige" Antisemit gibt zu, daß es „anständige" Juden gibt. Aber er hält sie für Ausnahmen, die nur die Regel bestätigen. Er wird aufhören, ein Antisemit zu sein, wenn wir ihm beweisen, daß die Juden, die fühlen wie er, nicht nur Einzelerscheinungen sind, daß sie eine starke Gruppe in der Gesamtheit der deutschen Juden bilden. Er wird bereit sein, mit uns zusammen gegen alle Feinde des Deutschtums, jüdische wie nichtjüdische, zu kämpfen, wenn wir ihm dartun, daß wir nicht eine Handvoll Über-

The first publication of the program of the V.n.J. as it appeared in the membership newsletter of the association in September, 1921. Presumably, this is one of the few surviving copies. The association itself has but one surviving member. *(Collection of the author)* litical organization capable of bringing about a "rebirth of Germandom." In appealing for German Jews to support the Nazis, Dr. Naumann asked German Jews to ignore what he called "the regrettable side effects" of Nazi anti-Semitism and to join the National Socialists "even if they behave as if they are our enemies."

This was the incident which prompted the creation of the legend of the placard-carrying Naumannites. Although the story is apocryphal, the sentiments do have a basis in reality, and it is hard to believe that only the political enemies of Dr. Naumann, particularly the Zionists, were responsible for the widespread currency of the story.

Rabbi Dr. L. Gerhard Graf of Cardiff, Wales, is apparently the last surviving member of the V.n.J. Dr. Graf, a member for "one or two years," denies that "we marched through the streets of Berlin carrying placards reading 'Down With Us' and 'We Are Our Misfortune.' " According to Dr. Graf (who did not leave Germany until 1939, the year of Dr. Naumann's death), the reports that Dr. Naumann was a Nazi supporter are "all utter rubbish and completely untrue,"[8] although the facts clearly prove otherwise. This view is also held by Professor Klaus J. Hermann, the great-nephew of Dr. Naumann.

The placard story was good copy, and it found its way into two best-selling books of the time. Both Jewish-American journalist Robert Gessner and American Rabbi Dr. Lee J. Levinger helped spread the allegations on this side of the Atlantic.[9] Forty years later, the story is still being quoted and widely believed.

A recent book by Rabbi Dr. Raphael Patai,[10] a prolific writer and philosopher, refines the rumor by stating that V.n.J. "members joined the Nazis in their street parades carrying banners" bearing the slogans. Although Dr. Patai hastens to reassure us that the V.n.J. did not "actually ever parade" with such slogans, he follows this with a qualifying statement eerily reminiscent of one made forty-one years earlier by Gessner.

First, Gessner in 1936:

"Whether the Jewish Nazis [sic] demonstrated this sentiment is incidental to the actual existence of the sentiment in
certain quarters where expressions of loyalty are repeatedly
made."

Then Dr. Patai in 1977:

"But the acceptance by *any* Jewish group, even a small and
insignificant one, of any part of the Nazi anti-Semitic diatribe
speaks volumes about the inability of some Jews to escape the
impact of vicious anti-Jewish propaganda."

Could it just be that no one from the Nazi Party ever
thought of asking the V.n.J. members to march in their parade? They probably repelled even the Nazis!

Gessner pulled no punches about his response to the V.n.J.
He wrote that "observing the please-tread-on-me attitude of
the middle-class wealthy Jews disgusted me." He described
the V.n.J. as "this association which regards itself as a storm
troop for Germanism among Jews living in Germany." Gessner
quotes Naumann as having said that even if the Jews in Germany had to starve more than they do at present, he and his
followers would still remain loyal to the anti-Semitic program.

Why should anyone have been surprised by Naumann's endorsement of National Socialism? Any astute observer of his
philosophy would recall his hope that German racists look to
the example of Mussolini's Italy "where Jews are part of the
Fascist movement and Mussolini has declared his opposition
to Zionism." And Naumann's attitude wasn't tempered in the
least once the Nazis came to power. The V.n.J. continued to
demonstrate its willingness to reach an accommodation with
racial anti-Semites, particularly if they were leading officials
of the Hitler regime.

Of course, some Nazis weren't all that displeased by Naumann's attacks upon Jewish intellectuals, like journalist and
author Kurt Tucholsky and politicians who had openly sympathized with left-wing causes during the Weimar Republic.
To the V.n.J., these individuals had reinforced the popular
image of the rootless, cosmopolitan Jew, another image the

Nazis were quick to pick up on for their own purposes. Throughout its existence, the V.n.J. hoped to force the German right to admit that a distinction had to be made between the "vast majority of German Jews who were thoroughly German in feeling" and a minority who, because of their affinity to Zionism or Marxism, "were unworthy of continued participation in German life."

Such fine points meant absolutely nothing to the Nazis. Eventually, even they tired of Naumann. He was arrested by the Gestapo and held at the infamous Columbia House, the dreaded SS special prison in Berlin, for two weeks in November 1935. After his release, he was never again detained. Just prior to his arrest, Naumann's own organization had booted him out as its leader. Dr. Naumann called in one of his last I.O.U.'s from the Nazi Party hierarchy, who then "persuaded" his replacement to step down and saw to it that Naumann was reinstated to his post.

But even this was temporary. Once the Nazis saw they could easily accomplish their anti-Semitic tasks without the aid of Jewish apologists, they dissolved the V.n.J. and seized the group's membership records and papers.

Today, these are not to be found in any West or East German archive. Frau Baumann, the non-Jewish former executive secretary of the V.n.J. (she was also Dr. Naumann's mistress), smuggled a duplicate set of the membership roster out of Germany when she emigrated to England in 1939. Ironically, that set was destroyed by the Nazis when the Germans bombed London in 1940.

As for Dr. Naumann, he died at his home in Berlin in May 1939 of natural causes (stomach cancer). But his enemies will tell you today that he died in a concentration camp as a result of injuries received in a beating by the Gestapo. Apparently even in death, there can still be no middle ground for Dr. Max Naumann.

Psychoanalyst Kurt Lewin considered Dr. Naumann to be a prime example of Jewish self-hate. In his classic study of the subject, Lewin wrote, "A few Jews, such as the infamous Captain Naumann in Germany, have become fascistic themselves under the threat of Fascism."[11]

Dr. Raphael Patai used a memoir to make his point about Naumann in a 1977 essay on Jewish self-hate.[12] "It was in 1929 or 1930," wrote Patai, "that, as a young student in Breslau, Germany, I first became aware of the way in which anti-Semitic stereotypes could insinuate themselves into the Jewish mind. The National Socialist Party was engaged in a concerted effort to increase its following in Germany, and I learned to my surprise that among my colleagues at the Rabbinical Seminary there were two who sympathized with, and supported, the Nazi Party. They belonged to the Verband National-deutscher [sic] Juden, which was founded in 1921 by Max Naumann and whose platform acknowledged the truth of some anti-Semitic charges and demanded that the Zionists be deprived of German citizenship. The Verband had its own youth movement, which had approached the Hitlerjugend [Hitler Youth] and tried—in vain, of course—to identify and ingratiate itself with the Nazi Party."

Although the V.n.J. did have a youth movement (Günther Ballin was Bundesführer of the 400-member Schwarzes Fahnlein, which apparently had some connection with the Boy Scouts), what Dr. Patai has done is confuse it with another right-wing German-Jewish movement of the era. It was the Deutscher Vortrupp, the Nationalist Zionist youth group led by Hans-Joachim Schoeps, which approached the Hitlerjugend.[13] Almost certainly, the Schwarzes Fähnlein (like Werner Goldberg) would have been cast aside when the Boy Scout movement was merged into the Hitlerjugend.

The uniforms worn by the Deutscher Vortrupp closely resembled those of the Hitlerjugend. They were equipped with shoulder straps and leather belts, these items being at that time the exclusive privilege of all Nazi organizations from the Hitlerjugend to the SA and SS. They were therefore the ideal and dream of all boys between the ages of ten and fourteen.

To Hanns Rehfeld, being a Mischling only brought all the disadvantages of being an outsider. "We were not allowed to join the Hitler Youth," says Rehfeld, "and if you lived in a nation where you were excluded from what everyone else participated in, it could be a most bitter experience."[14]

The Schoeps youth group was clearly meant to serve as an ersatz Hitler Youth for full Jewish boys who, according to historian John K. Dickinson,[15] were also heartbroken because they could not join the Nazi organization. Their routines even featured the same type of snappy heel-clicking discipline as did the Hitler Youth. But all it really created was a fatal illusion that its Jewish members belonged to both cultures. Just how much this may have contributed to the almost total lack of awareness among these Jews of the gravity of their situation is tragic to contemplate.

The Nazi equivalent of the Hitlerjugend for girls was the Bund Deutscher Mädel or B.D.M. (League of German Maidens). No effort was made to establish a parallel association for full Jewish girls, who apparently were not encumbered by the leather fetishes of their brothers.

When challenged, Dr. Patai was unable to produce the names of his two allegedly Nazi-sympathizing colleagues at the Breslau Rabbinical Seminary.[16] However research has identified them as Rabbi Franz (later Frank) Rosenthal and Rabbi Bernard Wechsberg, both of whom later emigrated to the United States.[17] Dr. Wechsberg, who is rabbi to a southern California congregation, was definitely a member of the Schoeps group. This was confirmed by Schoeps who later received postwar renown as a popular German historian.[18] It is extremely doubtful that either Rabbi Rosenthal (who died in 1979) or Rabbi Wechsberg belonged to the V.n.J. as Dr. Patai has claimed.

But Rabbi Wechsberg had another interesting affiliation. According to Dr. Alfred Jospe,[19] for many years national director of the B'nai B'rith Hillel Foundation, Rabbi Wechsberg was a member of yet another of the numerous contemporary right-wing German-Jewish organizations: the Kartellconvent deutscher Studenten judischen Glaubens (or K.C.), an anti-Zionist student group which emphasized its German character and loyalty. Not anywhere as extremist as the Naumann group, this association would never "sympathize with and support" the Nazi Party.

And now we come to Georg Kareski. He was a former Berlin banker who emigrated to Palestine in 1937 and there appeared before a rabbinical court inquiring into charges that he had collaborated with the Gestapo.[20] New light has been cast upon this epochal case by discovery of a summation of the findings of the court. This treasure trove was located in the archives of the Yad Vashem Holocaust Memorial in Jerusalem.[21] With this documentation, it is clear that once again, the distortions of history have obscured the facts.

Although Kareski appears as a pivotal figure in the story, a recent Pulitzer Prize-winning biography of Rabbi Leo Baeck makes absolutely no mention of the trial. And wherever the trial is referred to, usually in obscure German texts, the facts are hopelessly garbled. To set the record straight:

1. It was not a secret trial.
2. Kareski himself was not actually on trial.
3. Kareski was defending himself against published charges of his collaboration with the Nazis, and the charges were upheld.
4. Kareski instituted the trial and those who accused him were acquitted of slander.

It has become increasingly popular among Holocaust historians to use Kareski as a means of explaining away several Nazi "concessions" made to the Zionists. On the basis of an interview with Kareski which appeared in *Der Angriff* (*The Attack*), personal newspaper of Reich Propaganda Minister Dr. Joseph Goebbels, and headlined as "The Nuremberg Laws Also Satisfy Old Zionist Demands," Kareski has been both blamed and credited for the appearance of several repressive measures. Chief among these is the provision in the Nuremberg Laws which gave Jews the "right" to fly the Zionist flag while depriving them of flying the German national flag—the swastika. To credit Kareski for this brilliant maneuver, designed to further isolate and identify the Jews, is to unfairly denigrate the Nazi mentality. They simply did not need a Jew to tell them about this tactic.

Kareski is also alleged to have personally lobbied the Nazis against the moving of the Mischlinge out of the Jewish column by the Nuremberg Laws. This too is pure folly. The very last thing that the Nazi Party needed was to have a Jew come out in support of an argument which they were already losing—to their own bureaucrats. Certainly Kareski and the more radical Zionists wanted to see all fractional Jews counted as full Jews. Why? Because their avowed objective was to get as many German Jews as possible out of Germany and resettled in Palestine. The Nazi goal was to get the Jews out—period. Where they went didn't much matter. If any movement could get rid of Germany's Jews, the Nazis would give it their passive support.

Where then did the fractional Jews figure in all this? From the standpoint of political pressure, Kareski felt that if Germany were to consider all fractional-Jews as full Jews (they were then still in the "non-Aryan" catch-all which had led to great confusion), the Jews would see this as a sign that the Nazis meant business. Surely the Jews would then realize they were not wanted in Germany. Kareski hoped the Jews would all decide to emigrate to Palestine. It was as simple as that: the culmination of the Zionist Dream aided by the Nazi nightmare. And it might have worked.

If you remember, the battle lines for the first skirmish for possession of the Mischlinge had already been drawn by November 1935. To the Jews, the soon-to-be-called-Mischlinge were "goyim" since the majority were not being raised in the Jewish faith, while to the Zionists, they were Jews, and a

potential form of leverage. Of course, to the Nazi Party, they
were Jews, regardless. But to the civil servants of the bureaucracy, who won the battle, they were Germans above all!

Had the Nazi Party, and the Zionists, won, the Jews of
Germany might have started an exodus in 1935 that would
not only have rivaled that of Moses from Egypt, but would
have left Germany Judenrein—Jew-free—without a single
drop of Jewish blood having been spilled in the process.

One thing that the Nazis *did* need the services of Georg
Kareski for was the *Der Angriff* interview. It was to be the
first and only time that a Jew was to be asked for an official
opinion by a Nazi. It was the misfortune of Georg Kareski to
be that Jew.

Spurned by the regular Zionist organizations as a leader,
Kareski formed his own extreme Nationalist-Zionist splinter
group. He had first proven his worth to the Nazis when, early
in 1935, he allowed his Volksbank Iwria (a small national cooperative bank used predominantly by middle-class Berlin
Jews) to provide funds for a German Jew sent to England as
a spy for the Gestapo. The funds from the Gestapo were
"laundered" through Kareski's bank in much the same method
as would later be employed in the United States by the Wa-
tergate conspirators and organized crime figures.

Dr. Dr. Erwin Goldmann (the double doctorate is not a mis-
print) was a Mischling—some say he was even an Honorary
Aryan—who later became a postwar spokesman for the extreme German right. He tells an illuminating anecdote about
Kareski in his memoirs, dating it shortly before Kareski's emigration to Palestine. Goldmann says that one of his medical
patients, an "official of the Gestapo," told him during a routine
office visit that "a certain Georg Kareski, a staunch Zionist,"
had repeatedly proposed to the appropriate authorities in
Berlin the wearing of the Star of David by *all* Jews, presumably including Goldmann. That disturbed him to such a degree
that he met with Kareski in an attempt to dissuade him. "We

had such conflicting views," Goldmann wrote, "that it was hard
to say who would have liked to shoot whom first." Memorable
first impressions aside, the proposal to mark the Jews *was*
proposed by Heydrich in a conference on 12 November 1938,
about a year after the meeting described by Goldmann.[22]

Only a few months after the *Der Angriff* interview appeared, Kareski officially announced *his* emigration plan. It
called for the annual resettlement of 25,000 German Jews to
Palestine. Under the Kareski Plan, this massive, but con-
trolled, migration would be handled by an organization which
Kareski would head. This organization—meaning Kareski—
would have absolute control over all property owned by the
Jews in Germany. Since in 1933, three years earlier, there
were 600,000 Jews and Mischlinge (even after the Nuremberg
Laws, the latter were still being counted as Jews by Kareski!)
in Germany, this would easily provide Kareski with a lifelong
source of income. The British, who administered Palestine
under the terms of the League of Nations Mandate, and who
strongly resisted and feared any mass Jewish immigration
movement, were neither consulted nor, one supposes, amused.

The interview in the 23 December 1935 *Der Angriff* was
flashed around the world. It was Dr. Goebbels' Christmas gift
to the universe. The Nazis had found the perfect dupe in Kareski. The interview is worth quoting in part.[23] It begins with
an introduction:

"The Jews are by no means as united as the international
yellow press tries to portray them with regard to the question
of whether or not the legislation regarding Jews, for which
the Nuremberg Laws provided a solution, should be rejected
or not. On the contrary, a considerable number among them
do not at all deny the existence of a separate Jewish race and
want to be treated according to this idea just as they will act
upon it themselves. . . . We have therefore provided space
for a very interesting interview of a German editor with the
president of the National Zionist organization, Georg Kareski–

Berlin, which took place with the approval of the competent authorities in charge of the supervision of Jewish cultural affairs in Germany. Kareski, who is an internationally known personality of the Zionist movement and who was also just named the leader of the Reichverbandes der jüdischen Kulturbünde in Deutschland [Association of Jewish Cultural Associations *in Germany*—emphasis supplied. Actually that wasn't quite true. Kareski's ambitions to supplant Dr. Kurt Singer as leader of the Kulturbünde were thwarted], expresses his views regarding a number of questions connected with the Nuremberg Laws in the following way:

"First question: Herr Direcktor Kareski you know that our leader and Chancellor of the Reich [Hitler] expressed the hope, when explaining the Nuremberg Laws, that this unique, secular solution might yet provide a basis on which it might be possible for the German people to establish a tolerable relationship with the Jewish people. As a leading personality in the National Zionist movement, you have always supported a strict separation between the German and the Jewish culture, based on mutual respect.

"Answer: That is correct, for many years I have regarded a clear demarcation between the cultural affairs of two peoples that live together as a prerequisite for their living together without conflict, and I have long supported such a demarcation. . ."

And Kareski goes on. Not since the exploitation of Marianus van der Lubbe at the Reichstag fire trial had the Nazis found so willing a victim. Kareski even defends the Nazi prohibition on intermarriage. This sparkling exchange of repartee appears under a subhead reading "Mixed Marriages Also a Jewish Concern."

Here is what Kareski had to say on that issue:

"Seventh question: As an expert of National Socialist ideology you know, Mr. Kareski, that according to the German point of view the marital relationship of two people is a high, moral duty as well as a cultural element of the highest order.

Therefore, the prohibition of mixed marriages, quite apart from their importance for race politics, also has an important cultural aspect. What do you have to say about this from the jüdischvölkisch [National-Jewish] point of view?

"Answer: On the Jewish side, there is no need to emphasize the enormous importance of a healthy family life. The fact that the Jewish people survived until today for two thousand years, even after the loss of their national sovereignty and despite the lack of a settled community and linguistic unity, can be attributed to two factors: their race [sic] and the strong position of the family in Jewish life. The loosening of both of these ties during the past decades gave rise to serious concerns on the Jewish side as well. The interruption of this process of disintegration that affected wide Jewish circles and which was advanced by mixed marriages, must therefore be welcomed without reserve from the Jewish point of view."

For the grand finale, Kareski was told, "You are familiar with the views of competent authorities in Germany that the racial laws and the national character of the Germans do not intend to fundamentally defame the Jewish people as a whole. Once the overgrowth of foreign thought in Germany everywhere has been overcome, the true cultural achievements on the Jewish side will, once again, be appreciated without prejudice, if they receive interest and if they abandon any disguises which are rightfully regarded as unprincipled in Germany. Do you believe that the boundaries created by the clear separation of both of the cultural spheres will, in future, be respected by the Jewish side as well?"

Naturally, Kareski agreed. He did not disappoint his masters. The worldwide outrage this interview created was the same as one imagines it might have been had a militant leader of the American Black Separatist movement (like Stokely Carmichael or H. Rap Brown) publicly endorsed the segregationist policies of Alabama Governor George C. Wallace in 1963 because both were working toward the same objective. But Kareski ignored the furor. He angrily refused a request from an American Zionist newspaper to either refute the *Der Angriff* interview or resign from the Zionist movement.

Surprisingly, it wasn't even this incident that eventually brought total disgrace to Kareski. Emboldened to the point of becoming feckless by what he perceived as his success in encouraging cultural and racial rapproachment, Kareski in one fell swoop burned all his Jewish bridges behind him. He sought, and accepted, the support of the Nazis in a move to take over the leadership of the Reichsvertretung der deutschen Juden (the National Council of the German Jews—then, along with the Kulturbünde, still under Jewish control). The Gestapo supported Kareski because they knew they could control him, he would be "their man." Despite (or because of) his Gestapo backing, Kareski failed to displace Dr. Leo Baeck as titular leader of the Jews of Germany. Baeck's biographer, Leonard Baker, calls Kareski "the first Jewish quisling, the man who sold out to the Nazis."[24]

Shortly afterward, Kareski's bank failed and thousands of Jews found themselves penniless overnight. Strangely enough, this event was not reported in either *Der Stürmer* or *Der Angriff* where presumably one would expect to find gloating coverage of real-life Jewish financial chicanery splashed all over the front page. It was then that Kareski decided to practice what he had so often preached. He began to make plans to emigrate to Palestine.

While Kareski was on a preliminary visit to Palestine in the autumn of 1937, he picked up a piece of startling reading matter. The Hitachduth Olei Germania (H.O.G.—a somewhat unfortunate acronym for a Jewish organization), the Palestine association of immigrants from Germany, had published four highly damning allegations about Kareski's behavior in Germany in their October 1937 news organ. Kareski attempted to suppress publication of the accusations, but since this was Palestine not Germany, he had no friends in high places to come to his rescue. Kareski then filed a defamation suit against the H.O.G., but there was never anything secret about his action. Rather than have the case heard in the Palestine civil courts which were administered by the British—who would be none too pleased to hear from an "internationally known" advocate of increased Jewish emigration to Palestine—Kareski opted for the rabbinical court. It is an option available to Jews everywhere.

The case was heard in October and November of 1937. The court was greatly hampered in reaching its verdict because much of the material that had been submitted against Kareski could not be used in open court, where it would have endangered the lives of Jews who were still in Germany.

There were four parts to Kareski's suit. The first concerned the H.O.G.'s charge that Kareski attempted to "impose himself as leader of the Jews by means of non-Jewish authorities and against the will of all the Jewish organizations and of the entire Jewish community in Germany." It was here that Kareski's interview figured. Testimony revealed that in the course of seeking "the help of the National Socialist authorities," Kareski held three meetings with the Reich Commissioner Hans Hinkel (later of the Propaganda Ministry), the "competent authority in charge of the supervision of Jewish cultural affairs in Germany," as he was referred to by *Der Angriff*. But there never was an interview. It was a typical Nazi sham; a pre-arranged statement by Hinkel and Kareski, the publication of which, in the verdict of the court, was to "achieve his [Kareski's] appointment with the help of non-Jewish authorities." Kareski argued that the "interview" was "intended for the benefit of the Jews," but the court was unimpressed, finding that "the statements of the H.O.G. cannot be considered to be contrary to the truth."

And so it went on the second round. The H.O.G. alleged that after Kareski had been expelled from the mainstream German Zionist organization in May 1933, he attempted to destroy the organization by denouncing it publicly as "a Marxist stronghold and a breeding ground for international Marxist ideology." Kareski denied the charge, but he did admit that to call an organization Marxist in Nazi Germany meant endangering it. Kareski defended himself by stating that his comments could not have been considered as a denunciation as "the government already knew that there were Marxist elements in the Zionist organization." In response to this, the court ruled that "whether the government believed this to be the case or whether a Jew, and an experienced politician, publicly emphasized it are two different things," and thus again upheld the H.O.G.

Kareski fared just as poorly on the third allegation: that he permitted the publication of a murder threat against the then president of the Zionist Organization of Germany, Dr. Siegfried Moses (later State Comptroller of Israel) in his (Kareski's) newspaper, *Das Jüdische Volk* (*The Jewish People*). The questionable statement read, "It is a relief for us to know that Dr. Moses will soon be in reach of the Jewish people. Since time immemorial there has only been one punishment for high treason." The court believed the statement "must be regarded as a threat, which could incite a youthful fanatic to commit murder." Kareski denied that he was the editor responsible for the newspaper, which was true, but he admitted to not only having read the article before publication, but to playing out a charade involving allegedly striking the offensive quote which he said "inadvertently remained as before." The court once more ruled in favor of the H.O.G.

The final allegation concerned the failure of the Volksbank Iwria. In the eyes of the H.O.G., the bank failed because "the board of directors and the members of the executive granted themselves loans of such high amounts that they surpassed the available funds of the bank." Kareski vehemently but unconvincingly denied the accusation and the court once again upheld the validity of the charge. The H.O.G. was fully vindicated. The unanimous decision of the rabbinical court against Kareski on all four points was to succeed where previous attempts at public vilification had failed, for nothing more would ever be heard from Kareski again. It is known that he remained in Palestine, but authorities in Israel are uncertain even as to the date of his death.

The chief dayan (judge of the rabbinical court) was Palestine's Chief Rabbi, Dr. Isaac Herzog. (In 1983, his son, Genferal Chaim Herzog, a former Israeli ambassador to the United Nations, was elected President of Israel.) Appointed to the post only the year before, this was the first major ruling handed down in Palestine by this former Chief Rabbi of Dublin and later of the entire Irish Free State. Rabbi Herzog and the other dayanim (judges of the court) are identified on the transcript only by their initials, which has contributed to the aura of secrecy surrounding the proceedings. Rabbi Herzog's co-adjudicators were Rabbi H. Brody of Prague and the former rabbi of the Mannheim, Germany, Gemeinde, Dr. Isaak Unna.

The psychological damage inflicted upon their fellow German Jews by men like Dr. Max Naumann and Georg Kareski remains difficult to fully assess today. But it pales by comparison with the evil shown by one man who, after managing to save his own life by emigrating to the United States, expressed his gratitude by helping send 25,000 German-Jewish children to their deaths.

Dr. Franz Kallman is the German psychiatrist hailed today as "the father of biological psychiatry."[25] Kallman was born in 1897, the son of a German physician who had converted from Judaism to Christianity. A doctor himself, Kallman was drawn to genetics and in 1931 began exploring the then-unknown field of hereditary mental illness. At the notorious 1936 German Psychiatric Congress, Kallman proposed the sterilization of the parents, siblings and children of all schizophrenics. This was a move too drastic for even the Nazis to stomach. Two Nazi doctors lept to their feet and expressed their indignation and dissent.

Although Dr. Kallman did not consider himself a Jew, he feared that the Nazis might. It is not clear whether his father had married a Christian, so Kallman may not have held Mischling status. As the child of Jewish parents, regardless of whether his father had been baptized, he was still a Jew.

Kallman left Germany for the United States, where he arrived in time to lobby successfully against the passage by Congress of the Child Refugee Bill. His attacks on the pending legislation, which would have allowed the immigration of 25,000 German-Jewish children to the United States on the very eve of the Second World War, torpedoed the bill with the deadly accuracy of a U-boat commander.

Dr. Kallman died in 1965.

The 25,000 children died in the ovens of Auschwitz.

Epilogue

The story could have ended differently. What if the Nazis had won the war? What then would have been the fate of the Mischlinge? Would the Mischlinge Problem have required its own Final Solution? Some of the Mischlinge, like Hanns Rehfeld, think so. "They were going to kill us," Rehfeld flatly states. He has come to this conclusion from careful study of the minutes of the 1942 Wannsee Conference. Rehfeld sees the Mischlinge as being Adolf Eichmann's unfinished business. Certainly, other Mischlinge lived with this fear throughout the war years, never knowing whether they indeed would be the next to die. The one thing they knew all too well was the fate of the Jews. However, it is worth remembering that when some of the Mischlinge were sent to camps in the last months of the war, they were sent to labor camps and not to the death camps.

Many of the Mischlinge have received Wiedergutmachung —the official restitution monies—from the West German government—but only under the one category covering "impairment of professional or economic advancement" under the Nazis. When the Mischlinge were prohibited from continuing their higher education, some, like Werner Goldberg and Heinz Elsberg, saw their dreams of becoming lawyers or doctors evaporate into the German air. To Rehfeld, "There obviously was no need to educate us if they were going to kill us anyway. It would have just been a waste of money." To the credit of many German teachers, a number of the Mischlinge, and even

some full Jews like Charlotte Lehmann's half brother Herbert
Stein, continued to receive at-home tutoring by their professors, at the gravest personal risk to all involved.

The Mischlinge have lobbied intensely to be included among
those eligible to receive other categories of restitution monies.
And each year, their efforts have failed. Put simply, they can
not collect damages for categories of "suffering" that are restricted to Jewish applicants, specifically those who were deported, lived in hiding or in the ghettos, wore the Star, or
lost their homes and property. Nor do they qualify under the
category of Germans who were persecuted for their political
beliefs. Persecution for one's religious beliefs is interpreted
to mean those who were Jews, in the full Nazi definition of
the term. Because the Mischlinge had to be Christians in order
to survive, they are not eligible under these official rules. Instead we are asked to accept the obvious fallacy that the Nazis
did not overtly persecute those who believed in and practiced
the tenets of Christianity.

Once again, after forty years, the Mischlinge find themselves to be neither Jew nor German in the eyes of their own
government. If as Hanns Rehfeld has stated, the ultimate result was to have been the destruction of the Mischlinge, that
goal has been accomplished. Should anyone be surprised that
it has been done bureaucratically?

The survival of the Mischlinge, as well as that of the Jews
in mixed marriages, handed Adolf Hitler his greatest personal
defeat. Once the other Jews were forced to wear the Star,
they were lost. They abandoned all hope for survival by
proudly pinning on their "yellow badge with pride" (as they
had been exhorted to do in an editorial by Dr. Robert Weltsch,
editor of Berlin's *Jüdische Rundschau*). When the Final Solution became a nightmare of reality, the Mischlinge and the
privileged mixed marriage Jews, both certainly among the
likely candidates for deportation, stayed behind. As long as
they remained alive, Hitler's Reich was never completely Ju-

denrein. Although six million died, these Jews lived. And through their lives Hitler lost his war against the Jews. Jewish blood was spilled, but it was not eradicated.

Notes and Sources

FOREWORD

1. Novelist Meyer Levin, a war correspondent, and Rabbi W. Gunther Plaut, were among the first Americans to enter Germany with the U.S. Army in 1945. Levin's *In Search: An Autobiography* (Paris: Author's Press, 1950), p.227, recounts that in Cologne and Bonn, "the few survivors were Jews married to Aryans." Of the first Jew found in Germany by the American army, Levin writes (pp.197–199), "she was the daughter of one of the wealthy old Aachen textile-mill families, but married to an Aryan. . . . a few years ago the Nazis had ordered her husband to divorce her, but he had refused, and his brother, a high Nazi, had managed to protect them. . . . yes, her kind had even survived the Nazis." This woman was hired as an interpreter and secretary by the first U.S. military government unit to be established in occupied Germany.

CHAPTER ONE

1. Werner Goldberg was personally interviewed by the author in Am Grunewaldsee, German Federal Republic, 5 March 1982. The interview took place over lunch at Forsthaus Paulsborn, once used by Reichsmarschall Göring as a retreat and hunting lodge.

2. Nora Levin, *The Holocaust: The Destruction of European Jewry 1933–1945* (New York: Thomas Y. Crowell Co., 1968), p.476. See also Gerald Reitlinger, *The Final Solution: The Attempt to Exterminate the Jews of Europe 1939–1945* (New York: Beechurst Press,

1953), p.164, who puts the figure at 33,000. He identifies Frankfurt as one of a half-dozen cities where privileged Jews remained.

3. Raul Hilberg, *The Destruction of the European Jews* (Chicago: Quadrangle Paperbacks, 1967), p.26. See also Levin, p.474, p.501, who uses the figure of 150,000 Mischlinge and intermarried Jews in the Reich-Protektorat.

4. George E. Sokolsky, *We Jews* (New York: Doubleday, Doran, 1935). He may have meant all fractional-Jews. By comparison, there were no more than 600,000 full Jews in all Germany. On p.103 he states, "There were, in Germany, five times as many persons of mixed Jewish-Christian origin as there were Jews when Hitler came to power."

Professor Dr. Klaus J. Herrmann in his *Das Dritte Reich und Die Deutsch-Jüdischen Organisationen 1933–1934* (Köln: Carl Heymanns, 1969), quotes statistics at the time of the Nuremberg Laws showing 750,000 fractional-Jews in Germany. These statistics put three-quarter Jews into the Jewish category and still showed only 450,000 full Jews in the Reich.

The confusion over determining an accurate total of Mischlinge in Germany is further compounded by the fact that a Federation of German Christians, organized before the promulgation of the Nuremberg Laws, claimed a membership of two-and-a-half million Germans who were "not Jews and not Aryans."

5. Hilberg, p.268.

6. A Nazi report, typed by a "Frau Slottke," and titled *Entwicklung der Judischen Ruckstellungsgruppen in den Niederlanden*, gives the following October 1941 figures on p.8. For Halbjuden (half-Jews), 14,895. For Vierteljuden (quarter-Jews), 5,990. The cover page of this report on Jewish Stay-Behind Groups uses "ca. 20,000." This figure has been perpetuated by those who apparently never looked inside. The document is in the archives of the Rijksinstituut voor Oorlogsdocumentatie, Amsterdam. A photocopy of the entire document is in the collection of the author.

7. Hilberg, p.377. See also *Entwicklung . . .*, pp.4–7.

8. There were between 2,000 and 3,000 privileged Jews in Sofia, Bulgaria's capital. Hilberg, p.983.

9. And maybe even earlier! Certainly the Einsatzgruppen (mobile killing operations) didn't take time to bother with definitions. If a half-Jew was denounced as a Jew, he was killed as a Jew. A similar situation existed in Frankfurt in 1943, where even Jews in mixed marriages were, for a time, deported. Those who complained were told "we make our own decrees." Reitlinger, p.164. The same author states that some Russian Jews in mixed marriages were sent to the "privileged" ghetto of Theresienstadt. One wonders what the Nazis would have done had they conquered Russia: Joseph Stalin's third wife, the former Rosa Kaganovich, was the sister of Lazar M. Kaganovich, one of the highest ranking Jews in the Soviet Communist Party.

Sol Littman, in an otherwise undistinguished book, *War Criminal on Trial. The Rauca Case* (Toronto: Lester & Orpen Dennys, 1983), tells on pp.94–97 of a Lithuanian full Jew who passed as a Mischling in order to live outside the soon-to-be-liquidated Kaunas ghetto. The story was told to Littman by Mickolas Yatzkevichis, Foreign Minister of the Lithuanian Soviet Socialist Republic. It would certainly indicate that the exemptions for Mischlinge extended to the Nazi-occupied Baltic regions as well. Hilberg, p.388, cites "the existence of a privileged class, which included . . . the intermarried Jews" in Belgium.

10. Scholars of the Bible have long cited references to the marriages of Joseph and Moses to the daughters of pagans and the subsequent acceptance of their sons as full-fledged Jews. Interestingly, the concept of defining Jewishness on the basis of the mother's status developed from a reflex action against the rising tide of intermarriage— in the 6th Century B.C.E.(!) A decree banishing "foreign" wives and their children contains the redefinition of descent in matriarchal terms. See the *Jewish News* (Detroit), 20 January 1984, p.46.

11. See *Newsweek*, 28 March 1983, p.50. See also the *Jewish News* (Detroit), 25 March 1983, p.16. The use of "presume" to determine the status of one's religious ancestry can also be found in the April 1933 "Aryan" laws.

12. Michael Wolfson, an Israeli-born professor of history in Hamburg, West Germany, is the source of the European statistic. The *Jewish News* (Detroit), 20 January 1984, p.12.

13. Leonard Baker, *Days of Sorrow and Pain: Leo Baeck and the Berlin Jews*. (New York: Oxford University Press, 1980), p.96. A 1983 "demographic survey" chillingly underlines the 1911 prediction in Baker's book. It foretells a shrinkage of the world's Jewish population (outside Israel) by up to one-fourth by the year 2000 because of intermarriage, cultural assimilation, and a new evil: reduced fertility among Jews. *Detroit Free Press* 15 May 1983. See also Alan Abrams, "Keeping the Faith," *The Windsor* (Ontario) *Star*, 26 November 1983, p. B-4.

It is worth noting that all three of the most revered names in the creation of Zionism and the modern state of Israel—Theodor Herzl, Chaim Weizmann and David Ben-Gurion—had children who intermarried. Herzl's son Hans was baptized in the Catholic faith in 1924. See Rosalie Marie Levy, *Why Jews Become Catholics* (New York: The author, 1924), p.194.

14. And many of them, including the Jewish-born Catholic philosopher Dr. Edith Stein, died in Auschwitz. Dr. Stein had been among those who unsuccessfully sought to have Pope Pius XII issue an encyclical on the Jewish question.

15. Arthur Ruppin, *Jews in the Modern World* (London: The Macmillan Co., 1934). An authority on Jewish demography, Ruppin was director of Zionist colonization in Palestine.

16. Hilberg, p.115.

17. Albert I. Gordon, *Intermarriage: Interfaith, Interracial, Interethnic* (Boston: Beacon Press, 1964), p.179.

18. Bruno Blau, "Die Mischele in Nazireich," *Judaica*, Heft 1.1 (Zurich: April 1948). Curiously, Josef Kastein, *History and Destiny of the Jews*. (New York: Garden City Publishing Co., Inc., 1936), p. 437, gives that fraction for *all* of Germany between 1900–1927 (33,800 out of 103,000 marriages).

19. Ernst Christian Helmreich, *The German Churches Under Hitler: Background, Struggle and Epilogue* (Detroit: Wayne State University Press, 1979), p. 330. These were the Mischlinge of the First Degree. Only 392, or 1.6 per cent of the Mischlinge of the Second Degree, were brought up as Jews (at the time of the survey) thus raising the combined total for both grades of Mischlinge to 11.5 per cent.

20. Hilberg, p. 45.

21. Told by Globke to journalist Rolf Vogel and repeated by Vogel to the author during an interview in Bonn-Röthken, Federal Republic of Germany, 1 March 1982.

Reitlinger, p. 173, says, "These men [Stuckart, Lammers, etc.] sought to create a privileged class of Jew out of those who were nearest to their own way of life," as well as those married to people in their circle.

22. Hilberg, p. 46. Blome later became Deputy Reichsärzteführer (chief medical officer of the Reich). After the war, he was tried and acquitted by a U.S. military tribunal.

23. The Gemeinde has no equivalent in the Ausland (the rest of the world). All Jews except those who had formally converted to Christianity belonged to the Gemeinde of the city in which they lived. They paid taxes to that Gemeinde, which were usually collected by the state along with their secular taxes. Baker, pp.93–94.

24. This definition is also used by John K. Dickinson in his *German and Jew* (Chicago: Quadrangle Books, 1967), p.256. This was not the first application of a "barnyard" term to Jews. "Marrano," the Spanish name for Christianized Jews, means "pig." Sokolsky, p. 11.

25. Found in a computer search on the Datapac information base at the library of the University of Windsor, 28 May 1982.

26. Salinger, Sorensen, Schlesinger and Hawn are in fact included in *The Jewish Lists* (New York: Schocken Books, 1979), compiled by Martin H. Greenberg. The others also make no secret of their Jewish lineage.

27. For more on the marriage of Diana Ross, see Peter Benjaminson, *The Story of Motown* (New York: Grove Press, Inc., 1979), p.123.

28. The commonly used translation of "Artikel 7" is: "The Führer and Reich Chancellor may grant exemptions from the stipulations of implementory ordinances." Raul Hilberg, *Documents of Destruc-*

tion: Germany and Jewry, 1933–1945 (Chicago: Quadrangle Books, 1971), p. 21. It was first reported in *Reichsgesetzblatt* (Reich Legal Gazette) 1935, 1, 1333.

Dickinson refers to it as "the power granted to Adolf Hitler to free individuals from the definition of Jew. In other words, a Jew could be rated a non-Jew if Hitler felt that this was, for any reason, desirable." p.191.

29. Hannah Arendt, in *Eichmann in Jerusalem* (New York: Penguin Books, 1977), p.133, uses that wording which is generally attributed to Himmler's 4 October 1943 speech. Hilberg translates the phrase as "first-class Jews." See *Destruction*, p. 660.

30. Hilberg, p. 273.

31. Told in Walter C. Langer, *The Mind of Adolf Hitler. The Secret Wartime Report* (New York: New American Library, 1978).

32. The text of the Seyss-Inquart letter to Bormann was introduced as an exhibit at the Eichmann trial. It is Israel Police Document 1439. It also appears in Hilberg, *Documents*, p.149.

33. Hilberg, *Destruction*, p. 275.

34. Privileged and non-privileged mixed marriages are explained in Hilberg, *Destruction*, pp.115, 274–275. The concept I followed for my explanation is taken largely from Blau's *Judaica* article cited above.

35. The Reichsvereinigung was originally the Reichsvertretung der deutschen Juden (The National Council of the German Jews) when it was organized in September 1933. This was the organization which the Nazis wanted Georg Kareski (see Chapter Nine) to head. By the time it became a part of the framework of the Nazi destruction process, the emphasis had shifted from "German Jews" to "Jews in Germany." And so had the status of its members.

36. The exemption of mixed marriage Jews from membership in the Reichsvereinigung also appears in Hilberg, p. 327.

37. By the time of the Star decree, privileged mixed marriage Jews even included those married to Mischlinge of the Second Degree— one-quarter Jews. Hilberg, p. 274.

38. Identification cards bearing both the closed and open "J" were examined by the author at the Rijksinstituut voor Oorlogsdocumentatie in Amsterdam. Photocopies in collection of the author.

39. For more on von Preysing's role, see his pastoral letter of 13 December 1942. Other leaders among German Christian churchmen who protested against the compulsory divorce scheme were Cardinal Adolf Bertram of Breslau and Bishop Theophil Wurm of the Protestant Church of Württemberg. Helmreich, p. 362, believes that the protest demonstration by Aryan spouses (witnessed and described by Werner Goldberg) also played an important role.

Levin, p. 501, says the "major churches of Germany were passive throughout the extermination of German Jewry . . . church intervention, when it occurred, was limited to the Mischlinge or partners in mixed marriage."

40. Hilberg, p. 277; Levin, p. 476.

41. Hans-Otto Meissner, *Magda Goebbels: First Lady of the Third Reich* (Scarborough, Ontario: Nelson Canada Limited, 1981), p.14. The book was originally published in West Germany in 1978. The Goebbels letter is quoted by Reitlinger, pp.161–162.

42. Werner Goldberg personal interview cited above. Ironically, at virtually the very same time that this protest demonstration began, another massive demonstration against the Nazi arrests of Jews was taking place in New York's Madison Square Garden. On the first day of March 1943, more than 100,000 people turned out for the "Stop Hitler Now Rally" which adopted a resolution calling upon President Franklin D. Roosevelt and the United Nations to take immediate action to rescue as many as possible of the Jews living under Nazi terror. As no such action was ever undertaken, this demonstration can hardly be considered as successful as the one taking place simultaneously in Berlin. For more, see Leah Esther Weil, "As the World Stood By and Watched": *The Voice of the Second Generation* (Los Angeles: Holocaust Documentation Committee of the American Congress of Jews from Poland and Survivors of Concentration Camps, 1983), p.14.

By contrast, the Berlin protest demonstration rates but one paragraph in a pictorial guide to key sites of the German anti-fascist resistance movement, 1933–45, in East Berlin, published several years ago. Copy in collection of the author. The Rosenstrasse site is about midway between the Alexanderplatz and the Marx-Engels-Platz in East Berlin.

43. The eldest daughter of Army Generalmajor Riemann, Frau Dr. med. Hils, still lives in Berlin. She declined to be interviewed as presumably she intends to write her own book some day. The information about her father surfaced in an interview with Dr. Waltraud Rehfeld conducted in Berlin, German Federal Republic, 3 March 1982.

44. The Wannsee Conference is extensively covered by Hilberg, Levin and Arendt. The Eichmann quotation appears in the latter.

45. Reitlinger, p.179.

CHAPTER TWO

1. "The Perfect Aryan Soldier" document in collection of Werner Goldberg, Berlin. Data from personal interview cited earlier.

2. A similar story is told by Auschwitz survivor Marc Berkowitz of New York. Because Berkowitz had blue eyes and blond hair, Dr. Josef Mengele pronounced him a "Perfect Aryan" specimen and gave him a signed certificate stating so. Mengele dressed the then twelve-year-old Berkowitz in a Hitler Youth uniform and allowed him to swim in the SS swimming pool. Mengele allegedly planned to introduce Berkowitz to Hitler as proof of the possibility of "rehabilitating" Jews via genetic manipulation. Interview with Berkowitz in the *Windsor* (Ontario) *Star*, 14 November 1983.

3. The full text of Keitel's order, and of all other orders cited here, is found in a compilation by Rolf Vogel, *Ein Stück von uns. 1813–1976. Deutsche Juden in deutschen Armeen. Eine Dokomentation* (Mainz: v. Hase and Koehler Verlag, 1977). Vogel also provides a full text of the Nuremberg Laws.

4. Arthur Müller (Miller) was personally interviewed by the author in Berlin, Federal Republic of Germany, 4 March 1982.

5. The Rolf Vogel interview has been previously cited.

6. Dr. Hans Salomon was personally interviewed by the author in Berlin, Federal Republic of Germany, 5 March 1982.

7. Hans Faust was personally interviewed by the author in Berlin, Federal Republic of Germany, 4 March 1982.

8. The title of the Heil de Brentani book is *Lorie auf der brücke.* His identification on the title page reads "Offizier für nationalsozialistsche führung, 1944." A listing of this and several other wartime titles by Heil de Brentani can be found on p. 242 of the *L(ibrary) (of) C(ongress)-N(ational) U(nion) C(atalogue) Author Lists, 1942–1962.*

9. Much of the information about von Brentani came from Professor Dr. Klaus J. Herrmann who was personally interviewed by the author in Montréal, Québec, 18 December 1981. It was later verified in a series of letters from Gerhard Moest of Leipzig, German Democratic Republic. The letters are cited below. Other members of von Brentani's family who remained in Europe have continued to use the Heil de Brentani name.

10. Specific allegations of wrongdoing by von Brentani appear in a letter from Moest dated 12 December 1982. These confirm the information independently acquired by the author. Further details are given in a letter of 1 January 1983. Both letters are in the author's collection.

11. Information regarding von Brentani's art appears in a trilingual publication *Mario von Brentani: The World Renowned Painter of the Canadian Eskimoes* (Montreal: Maison d'edition Bert Waigel, n.d.), identified from internal evidence as circa 1974. Collection of author.

12. A copy of the Trudeau letter, dated 27 February 1978, and a second letter, in French with a holograph salutation and closing by Trudeau, dated 19 June 1979, are in the collection of the author. Copies of both letters had been examined by the office of former Canadian federal Minister of Justice Mark MacGuigan, and their authenticity established beyond doubt. A request by an aide to MacGuigan that the author refrain from publishing both letters

served as a reinforcement of their authenticity. Some of the information about von Brentani's dealings with the Canadian government was subsequently received from this aide on the condition that it remain non-attributable. On 30 June 1984, Trudeau stepped down as Prime Minister of Canada after sixteen years in office. Although MacGuigan frequently had been touted as a possible successor to Trudeau, he could not marshal enough support at the Liberal Party leadership convention to even pose a serious threat to former Finance Minister John Turner. MacGuigan resigned from the cabinet and on Trudeau's last day in office was appointed to a judgeship on the federal Court of Appeals.

13. The *Der Spiegel* story is also dated on the basis of internal evidence. The copy in the collection of the author was apparently reprinted for private distribution within the German-Canadian community. It was obtained from the former editor of Winnipeg's *Kanada-Kurier*, Bernd Längin.

14. Copies of von Brentani's award from the GDR and his obituary from GDR publications are in the collection of the author.

15. The obituary of von Bolschwing appeared in the Toronto *Globe and Mail*, 10 March 1982, p. 20.

16. Copies of von Brentani's Nazi Party membership papers and the other official documents cited were obtained from the archives of the Berlin Document Center, Berlin, Federal Republic of Germany. Mrs. von Brentani supplied the Hitler document. A photographic copy is in the collection of the author.

17. Mrs. Ruth von Brentani was interviewed by the author from her home in Huntingdon, Québec, 9 February 1982. Tape of conversation in collection of author. Further elaboration of her story is taken from a series of subsequent query letters, also in collection of author.

18. Charlotte Lehmann was personally interviewed by the author at her home in Bad Godesberg, Federal Republic of Germany, on 1 March 1982. The recreated conversation between her father and the Wehrmacht officer is based upon information she later received from Valerie Stein.

19. A photocopy of Werner Goldberg's 1939 Christmas poem is in the collection of the author.

20. The Schneersohn story is told by Vogel, pp. 310–313.

21. In late 1983, a source close to British intelligence confirmed that Admiral Canaris passed Nazi military secrets, including plans for the invasion of the Soviet Union, to the Allies throughout the war. *Detroit Free Press*, 17 October 1983, p. 1-A.

22. For more on Dr. Jovy, see the *Jewish News* (Detroit), 20 January 1984, p. 22.

CHAPTER THREE

1. Jürgen Landeck, whose quotation opens this chapter, was interviewed by the author in Berlin, Federal Republic of Germany, 3 March 1982.

2. The marriage regulations for Mischlinge are cited in Hilberg, *Destruction*, p. 108.

3. The Paulus-Bund was also organized in 1937.

4. The advertisements quoted in this chapter appear in the *Mitteilungsblatt Der Vereinigung 1937 e.V.*, December 1937/January 1938, No. 12/1. An original is in the collection of Werner Goldberg, Berlin. A photostat of the page of advertisements and a photocopy of the entire issue are in the collection of the author.

5. The "Jewish" origin of the old German Gothic script is mentioned by Helmreich, p. 329.

6. The dates and places of the author's interviews of Miller, Goldberg, Salomon, Vogel and Lehmann have already been cited.

7. Hanns Rehfeld was interviewed by telephone in New York City, 10 March 1982.

8. The story about the Synodal baptism certificates was told to the author by C.J.F. Stuldreher of the Rijksinstituut voor Oorlogsdocumentatie in Amsterdam, The Netherlands, during an interview on 26 February 1982.

9. Information about the "cooperative Aryans" can be found in Dr. J. Presser, *The Destruction of the Dutch Jews* (New York: E. P. Dutton & Co., Inc., 1969), pp. 298, 308. On the latter page, Dr. Presser points out that the Dutch Bench "admitted quite irrelevant evidence and declarations about adulterous relationships, when everyone—advocates, judges and clerks—knew that the whole thing was nothing but perjury."

10. The quotation is found in Helmreich, p. 329.

11. About the hospital at Theresienstadt, Meyer Levin writes (p. 272), "it was quiet, clean, excellently equipped, for the able practitioners of Prague and Vienna and Berlin had been permitted to bring their instruments and part of their medical machinery here, and the hospital was of course staffed with some of the finest physicians and surgeons of three countries."

Levin also tells (pp. 227–228, 272–273) a story about the liberation from Theresienstadt of a mixed marriage Jew which is similar to the stories told about their mothers by Rolf Vogel and Dr. Hans Salomon. Interestingly,the woman had a son that Levin thought was "probably in the German forces." Even in 1950, Levin apparently still did not know that almost all of the Mischlinge were officially severed from the German armed forces in 1940.

12. Heinz Elsberg was interviewed by the author in Berlin, Federal Republic of Germany, 4 March 1982.

13. An editorial in the Detroit *Jewish News*, 3 June 1983, seriously recommended the return of the custom of sitting shiva in mourning mixed marriages. The suggestion appeared in the "Purely Commentary" column of Philip Slomovitz, who although legally blind, and now 87, is still widely regarded as the most erudite (and respected) of English-language Jewish-community newspaper journalists. Mr. Slomovitz is founding editor and editor emeritus of the paper, now edited by Gary Rosenblatt. For an excellent depiction of the custom of sitting shiva to mourn the loss of a son in a mixed marriage, see Sholem Asch's classic Yiddish-English novel *East River*. One of the most famous real life personalities to use shiva as a protest was the grandmother of English poet and author Siegfried Sassoon. Not content to merely sit shiva, Sassoon's grandmother placed a curse upon the offspring of the marriage of her Jewish son (the first of the Sassoon clan to intermarry) and his Christian wife. Siegfried was raised as a Christian and later formally converted to Roman Catholicism. Today, a significant number of the Sassoon family are Christians.

Actor and Screen Actors Guild president Ed Asner (television's "Lou Grant") has told of yet another form of parental protest. When his parents learned he was dating a gentile while at college, they stopped sending him money from home.

14. A photocopy of Albert Goldberg's medical history record is in the collection of the author. The original is in the collection of Werner Goldberg in Berlin. Werner Goldberg briefly touched upon several aspects of his life story in an essay. "Politischer Radikalismus weckt die Angst," which can be found in Henryk M. Broder and Michael R. Lang, eds., *Fremd im eigenen Land: Juden in der Bundersrepublik* (Frankfurt am Main: Fischer Taschenbuch Verlag, 1979), pp. 197–202. Another published Mischlinge memoir is Lili Hahn's *White Flags of Surrender* (Washington, D.C.: Robert B. Luce, 1974). The book was translated from the German by Sybil Milton. Dr. Milton is the Chief Archivist of the Leo Baeck Institute in New York and a past winner of the Jewish Book Award. The book, based on a diary, never uses the word, Mischlinge, although it is clearly the story of a Mischling of the Second Degree.

Angst zu Atmen, the childhood memoirs of Rolf von Sydow, another Mischling now active in West German theater and television circles, was published by Ullstein Verlag in late 1983. Early in 1984, the memoirs of Ingeborg Hecht, *Als unsichtbare Mauern wuchsen. Eine deutsche Familie unter den Nürnberger Rassengesetzen*, was published by Hoffman and Campe Verlag in Hamburg. Hecht's father was a Jew.

15. See footnote to the Foreword for another example of how the victorious Allies hired Mischlinge or their Jewish parents as interpreters and secretaries. Although the Allies trusted the anti-fascist credentials of the Mischlinge and the mixed marriage Jews, they must have been more than a little amazed to find both groups still free and alive after the fall of Hitler. Interestingly, the U.S. Army authorities considered the surviving Jews in Germany as Germans, and any fraternization with "the enemy" was strictly prohibited. Contrast this attitude with that of the Soviets as reported here by Werner Goldberg and in Chapter Four by Klara Riesenburger.

16. Regarding Globke's "Jews like us" quote, it is again worth repeating the reference in Reitlinger, p. 173, to the effect that "these men [the Nazi Interior Ministry bureaucrats] sought to create a privileged class of Jew out of those who were nearest their own way of life."

CHAPTER FOUR

1. The quotation by Moses Hess which appears as the epigraph for this chapter is found in Jörg v. Uthmann, *Doppelgänger, zu bleicher Geselle. Zur Pathologie des deutsch-jüdischen Verhaltnisses* (Stuttgart: Seewald Verlag, 1976), p. 10. Hess, a Jew, was married to a Christian prostitute. Author von Uthmann, a West German diplomat, was posted at the German embassy in Israel from 1965 to 1969.

2. Klara Riesenburger was interviewed by the author at her home in Berlin, German Democratic Republic, 6 August 1981.

3. One of those buried by Martin Riesenburger in 1943 was Theodor Wolff, the noted journalist and former chief editor of the *Berliner Tageblatt*. The usually objective, highly respected American churchman George N. Schuster, in his *Like a Mighty Army: Hitler versus Established Religion* (New York: D. Appleton-Century Company, 1935), p. 85, uncharitably called Wolff's *Tageblatt* "little more than a clever Semitic organ of propaganda."

4. Many of the details in Klara Riesenburger's story have been verified against Martin Riesenburger's memoirs, *Das Licht Verlöschte Nicht: Dokumente aus der Nacht des Nazismus* (Berlin, German Democratic Republic: Union Verlag, 1960).

5. The historical precedent is cited by Baker, p. 52. The story of von Laue's attendance at Arnold Berliner's funeral at Weissensee is told by P. P. Ewald in "Max von Laue," *Biographical Memoirs of the Fellows of the Royal Society 6* (1960), pp. 135–156 as cited by Alan D. Beyerchen, *Scientists Under Hitler. Politics and the Physics Community in the Third Reich* (New Haven, Connecticut: Yale University Press, 1977), p. 65.

6. The sanctuary aspect of Weissensee is mentioned in an article, "East Germany Guards Its Jewish Heritage," Toronto *Sunday Star*, 16 November 1980.

7. Further details of Klara Riesenburger's story were verified against a book about Weissensee: Alfred Etzold, Dr. Peter Kirchner, Heinz Knoblock, *Jüdische Friedhöfe in Berlin*, Heft 1, *Historische Friedhöfe in der Deutschen Demokratischen Republik* (Berlin, German Democratic Republic: 1979). Klaus Gysi has contributed the afterword. The book has a photograph of the grave of Michael Bodjana on pp. 51–52. Rabbi Leo Baeck was buried at Weissensee in 1956.

8. Rabbi Plaut's autobiography, *Unfinished Business*, was published in Toronto by Lester & Orpen Dennys in 1981. The references to Rabbi Riesenburger are on pp. 309–310. Elsewhere in the book, (pp. 124–125), Plaut gives a description of mixed marriage Jews who survived the war surfacing to attend Jewish services in Cologne in 1945. On p. 137, he makes a similar reference to encountering surviving half-Jews. Yet all of this must have somehow escaped Plaut's attention when he wrote "There was no room in the Nazi system for any Jew," in a book review for the Toronto *Globe & Mail*, 18 July 1981. (His autobiography had not yet been published.)

9. The information about Gysi and Norden was revealed to me over lunch at East Berlin's fashionable Prag Restaurant by a high ranking official of the Foreign Office-affiliated Internationales Pressezentrum, 11 August 1982.

10. Brecht's "Rechtsfindung" appears in *Aufbau*, Oktober 1945, Heft 2. The publisher is Aufbau Verlag GMBH, Berlin. Copy in collection of the author.

11. Dr. Peter Kirchner was personally interviewed by the author in Berlin, German Democratic Republic, 6 August 1981.

12. A photocopy of Dr. Peter Kirchner's "Peoples and Professions" questionnaire is in the collection of the author. The original is in the collection of the Bibliothek der Jüdischen Gemeinde, Berlin, German Democratic Republic.

13. It was Klaus J. Herrmann who had examined Dr. Kirchner's report card coincidentally only one day before my own visit to Kirchner's office.

14. The interview with Charlotte (Lotte) Lehmann has already been cited.

15. Apparently there is a credible scientific hypothesis which contends that vocal characteristics are hereditary and genetically transmittable from parent to offspring.

16. Cristal Senda was interviewed by telephone in San Francisco, California, 6 February, 1983.

17. Klaus Peter Scholz was interviewed by telephone in Montréal, Québec, 8 April 1983.

18. Until recently, the only rabbi in Canada willing to officiate at a mixed marriage ceremony was Temple Emanu-El's Rabbi Stern. The willingness of some Reform rabbis to perform mixed marriage ceremonies is still a touchy issue in Judaism. Rabbi Alexander Schindler, president of the Union of American Hebrew Congregations (UAHC), in a November 1983 speech criticized Reform congregations that "judge the eligibility of rabbis they wish to engage first and foremost by the fact of whether he or she does or does not officiate at mixed marriages." (The UAHC is a Reform organization.) Reported in the *Jewish News* (Detroit), 20 January 1984, p. 53.

CHAPTER FIVE

1. The epigraph for Chapter Five is taken from the Ann Landers column (Field Newspaper Syndicate) as it appeared in the *Windsor* (Ontario) *Star* 5 February 1982. Landers, née Esther Friedman, is herself a Jew. (Greenberg, p. 50.)

2. For more on this aspect of the Lublin Aktion, see Hilberg, *Destruction*, pp. 273–74, 296 (footnotes).

3. The Organization Todt was Speer's construction agency. It was named after Fritz Todt, the German engineer who built both the German system of autobahns and the Siegfried line of defense. Hilberg, p. 419, says, "The Jews in mixed marriages were to take the place of deportable Jews in camps of the Organization Todt (in France)."

4. For more on Ida Schneidhuber, see Ralph Oppenhejm, *An der Grenze des Lebens: Theresienstädter Tagebuch* (Hamburg: Rütten & Loening Verlag, 1961), p. 203. For her husband, see Karl Dietrich Bracher, *The German Dictatorship. The Origins, Structure and Effects of National Socialism* (New York: Praeger Publishers, 1970), p. 137; and Alan Bullock, *Hitler, A Study in Tyranny* (New York: Harper Torchbooks, 1964), pp. 302, 305.

5. For von Hirsch, see Oppenhejm, p. 192.

6. Meyer Levin, p. 271. Levin followed this observation about Theresienstadt with, "Again it may be felt that such things as I have to tell here should be kept 'amongst ourselves' in the Jewish world. But this is more than a book about the Jews; it seeks to touch the human spirit, and my Jewish experience is the probe." Levin and Rabbi W. Gunther Plaut were among the first Americans to enter Germany with the U.S. Army in 1945 (see notes to Foreword). Levin, like Plaut (see notes to Chapter Four) found that the Jewish survivors of the Holocaust were those who had lived in mixed marriages or were Mischlinge. These were the Jews that Levin saw as the rebuilders of European Jewry. His findings in that respect are shared by Bruno Blau, who is cited in Chapter One. Levin, incidentally, was married to a gentile. On p. 79 he says, "I had never felt that there was in our time a danger of the Jewish fold being dissolved through intermarriage." Contrast this with the statement by Rabbi Naftali Halberstam as also cited in Chapter One.

7. For Helene Mayer, see Greenberg, p. 255. For the stamp, see Ariah Lindenbaum, *Great Jews in Stamps* (New York: Sabra Books, 1970), p. 31. A somewhat conflicting version of the Mayer story is told by Stanley B. Frank in *The Jew in Sports* (New York: The Miles Publishing Company, 1936), pp. 16–17. Although Mayer was a Mischling, she is included among those honored in the "Jews in Germany Under Prussian Rule" exhibit developed by Dr. Roland Klemig, director of the Picture Archive of Prussian Culture in Berlin,

Federal Republic of Germany. The exhibit debuted in North America at the Holocaust Memorial Center in West Bloomfield, Michigan, in March 1984.

The Jewish claims on Mayer are especially interesting in view of the fact that it was her father, and not her mother, who was a Jew.

8. The Jürgen Landeck interview has been previously cited.

9. For Rudolf Ball, see Alan Abrams, *Why Windsor? An Anecdotal History of the Jews of Windsor and Essex County* (Windsor, Ontario: Black Moss Press, 1981), p. 100, for an entire chapter detailing the hitherto unknown participation by Jewish athletes in the 1936 "Aryan" Olympics.

10. Information on Lewald was supplied in a letter from Professor Klaus J. Herrmann, 3 February 1982, collection of the author. According to Dr. Herrmann, there allegedly exists a postwar-published autobiography by Lewald which further confirms this information, but a search of both the *National Union Catalogue* and the *British Museum Catalogue* failed to turn up any trace of it. Frank, p. 12, calls Lewald the head of the German Olympic Committee, but says nothing about his ancestry. Lewald is included in Ernst G. Lowenthal's *Juden in Preussen* (Berlin: Bildarchiv Preussicher Kulturbesitz, 1981), p. 136. This biographical directory of Jews in Prussia treats Lewald as if he were a full Jew. This book became the basis of the touring 1984 exhibition "Jews in Germany Under Prussian Rule." The book lists Helene Mayer on p. 152. Lewald however did write the official history of the German participation in the 1904 St. Louis World's Fair, for which he apparently held some official responsibility. He was born in 1860.

11. For Quaatz, see Bernt Engelmann, *Deutschland ohne Juden* (München: Schneekluth Verlag, 1970). Engelmann is himself the child of a mixed marriage—his father was a Jew.

12. For Emil Maurice, see Walter Hagen, *Die geheime Front. Organisationen, Personen und Aktionen des deutschen Geheimdienstes* (Wien/Linz, 1950). Hagen/Höttl thought Heydrich may have been as much as a three-quarter Jew! But he was also practically certain that even Himmler had a Jewish relative. See also Bracher, pp. 128, 241; and Bullock, pp. 72, 121, 302, 393. For the quotation from Eichmann, see Arendt, *Eichmann*, p. 178.

13. For Düsterberg, see Bracher, p. 222; v. Uthmann, p. 44; Fredrik Böök, *An Eyewitness in Germany* (London: Lovat Dickson Limited, 1933), p. 135; and also Engelmann. Professor Böök was a controversial juror on the Nobel Prize in Literature committee during the 1930s.

14. For Gottheiner, see v. Uthmann, p. 44.

15. For Kaufmann-Asser, see Engelmann.

16. For Trebitsch-Lincoln, see v. Uthmann, pp. 46–47.

17. The letter from Albert Speer, 25 July 1981, is in the collection of the author. Speer died on 2 September 1981.

18. The Charlotte Lehmann interview has been cited earlier.

19. The Strauss biographical sketch appears in Justin Wintle, ed., *Makers of Modern Culture* (London: Routledge & Kegan Paul, 1981), pp. 505–506. It was contributed by Strauss's biographer, Alan Jefferson.

Another curious case is apparently that of German art historian Wilhelm Fraenger (1890–1964), who is best known for his posthumously published (1975) monumental study of Hieronymus Bosch. In the 4 December 1983 *New York Times Book Review*, p. 13, John Russell, reviewing the American edition of Fraenger's magnum opus, comments, "Somehow or other, Fraenger managed not only to survive the next twelve years [the Nazi era] in Germany but to devote himself to a form of study that was highly unpopular at the time— the Gnostic-Jewish ferment as it expressed itself in the lifetime of Bosch . . . Fraenger burrowed away at it [the book], even in a period when the very idea of harmonious intellectual collaboration between Jew and gentile was anathema in Germany." Almost certainly Fraenger was allowed to live and continue his work unmolested by the Nazis because he presumably lived in a privileged mixed marriage and may even have been under the added protection of someone highly interested in his work—the Foreign Office perhaps, or even Göring.

20. Information on *Ehe im Schatten* was supplied from the Archives of DEFA-Studio für Spielfilme, Potsdam, German Democratic Republic. The film was directed by Petra Czisch and starred Hans Wieland and Elizabeth Maurer.

21. The Jochen Klepper story was told by Charlotte Lehmann.

22. For more on Raeder's assertions, see Grand Admiral Erich Raeder, *My Life* (Annapolis: United States Naval Institute, 1960), pp. 263–264.

23. Professor Peter C. Hoffman, author of the highly regarded *History of the German Resistance* 1933–1945, was interviewed by telephone in Montréal, 2 February 1982.

24. The letter from Professor Klaus-Jurgen Müller, 14 March 1982, is in the collection of the author.

25. The letter from Kapitän zur See a.D. Hans Heinrich Lebram, 6 May 1982, is in the collection of the author.

26. For the Mailander obituary, see the *Los Angeles Times*, 21 January 1980, p. 20 of section 1, and the Detroit *Jewish News*, 25 January 1980, p. 62.

27. The Speer letter has already been cited.

28. Magnus von Braun was interviewed by telephone in Sedona, Arizona, 29 June 1981.

29. The letter from Lee D. Saegesser, 22 July 1981, is in the collection of the author.

30. The letter from the Historian of the U.S. Department of State, 8 July 1981, is in the collection of the author.

31. Irma Mailander, the widow of Otto Mailander, was interviewed by telephone in Cupertino, California, 28 June 1981.

32. The letter from Mitchell Sharpe, 24 July 1981, is in the collection of the author.

33. The best book on Project Overcast is James McGovern, *Crossbow and Overcast* (New York: William Morrow & Co., 1964). Data on Otto Mailander's capture in 1945 could not be located in the records of the 44th U.S. Infantry Division at the General Services Administration, National Archives and Records Service, Suitland, Maryland. Nor could it be found in the Center of Military History, Department of the Army, Washington, D.C.

34. The letter from Magnus von Braun, 17 July 1981, is in the collection of the author.

35. Dolly Faust was interviewed by telephone in Boulder Junction, Wisconsin, 30 June 1982.

CHAPTER SIX

1. The epigraph for Chapter Six appears in Bracher, p. 254. He attributes the quotation to Lueger, but adds that it was "an idea Göring also toyed with, though in only a few scattered cases, as for example with respect to his State Secretary, Erhard Milch, technically of 'mixed blood.' "

2. Much of the background information for this chapter is based upon information found in Marrus and Paxton, *Vichy France and the Jews*. (New York: Basic Books, Inc., 1981). Especially useful were pp. 75–76, 92 and 151 on the *Statut des juifs*.

3. Letter of Robert O. Paxton, 6 April 1982, in collection of the author.

4. Letter of Michel Debré, 22 January 1982, in collection of the author.

5. For more about Beate Klarsfeld, see her *Wherever They May Be!* (New York: The Vanguard Press, 1975). Early in 1984, Mrs. Klarsfeld was twice briefly arrested and jailed in Chile while leading protest demonstrations urging the official expulsion of Walter Rauff, a former Nazi officer and alleged war criminal. Rauff, however, died in Chile in May 1984. For more on Mrs. Klarsfeld's arrest, see the *Jewish News* (Detroit), 3 February 1984, p. 1.

6. A copy of the Vichy police document prepared by Inspector Soustre on his investigation of Professor Robert Debré is in the collection of the author.

7. Marrus and Paxton, p. 190, offer a telling comment on the ideological composition of the French Resistance. They point out that *Cahiers O.C.M.*, an anti-Semitic organ of a conservative underground group, was written by Maxime Blocq-Mascart, "an economist of Jewish background."

8. Debré recounts details of his visit to Vallat in his *L'Honneur de vivre* (Paris: Stock 1974), p. 221.

9. Rueff's biographical sketch can be found on pp. 382–384 of the 1969 *Current Biography* yearbook.

10. The 187-page *Juden in Frankreich* was published in 1939 by Norland-Verlag, Berlin.

11. For more on General Darius-Paul Bloch-Dassault, see Pierre Assouline, *Monsieur Dassault* (Paris: Editions Andre Balland, 1983), 146, 174, 203. Greenberg, on p. 31, lists General Bloch as "Darius P. [sic] Dassault." Assouline, p. 168, reports that exemptions for Henri Bergson (who died in 1941), Dr. Robert Debré and Jacques Rueff, were requested by Marshal Pétain through Raphäel Alibert, the Vichy minister of justice whose office prepared the *Statut des juifs*, but were refused by the Occupying Authorities. Virtually every biographical source consulted for Bergson states he declined the Vichy exemption which was offered him. This could be the source of the allegation that Bergson "received support" from Vichy education minister Jérome Carcopino, which is found in Marrus and Paxton, p. 208. Certainly Bergson's widow had no qualms about receiving an exemption for herself.

12. Those seeking the actual text of exemptions can find the following in the *Journal Officiel* at the Bibliothèque Nationale, Paris:
> Bloch, pp. 6097–6098 (1940)
> Brisac, pp. 10–11 (1941)
> Garsin, p. 409 (1941)
> Meyer, pp. 669–670 (1941)
> Lion, p. 670 (1941)
> Berl, p. 1693 (1941)

Photocopies of the above are in the collection of the author, as well as a photostat of Rueff's exemption.

The corresponding listings in *Juden in Frankreich* are:
> Bloch, p. 133
> Berl, pp. 96, 105

13. For Berl's biographical sketch, see Jean-Albert Bèdé, William B. Edgerton, eds. *Columbia Dictionary of Modern European Literature* (New York: Columbia University Press, 1980), pp. 80–81.

14. For information on Berl's links to Vichy, see Marrus and Paxton, p. 45.

15. Berl is listed in *Juden in Frankreich* on pp. 124, 126, 129.

16. The allegation that Bènés and Joanovici received "special treatment" is found in a letter of Pierre Assouline, 28 August 1983, in collection of the author. Assouline is a journalist at *France-Soir* in Paris.

17. The Colette letter is quoted in Robert Phelps, ed., *Colette's Earthly Paradise. An Autobiography* (drawn from Colette's lifetime writings) (New York: Farrar, Straus & Giroux, 1966), p. 458. See also p. xxi.

18. Maurice Goudeket's autobiography is *Close to Colette* (London: Secker & Warburg, 1957). The quotation appears on p. 156.

19. Copies of the Dannecker discussion memo and Hagen's report on the 16 June 1942 meeting are in the collection of the author. Serge Klarsfeld supplied both. Herbert Hagen was tried and convicted by a Cologne court in 1980 and was sentenced to twelve years in prison on charges of ordering and administrating the deportation of Jews in Occupied France. The trial resulted mainly from the efforts of Serge Klarsfeld. The Hagen report may have been one of the documents assembled by Klarsfeld for his Hagen dossier. For more about Klarsfeld's efforts, see Brendan Murphy, *The Butcher of Lyon. The Story of Infamous Nazi Klaus Barbie* (New York: Empire Books, 1983).

20. Information on Bertrand de Jouvenel and the Zeev Sternhell book was supplied by Pierre Assouline in a letter of 18 October 1983 and a subsequent cable of 2 November 1983. Both are in the collection of the author.

21. Marrus and Paxton establish the 13 July 1942 date on p. 237 (footnote).

22. Information on the wartime activities of de Beauvoir and other French intellectuals can be found in Herbert R. Lottman, *The Left Bank* (Boston: Houghton, Mifflin & Co., 1982).

23. The additional exemptions can be found in Marrus and Paxton, pp. 17, 85–87, 213, 237. See also Reitlinger, p. 314.

24. For more on the activities of Schellenberg, see Ladislas Farago, *The Game of the Foxes. The Untold Story of German Espionage in the United States and Great Britain During World War II* (New York: David McKay Company, Inc., 1971), pp. 4, 604, 609. See also Murphy, pp. 47–48, 140–141.

25. For more on the "Blue Knights," see Presser, p. 311. See also Reitlinger, pp. 337–338.

26. For more on the NSB and Mussert, see Presser, p. 356, where he also discusses Jewish traitors.

27. The source and full title of the Slottke list has been cited earlier.

28. For the Flatow brothers, see Greenberg, p. 256. The conclusion is the author's.

29. Dr. Cohen's identification document bearing the "ongeldig" stamp, was originally kept in the Central Archives in the Hague. The original was examined at the Rijksinstituut voor Oorlogsdocumentatie, Amsterdam. A photostat is in the collection of the author.

30. For Flesch, see Hans Keller, ed. and trans., *The Memoirs of Carl Flesch* (London: Rockcliff, 1957). C. F. Flesch, the violinist's son, cites the assistance of several noted musical personalities like Wilhelm Furtwängler, Géza von Kresz, and Ernst von Dohnányi. But, of course, he knows nothing about the "Blue Knights" status of his parents.

31. For more on Göring and his relationships with Jewish art dealers, see Leonard Mosley, *The Reich Marshal. A Biography of Hermann Goering* (New York: Dell paperback, 1975), pp. 319–320, 324.

32. For Emmy Göring's comments on Milch, see Mosley, p. 447 (notes).

For more on Milch's ancestry, see Chapter Eight.

33. The Ballin story is found in Mosley, pp. 282–283.

34. The Blech-Göring relationship appears in Fred K. Prieberg, *Musik im NS-Staat* (Frankfurt am Main: Fischer Taschenbuch Verlag, 1982).

35. See Mombert's biographical sketch in Bèdé and Edgerton, p. 542.

36. Sigrid Schultz is quoted by Joan Givner in her *Katherine Anne Porter: A Life* (New York: Simon and Schuster, 1982). p. 260.

37. This may have been the father of Gabriela von Goldschmidt. She married Waldemar Baron von Oppenheim after World War I. Although a member of one of the oldest and most powerful German-Jewish banking families, von Oppenheim became one of the Abwehr's most important operatives. For more about him, see the following chapter.

38. For more on von Epenstein, see Mosley, pp. 22–23.

39. The story of Dr. Emanuel was told to me by Werner Goldberg in a letter dated 7 May 1982. Collection of the author. Dr. Emanuel died in Berlin in 1952.

40. Hilberg, *Destruction*, p. 600.

CHAPTER SEVEN

1. The epigraph for Chapter Seven can be found in v. Uthmann, p. 82. It originally appeared in a letter from Varnhagen to her brother.

2. For more on von Oppenheim, see Farago, pp. 532–537.

3. The von Papen quotations can be found in his *Memoirs* (London: Andre Deutsch, 1953), pp. 276–277.

4. The Bandi Gross story is admirably told by Amos Elon in *The Timetable: The Story of Joel Brand* (London: Hutchinson, 1981).

5. The quotation is found in Robert Gessner's *Some of My Best Friends are Jews* (New York: Farrar & Rinehart, Inc., 1936), pp. 82–83. Gessner, known for his later work at *Esquire*, was a Jew.

6. For the Hanfstängl quotations; see his *Hitler: The Missing Years* (London: Eyre & Spottiswoode, 1957), pp. 80–81. For information on Hanfstängl's alleged Jewish ancestry, see v. Uthmann, p. 46.

7. For the Meyer Levin quotation, see *In Search*, p. 199. However, Levin balances this story by telling, on the very next page, about a half-Jew he talked to in the Netherlands, "a lawyer, who had hidden Allied fliers as well as fleeing Jews in his home, helping them to slip across the border into Belgium on their way out of Europe."

8. The assertion is made by Leonard Gross in *Last Jews in Berlin* (New York: Simon and Schuster, 1982).

9. The Hans Faust interview has been cited earlier.

10. References to Jewish spies and traitors are found in a number of sources. Yehuda Bauer, *American Jewry and the Holocaust. The American Jewish Joint Distribution Committee, 1939–1945* (Detroit: Wayne State University Press, 1981), p. 253, refers to Jewish traitors in France.

Marrus and Paxton, p. 347, quote Walter Laqueur as establishing that reports of the mass killings of Jews were carried to the West by a number of sources, "even Gestapo agents, some of whom were Jews." This is eerily reminiscent of the Eichmann claim about Jews in the SS (see Chapter Five).

11. Information on Max Warburg can be found in Gessner, p. 79. See also Sokolsky, p. 133, who says "even in Hitler's Germany certain Jews, like the firm of Max Warburg in Hamburg, were exempted from persecution." See also the chapter on M. M. Warburg & Co. in David Farrer's *The Warburgs: The Story of a Family* (Briarcliff Manor, N.Y.: Stein and Day, 1975).

12. The quotation appears in Mike Gold, *Jews Without Money.* (New York: International Publishers, 1945), p. 8. Although Gold was a Communist writer, mainstream authors have made reference to the same theme. For instance, see Marvin Lowenthal, *The Jews of Germany. A Study of Sixteen Centuries* (New York: Longmans, Green and Co., 1936), p. 376, who says "certain Jewish firms were among the companies subsidizing National Socialism." Far more specific is Gessner, p. 151, who reports that the Viennese Rothschilds and Fritz Mandl, director-general of the munitions trust, were the biggest contributors to the Heimwehr, the Austrian Nazi movement led by Prince von Starhemberg. Lowenthal was associated with *The Menorah Journal.*

13. The Wasserman and Priwin quotations are found in Gessner, pp. 79–80. For more on the effects of the boycott, see Edwin Black's *The Transfer Agreement* (New York: The Macmillan Company, 1984).

14. For information on the American Warburgs, see Gessner, p. 360. See also Saul S. Friedman, *No Haven for the Oppressed.* (Detroit: Wayne State University, 1973). This book is far superior to the more recent and vastly overrated *None Is Too Many* by Irving Abella and Harold Troper.

15. For Otto H. Warburg, see his sketch in Greenberg, *Jewish Lists,* p. 240; and in Ernst G. Lowenthal, *Juden in Preussen,* p. 236.

16. Professor Warburg appears on the list of Jewish Nobel Prize Winners in *The Jewish Calendar 5738 (1977–1978)* as compiled by Michael Strassfeld and Richard Siegel (New York: Universe Books, 1977). But when Siegel coedited *The Jewish Almanac* (New York: Bantam Books, 1980) with Carl J. Rheins, Warburg's name was dropped from the list on pp. 495–496.

17. The reference to the activities of the German Citizens of the Mosaic Persuasion is in Marvin Lowenthal, *The Jews of Germany,* p. 382. However, he refers to the group as the "German Citizens of the Jewish Faith." Benton Arnovitz, editor of Isiah Trunk's award-winning *Judenrat: The Jewish Councils in Eastern Europe Under Nazi Occupation,* is the source for what he calls the only correct and intended translation of the name of the organization.

18. See Greenberg. Gustav Hertz is on p. 241, Heinrich on p. 109. Greenberg misdates Gustav Hertz's death as 1950, and it is he who claims Hertz converted to Christianity. Interestingly, Greenberg also includes a number of other Nobel Prize winners who were half-Jews. Three whose mothers were Jewish are: Niels Bohr (1922, Physics—the year after Einstein), Hans A. Bethe (1967, Physics) and Henri Moissan (1906, Chemistry). Niels Bohr's son Aage (1975, Physics), a one-quarter Jew, is also listed. Neither of the lists compiled by Richard Siegel (see note 16 above) include Hertz, although both of the Bohrs, Bethe and Moissan are listed.

19. See Beyerchen, p. 45: "Hertz was Jewish. . ." Beyerchen's fine work is the source for part of the biographical data on Hertz. Numerous standard biographical references were also consulted.

20. Beyerchen, p. 48.

21. Hilberg, p. 586.

22. The interviews with Klara Riesenburger, Ruth von Brentani and Rolf Vogel have previously been cited.

23. Hilberg, p. 286. Siemens also regularly received confiscated Jewish and captured economic holdings during the war.

24. The interview with Charlotte Lehmann has previously been cited.

25. The Killy story is told in Hilberg, p. 53. Unfortunately, the Bundesarchiv in Koblenz has returned the "liberation" document to the Killy family. Pity. It would have made a great illustration.

26. Hilberg, p. 53.

27. The references to the Ustashe appear in Levin, pp. 514–516. See also Arendt, *Eichmann,* pp. 183–184, and Hilberg, pp. 457–458.

28. By no means was this an isolated example. Among other twentieth-century heads of state with Jewish wives are Luis Alberto Monge, President of Costa Rica since 1982. His wife is the former Doris Yankelewitz. For more about her, see the *Jewish News* (Detroit), 20 January 1984, p. 78. Another was Cheddi Jagan, the first Premier of British Guiana (now Guyana), 1961-64. His wife is an American, the former Janet Rosenberg. Mrs. Jagan served, in her own right, as a key member of her husband's cabinet. And of course don't forget Joseph Stalin! (See citation nine, Notes and Sources, Chapter One.)

29. For Alexander Klein, see Hilberg, p. 457.

CHAPTER EIGHT

1. The epigraph for Chapter Eight appears in Hans-Joachim Schoeps, *Bereit für Deutschland! Der Patriotismus deutscher Juden und der Nationalsozialismus: Frühe Schriften 1930 bis 1939. Eine Historische Dokumentation* (Berlin, Federal Republic of Germany: Haude & Spenersche Verlagsbuchhandlung, 1970). It is also quoted in v. Uthmann, p. 45.

2. Edison McIntyre, "The Abraham Lincoln Battalion," *American History*, March 1983.

3. Information on Sam Carr is found in Erna Paris, *Jews: An Account of their Experience in Canada* (Toronto: Macmillan of Canada, 1980), p. 168.

4. Information on the participation by Jews in the Italian Fascist campaigns in Ethiopia and Spain, and particularly the "from the tops of our heads" quotation can be found in Gene Bernardini, "The Origins and Development of Racial Anti-Semitism in Fascist Italy," *The Journal of Modern History*, Volume 49, Number 3, September 1977. Bernardini cites Giorgio Pisano, *Mussolini e gli ebrei*, (Milan, 1967), Abramo Levi, *Noi ebrei*, (Rome, 1937) and Ettore Ovazza, *Il problema ebraica*, (Rome, 1938). Jews still served in the Italian army as late as 1943, the year of Mussolini's fall.

5. The Sanusi (or Senussi) Brotherhood are a sect of Islam of which the late King Idris I, Libya's first and only monarch, was hereditary leader.

6. For information on the Fascist exemptions for Jews see Arendt, *Eichmann*, p. 178. The exemption decree appears in *Il giornale d'Italia*, 20 September 1938. For Jung, see Greenberg, *Lists*, p. 25. For Farinacci, see Hilberg,*Destruction*, p. 412. For Toeplitz, see William Bolitho, *Italy Under Mussolini* (New York: The Macmillan Company, 1926).

7. Mussolini personally vacillated when it came to the Jews. In the fall of 1933 a group of American Jewish publications included Mussolini among twelve Christians who had been "most outstanding in their opposition to anti-Semitism." However, by 1938, Mussolini was being quoted as saying that the "Jews are the most racist people in the universe."

Mixed Jewish-Christian marriages were also quite common in Italy. In Trieste, half of all that city's Jews had Christian spouses. (Statistic quoted by Ruppin.) During the war, the Italians went out of their way to help the Jews, an episode of Holocaust history overlooked by many historians. References to "Angelo Donati, an Italian Jew with much influence in Rome" can be found in Marrus and Paxton, p. 319. The authors also detail the Italian efforts to provide protection for the Jews of Nice. The grateful Jewish community of that city raised three million francs as a donation to Italian victims of Anglo-American air raids. Further references to Donati can be found in Bauer, p. 252.

8. The early involvement by Jews in the Nazi party is documented in the records of the party in the Bundesarchiv in Koblenz. The file is identified as *Hauptarchiv der NSDAP*. These documents have been cited by Werner Maser, *Der Sturm auf die Republik. Fruhgeschilchte der NSDAP*, published in Germany by DVA. The Slovokian Neumann makes his appearance in Hilberg, *Destruction*.

9. Information on Count Anton Arco-Valley's gesture at Landsberg is found in Bracher, p. 117. Mosley, p. 72, says Arco-Valley allegedly was rejected for membership in the anti-Semitic Thule Society (whose members included Alfred Rosenberg and Rudolf Hess) "on the grounds that his mother was of Jewish descent, and decided out of pique to demonstrate how truly anti-Jewish he was." Siegel and Rheins in *The Jewish Almanac*, p. 202, apparently believe he was a member of the Thule Kampfbund, although they present his name as "Count Anton auf Valley Arco." The Freikorps, of which August Schneidhuber was a member, worked closely with this group.

10. For Wilhelm Marr, see Marvin Lowenthal, pp. 295–296.

11. For Trebitsch, see Solomon Liptzin, *Germany's Stepchildren*. (Philadelphia: Jewish Publication Society of America, 1944), pp. 189–194. Liptzin points out that Trebitsch was one of the first to use the *Protocols of the Elders of Zion* as the basis for his own writings.

12. For Wiesner, see Marvin Lowenthal, *loc. cit.*

13. The Wagner-Geyer story appears in numerous places, the best being v. Uthmann, p. 74.

14. For Weininger, see Marvin Lowenthal, p. 266. Liptzin, on p. 165, says Weininger was "a Jewish philosopher who undertook to prove scientifically the myth of Aryan superiority and the worthlessness of Semitic traits." He also deals with Weininger on pp. 184–190 and again on p. 194. See also Raphael Patai, *The Jewish Mind* (New York: Charles Scribners Sons, 1977), p. 463.

   The Jewish Soul, by Israeli playwright Joshua Sobol, a controversial play about Weininger, was first staged in Israel in July 1983. By January 1984 it was playing in London.

15. Calé, Steiner and Rée are all found in Marvin Lowenthal, p. 266. Rée is also found in Liptzin, p. 154.

16. For the Friedländer-Dühring story, see Marvin Lowenthal, *loc. cit.*

17. For more about Henry Ford and *The International Jew*, see Albert Lee, *Henry Ford and the Jews* (New York: Stein and Day, 1980), *the* definitive book on the subject of Henry Ford's anti-Semitism. The topic is also covered in another fine study: David L. Lewis's *The Publich Image of Henry Ford. An American Folk Hero and His Company* (Detroit: Wayne State University Press, 1976), pp. 143–159. See also Anne Jardim, *The First Henry Ford: A Study in Personality and Business Leadership* (Cambridge, Massachusetts: The Massachusetts Institute of Technology Press, 1970), pp. 140–155.

18. The author has in his collection a copy of *The Protocols and World Revolution. Including a Translation and Analysis of the "Protocols of the Meetings of the Zionist Men of Wisdom"* (Boston: Small, Maynard and Company, 1920). The book bears a warm presentation inscription on the front flyleaf to the Honorable J. W. Harreld from William H. Taylor dated January 27, 1921. At that time, John W. Harreld was United States Senator-elect from Oklahoma, and serving in Congress as a U.S. Representative from that state. Laid into the book is a carbon copy of a typewritten speech inspired by a reading of the *Protocols*. The speech singles out

American Jews like Samuel Gompers, Bernard Baruch, Louis D. Brandeis, Lillian Wald, Samuel Untermeyer, Jacob Schiff and Julius Rosenwald, all of whom are somehow linked to this Zionist conspiracy. Curiously, the list also includes William Randolph Hearst, who is described as being "worse than a German Jew." The speech points out that every one of the advisors to President Woodrow Wilson's friend and diplomatic troubleshooter Colonel E. M. House are "radicals and of the same race." Even half-Jews like William Christian Bullitt make this list.

Although it is not clear whether Harreld wrote or delivered this speech, it is quite apparent from the internal evidence that it was prepared by a U.S. Congressman in the weeks before the advent of the Harding administration and the new Republican-dominated Congress which met the first week of March 1921. Ironically, the speech assails Henry Ford for having met with Bolshevik emissaries who were seen as agents of this nefarious plot.

19. References to Brafman appear in Robert E. Conot, *Justice at Nuremberg* (New York: Harper and Row, 1983). See also v. Uthmann, p. 82.

20. For Bronnen, see v. Uthmann, p. 46.

21. For Borchardt, see Jürgen Rühle, *Die Schriftsteller und der Kommunismus in Deutschland* (Köln: Kiepenheuer & Witsch, 1960), p. 183. See also Liptzin, p. 183, and Bèdé and Edgerton, p. 102, and Ernst G. Lowenthal, p. 34.

22. Good sources on Milch are David Irving, *The Rise and Fall of the Luftwaffe. The Life of Field Marshal Erhard Milch* (Boston: Little Brown & Co., 1973), and Arendt's *Eichmann in Jerusalem*. The contrast between these two revisionist historians is fascinating.

23. Dr. Peter Kirchner interview cited earlier.

24. Milch's diary entry for 1 November 1933 appears in Irving, pp. 333–334.

25. Louis L. Snyder, editor. *Encyclopedia of the Third Reich* (New York: McGraw-Hill Book Co., 1976).

26. Udet's reference to "that Jew Milch" is found in Mosley, p. 345.

27. Interview with Arthur Miller previously cited.

28. Interview with Klaus J. Herrmann previously cited.

29. Dr. Waltraud Rehfeld interview cited earlier. The B.V.N., is also the Mischlinge Rights organization. Those interested in learning about their good work, can write Dr. Rehfeld at Mommsenstrasse 27, 1000 Berlin 12, Federal Republic of Germany. Their group needs all the support it can get. If I could figure out how to do it, Dr. Rehfeld and the B.V.N. are worthy candidates for the Nobel Peace Prize.

30. Dr. Robert M. W. Kempner, one of Milch's prosecutors at his Nuremberg trial, refused comment on the issue of Milch's Jewish ancestry. Letter of 23 June 1983 in author's collection. Dr. Kempner incidentally is a Jew.

31. The Jonas Wolk story is briefly touched upon by Conot. The source for most information was Klause J. Herrmann.

32. For Patrick Hitler, see v. Uthmann, p. 71.

33. The Heydrich essay is found in Michael Freund, *Deutsche Geschichte* (Gütersloh: Bertelsmann Lexikon-Verlag, 1973). The Bertelsmann publishing empire includes Bantam Books, the American mass market paperback house.

34. The Arendt quote about Heydrich and Milch is on p. 133.

35. The Hans Frank story is also in Arendt, *op. cit.*

36. Quoted by Patai, p. 281.

37. Quoted in Baker, p. 96.

38. The Heine quotation can be found in Marvin Lowenthal, p. 234.

39. Liebermann is quoted in v. Uthmann, p. 82.

CHAPTER NINE

1. The best source on Dr. Max Naumann and the V.n.J. is Carl J. Rheins, *The Verband National deutscher Juden 1921-1933*, *Publi-*

cations of the Leo Baeck Institute, Year Book XXV (New York, 1980). Valuable data on Dr. Naumann and his organization was provided by Professor Dr. Klaus J. Herrmann both in his *Das Dritte Reich* and in a series of interviews, telephone calls and letters. Dr. Herrmann is the great-nephew of Dr. Naumann. See also Baker, p. 153, although for some reason, he misspells both Naumann's name *and* the name of the organization.

2. Some of Dr. Naumann's quotations are taken from his *Vom nationaldeutschen Juden* (Berlin: Verlag von Albert Goldschmidt, 1920), which is the manifesto of the V.n.J. Collection of the author. Other Naumann quotations appear in various issues of *Der nationaldeutsche Jude* (some earlier issues are published under the title of *Mitteilungsblatt des Verbandes nationaldeutscher Juden e.b.*) 1921-1933. Issue number 1, September 1921, outlines the program of the V.n.J. It is again reprinted in the May 1933 issue. Collection of the author.

3. The quotations about "Jewish parasitism" are found in Patai, p. 458.

4. See Grace Humphrey, *Poland the Unexplored.* (Indianapolis: The Bobbs-Merrill Company, 1931), p. 274, an excellent example of how an innocuous appearing travel book can be used to spread the author's vicious racial and religious prejudices.

5. Although another Jew unfortunately said it later! Closely paralleling the public pronouncements of Dr. Naumann has been Bruno Kreisky, the Jewish former Chancellor of Austria, who also publicly labeled Zionism as a form of "Jewish racism." Kreisky has also described the Jewish people as being "a wretched people" and once said of Menachem Begin, a Polish Jew, "they think in such a warped way, these Eastern Jews." For more of Kreisky's public acts and utterances, see Siegel and Rheins, *The Jewish Almanac,* pp. 203–204.

Kreisky, incidentally, was a schoolmate of Robert G. Neumann, former United States Ambasssador to Saudi Arabia, Afghanistan and Morocco. Born of Jewish parents in Vienna, Neumann left the Jewish community at fourteen and converted to Catholicism at seventeen. That wasn't enough to keep him from being interned for two years at Auschwitz and Dachau. Like Kreisky, Neumann is considered to be an Arabist. He was forced to resign as envoy to Saudi Arabia after accusing the Reagan administration of being too soft on Israel. For more on Neumann, see the *Jewish News* (Detroit), 20 January 1984, p. 31.

6. There exists a historical precedent for this concept. The Reform (or Neologist) Movement in Hungary under Rabbi Yitzchak Einhorn had already replaced the traditional Sabbath observance with Sunday and even abolished the ritual of circumcision. See Rabbi Shlomo Zalman Sonnenfeld, *Guardian of Jerusalem. The Life and Times of Rabbi Yosef Chaim Sonnenfeld* (Brooklyn, New York: Mesorah Publications, Ltd., 1983), p. 54.

7. With all due respect to Professor Herrmann, it is positively uncanny how his writings sometimes read as if they had been penned by his great-uncle, Dr. Naumann. For instance, in an article titled "Canadian Jewry and the Duddy Kravitz Problem," *Le Chien d'Or/ The Golden Dog* (Montréal: November 1974), Number 4, Herrmann (who is a Reform Jew) discusses the introduction of ritual Hebrew prayers into Canada. Herrmann says that "what was styled as 'traditionally Jewish' chanting, was actually nothing more than the wailing of Ukrainean [sic] beggars' music, pitifully beseeching generous donors for the odd kopeck, but because the immigrant Ashkenasi [sic] Jews to Canada apparently felt it necessary to preserve this kind of dross, newly established Orthodox synagogues insisted on retention of these musical monstrosities."

A careful perusal of the article shows that Professor Herrmann stops somewhat short of calling for the establishment of a "Canadian God."

Dr. Herrmann also walks comfortably in the anti-Zionist footsteps of Dr. Naumann. Herrmann is an active member and supporter of the American Council for Judaism, the anti-Israel organization headed by the controversial Alfred Lillienthal. Hermann, an American citizen, has visited Libya as a guest of Colonel Qadhafi on several occasions, the most recent being in April 1983.

8. Letter of Rabbi Dr. Graf, 19 February 1982. Collection of the author.

9. The placard-carrying stories are found in Gessner, p. 81; Rabbi Lee J. Levinger, *Anti-Semitism, Yesterday and Today* (New York:

The Macmillan Co., 1936), p. 125; and also recur in George L. Mosse, *Germans and Jews* (New York: 1970), p. 113.

10. See Patai, *op. cit.*

11. See Kurt Lewin, "Self Hatred Among Jews," in *Contemporary Jewish Record*, IV, No. 3 (June 1941), pp. 218–232.

12. See Patai, *op. cit.*

13. For a comprehensive analysis of the Deutscher Vortrupp, see Heinemann Stern, *Warum hassen sie uns eigentlich? Jüdisches Leben zwischen den Kriegen Erinnerungen, herausgegeben und kommentiert von Hans Ch. Meyer* (Düsseldorf: Droste Verlag, 1970), p. 216. Some material in this section is drawn from Stern's description. (Stern died in 1957. The book is edited by Rabbi Dr. Meyer.)

14. The Hans Rehfeld interview has been previously cited.

15. See Dickinson, p. 247.

16. Letter of Dr. Raphael Patai to the author, 28 December 1981. Collection of the author.

17. Both identifications were confirmed in a letter of Dr. Alfred Jospe to the author, 14 January 1982. Collection of the author.

18. Regarding Weschberg's membership in the Schoeps group, the statement, "I know this fact from the late Schoeps himself," appears in a letter of Professor Herrmann to the author, 28 January 1982. Collection of the author.

19. See Patai letter cited above.

20. The Kareski story is touched upon by Heinemann Stern, pp. 360–364.

21. The summation of charges and the verdict of the court in the Kareski proceedings is based on material found in the Yad Vashem Archives, Jerusalem. The file number of the Kareski file documents is 01/112. The text is in German.

22. Dr. Dr. Erwin Goldman, *Zwischen Zwei Völkern—Ein Rückblick* (Königswinter: Helmut Cramer Verlag, 1975). See Hilberg, p. 120, for the Heydrich proposal.

23. For the entire text of the 23 December 1935 *Der Angriff* article (in German), see Herrmann, *Das Dritte Reich*.

24. The Kareski-Baeck conflict is reported by Baker, pp. 209–213.

25. Information on Dr. Kallman is based upon data appearing in an article on biological psychiatry in *Maclean's* (Toronto), 15 February 1982, p. 49.

Index